WARSHIPS
INSIDE OUT

WARSHIPS
INSIDE OUT

Robert Jackson

THUNDER BAY
P·R·E·S·S

San Diego, California

Thunder Bay Press
An imprint of the Baker & Taylor Publishing Group
10350 Barnes Canyon Road, San Diego, CA 92121
THUNDER BAY
P · R · E · S · S   www.thunderbaybooks.com

Amber Books Ltd
Bradley's Close
74–77 White Lion Street
London N1 9PF, UK
www.amberbooks.co.uk

ISBN-13: 978-1-60710-109-3
ISBN-10: 1-60710-109-2

Library of Congress Cataloging-in-Publication Data available upon request.

Printed in Thailand

1 2 3 4 5 14 13 12 11 10

Project Editor: Sarah Uttridge
Editorial Assistant: Kieron Connolly
Design: Nicola Hibberd
Picture Research: Terry Forshaw

Contents

Classic Ships 1859–1949

Modern Ships 1950–Present

Classic Ships 1859–1949

In 1860, the appearance of a new French warship caused great consternation in Britain. She was *Gloire*, and she was the first armoured warship in the world. Her deployment set off an arms race that was to last for decades.

Shikishima was still afloat at Sasebo the end of World War II, having somehow managed to escape American air attacks, but she had not moved under her own power for two decades. She was broken up in 1948.

The *Gloire*, and all the other warships that appear in this fascinating book, had one thing in common: they were built to fight, either on the surface of the sea or beneath it. In these pages, the reader will find a step-by-step guide to the development of warships over the past century and a half, each individual vessel featuring details of its internal workings as well as an in-depth account of its career.

In the last two decades of the nineteenth century, supremacy on the high seas unquestionably rested with Great Britain.

New ideas and inventions were emerging so quickly that a new vessel could be obsolete before it was launched. In the 1890s the Royal Navy, closely followed by other major naval powers, developed a new standard type of battleship later known as the "pre-dreadnought." In all, 42 pre-dreadnoughts were built for the Royal Navy up to 1904, and they laid down a firm pattern of capital ship construction that was quickly adopted by other seafaring nations.

MODERN NAVAL WARFARE

The era of modern naval warfare, however, began on 27 May 1905, on the other side of the world, when warships of the Russian Baltic Fleet – a force designated the 2nd Pacific Squadron – under Vice-Admiral Rozhdestvensky entered the Straits of Tsushima, at the entrance to the Sea of Japan, having completed an incredible seven-month voyage from its home base. The voyage was in the nature of a punitive expedition, mounted in response to a damaging Japanese attack on the Russian naval base at Port Arthur in the previous year. The Battle of Tsushima, in which the Japanese destroyed the Russian naval force, showed the world what modern warships, crewed by well-trained men, could achieve against obsolete vessels with conscript crews.

It was in 1905, too, that the shape of naval warfare was changed forever with the launch of a single British battleship. She was HMS *Dreadnought*, a vessel that made all other

If a proposal to upgrade the main armament to six 15-in (380-mm) guns in three twin turrets had been implemented, Scharnhorst *might have been a very formidable opponent, faster than any British capital ship.*

warships obsolete overnight. This was a time of innovation, a period that saw the debut of the battlecruiser, a hybrid warship that was to make its mark on the sea battles of the twentieth century.

BRITAIN'S SUPREMACY CHALLENGED

The years that led up to World War I witnessed Great Britain's naval supremacy challenged first by Germany and then Japan, but at the end of that conflict the German High Seas Fleet had ceased to exist and the principal maritime powers were Britain, Japan and the United States, with France and Italy also in the running. Russia's naval strength, shattered by the Japanese fleet at Tsushima in 1905, had never recovered from that humiliation, and its post-war reconstruction was delayed by the

economic effects of the Russian Revolution. The years between 1905 and 1935 were marked by undreamed-of technological innovation. Destroyers, once little more than coastal craft, were turned into hardy, seaworthy vessels with a role to play on the world's oceans, and World War I proved the destructive capability of the submarine beyond all doubt. During that war, Britain took the first tentative steps in the development of the aircraft carrier, the vessel that was to become the capital ship of the future. The carrier, perhaps, was the most significant naval design to emerge from the 1905–35 period; not only did it enable fleets to engage one another at distances far beyond visual range, but it also became a primary tool in hunting down the two

The battleship Bismarck *pictured during completion. Centre foreground, with his back to the camera, is Adolf Hitler, on a visit to the vessel. He was fascinated by battleships.*

Due to the cost-cutting policy that influenced her design, De Ruyter *was not quite up to her task. Her main battery (7 x 150-mm [5.9-in] guns) was inadequate, despite having an excellent fire control system.*

greatest naval threats of World War II, the commerce raider and the submarine.

Despite this, throughout the period of the 1920s and 1930s many traditionalists still remained convinced that any future naval battles would be decided by battleships, and at the beginning of World War II such vessels still represented the most powerful war machines made by man.

MOVING WITH THE TIMES

The attacks by torpedo aircraft on Taranto in 1940 and Pearl Harbor in 1941 changed the picture completely, proving that a battleship could not exist without control of the air space above it. The Pacific battles of 1942–45 saw the last major surface actions fought by

battleships, and proved conclusively that the aircraft carrier was at the core of modern naval warfare. That picture, too, would alter over the next two decades, with the advent of the nuclear submarine.

"The moral effect of an omnipresent fleet is very great, but it cannot be weighed against a main fleet known to be ready to strike and able to strike hard."

Lord Fisher, First Sea Lord

Gloire 1859

France's *Gloire* was the first armoured ship-of-the-line in the world, and the mother of all armoured warships that came after her. She caused great consternation in British naval circles, her appearance setting off a naval arms race that was to last for decades.

MACHINERY
The ship had a single-screw, return connecting-rod engine with eight oval boilers.

HULL
The wooden hull had armour plating. The two sister vessels were only armoured on the upper deck because French industry was unable to provide sufficient plating and armour for them to be built quickly with iron hulls, as demanded by the French Admiralty.

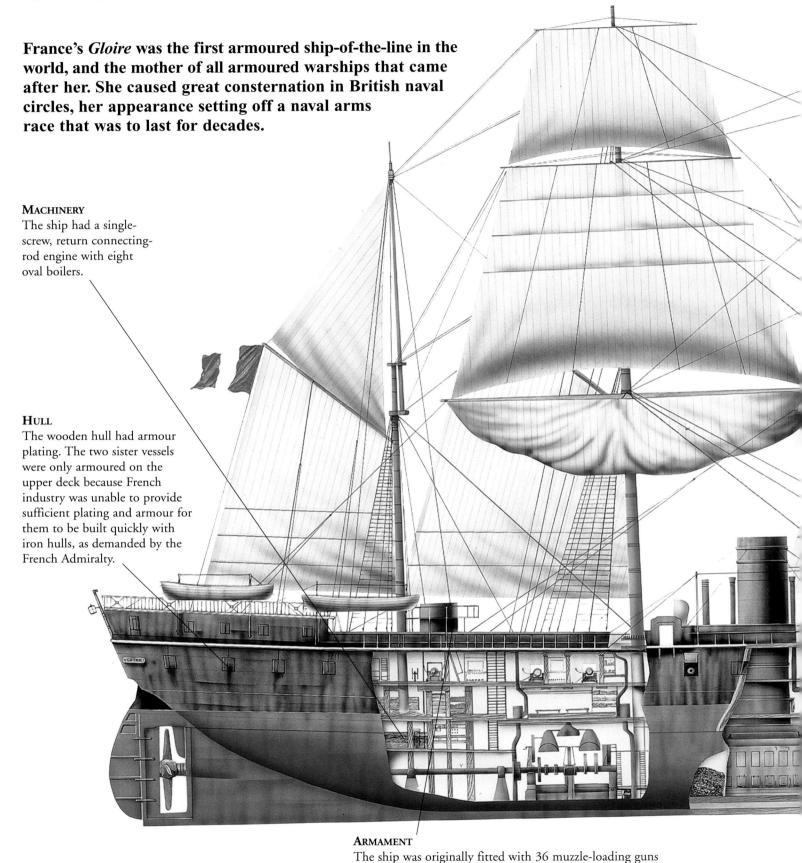

ARMAMENT
The ship was originally fitted with 36 muzzle-loading guns of 163-mm (6.4-in) calibre, but these proved to have very poor hitting power against armour. They were later replaced by more powerful breech-loaders.

ARMOUR
The armoured belt extended from stem to stern and from below the waterline to the upper deck, being backed by the wooden hull. The conning tower was unroofed, and there was an iron layer under the wooden upper deck.

RIG
Gloire was originally equipped with a light barquentine rig of 1096 sq m (11,800 sq ft), but to save on engine operating costs in peacetime this was changed to a full rig of 2,508 sq m (27,000 sq ft), much reduced at a later date.

F A C T S

- Launched 24 November 1859, completed July 1860.

- Two sister ships, *Invincible* and *Normandie*.

- Refitted and rearmed 1869.

- Discarded 1879, broken up 1883.

GLOIRE – SPECIFICATION

Country of origin: France
Type: Armoured frigate
Laid down: April 1858
Builder: Toulon, France
Launched: 24 November, 1859
Commissioned: August 1860
Decommissioned: 1879
Fate: Scrapped in 1883

Crew: 570 men

Dimensions:
Displacement: 5630 tonnes (6206 tons)
Length: 77.8 m (255 ft)
Beam: 17 m (55.8 ft)
Draught: 8.4 m (27.6 ft)

Powerplant:
Propulsion:
Sail: 1096 sq m (11,800 sq ft)
Machinery: Single-shaft HRCR (horizontal return) steam engine producing 1.9 mW (2,500 hp)
Boilers: 8 oval boilers
Speed: 13 knots
Endurance: 665 tonnes (733 tons) of coal

Armament & Armour:
Armament: 1858–60 model:
36 x 163-mm (6.4-in) rifled muzzle-loaders
after 1866: 8 x 239-mm (9-in) BL model 1864; 6 x 193-mm (7.6-in) BL model 1866
Armour: 110–119-mm (4.3–4.7-in) iron plates

CREW
Gloire and her sister ships had a complement of 570, existing in cramped and uncomfortable conditions. In July 1862, *Normandie* became the first armoured ship to cross the Atlantic to Mexico, but returned in the following year after a serious outbreak of yellow fever.

Gloire did not enjoy her prestige for long.
Quite apart from the fact that she was soon
overtaken by more modern designs, which
relied on steam power alone, the rapid
deterioration of her wooden hull components
meant that she had an active life of less than
20 years before she was stricken.

GLOIRE

The French were lucky in having the leading naval architect of the day, Dupuy de Lôme. He took the design of his outstanding two-decker *Napoleon*, built in 1850, and modified it to carry iron side-plating strong enough to withstand the impact of the latest explosive shells fired by the 25-kg (55-lb) muzzle-loading gun. The result was *Gloire*, the world's first armoured seagoing battleship. She was hardly a beautiful vessel, and she handled badly, but she temporarily gave the French a leading edge in warship technology.

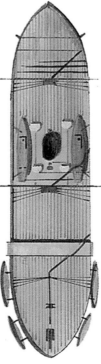

Gloire was a direct result of French Emperor Napoleon III's ambition to establish a French empire in Mexico, which would require considerable naval forces to maintain.

The British victory at Trafalgar in 1805 effectively meant the end of France as a major naval power for half a century. In the middle of the nineteenth century, however, the French Emperor Napoleon III laid plans to return France to her former glory by expanding her empire overseas. In 1848, the French launched *Napoleon*, the first battleship designed to be powered by steam. A few years later, the Crimean War reinforced a growing understanding that, when it came to evading counterfire from shore batteries, ships with engines were far more useful and manoeuvrable than those with only the power of sail.

Close-up

Gloire's design was based on that of the steam frigate *Napoleon*, with a full-length battery along the hull. She was the first armoured ship-of-the-line in the world and revolutionized naval warfare.

① **Masts:** *Gloire* retained masts and rigging. Her barquentine rig was later changed to full ship rig.

② **Lifeboats:** These were provided for the crew. Working conditions were hard on board because ventilation was poor and only oil lamps were available for lighting.

③ **Single funnel:** *Gloire*'s single funnel was one of her distinguishing features. She was more or less identical to her sister ships, *Invincible* and *Normandie*.

④ **Mainmast:** The ship was dominated by her huge mainmast. She had a short, tubby hull and was squat and ugly in appearance.

⑤ **Rigging:** The admirals of *Gloire*'s day refused to countenance warships without rigging, but within a few short years even they realized rigging was an unnecessary encumbrance.

⑥ **Hull:** French industry could not provide sufficient material for iron hulls quickly enough so the hull was wooden, with only the deck featuring armour plating.

The French Fleet in harbour, with Gloire *at centre. She is fitted with a bark rig in this picture. The ship on the right is* La Couronne, *which was a near sister ship, but with two gun decks.*

Naval firepower had also undergone a revolution in the first half of the nineteenth century. It began in 1822, when a French artilleryman called Henri Paixhans published a treatise on how the French Navy, shattered in its long war with Britain, could achieve parity with the Royal Navy without embarking on a massive and costly shipbuilding programme. His solution was to adapt the hollow cast-iron mortar bomb, which had been in use for many years, to be fired by naval guns. If such a shell penetrated a ship's timbers, it would explode with enormous force and start uncontrollable fires, leading to a huge blast. The tremendous explosion that had destroyed Admiral Brueys' flagship *L'Orient* at the Battle of the Nile in August 1798 was deeply embedded in French naval memory.

BRITISH IDEAS

The British had similar ideas. Both navies began using the explosive shell at about the same time, the French issuing their new shell in 1824 for use with their 25-kg (55-lb) guns, and the British issuing their own shell for use with the tried-and-tested 31-kg (68-lb) gun some two years later. Both navies continued to use solid shot, however, because the cannons that fired it were more accurate over long ranges.

By the 1840s most three-deckers carried a combination of 60 per cent solid shot cannon and 40 per cent shell guns. Shells were fitted with a wooden fuse, which was ignited by the flash of a black powder charge as the gun was fired. A simple time delay prevented detonation until the projectile struck its target.

THE FIRST OF HER KIND

The French took the next step when they built *Gloire*, a vessel capable of withstanding such missiles. She had some radical features, including a blunt bow with a convex stem, and she was not without her faults. She had a low freeboard, which made it difficult for her main deck gunners to achieve the desired accuracy in a seaway, and the gunports were too close to the waterline and to each other, making working conditions crowded and difficult for the gunners. She was also disadvantaged by being rushed into service – her timbers had not been allowed to season over the usual three-year period.

Nevertheless, she was the first of her kind, and she paved the way for more successful vessels. The fourth in her class, the somewhat larger *Couronne*, had an iron hull. Launched in 1861, she was not discarded until 1910, and she was still afloat in 1934, when she was broken up.

Warrior 1861

Britain's answer to the threat posed by the French battleship *Gloire* was *Warrior*, which was superior to the French vessel in most respects. *Warrior* was the first seagoing iron-hulled armoured warship, having wrought iron on a backing of teak.

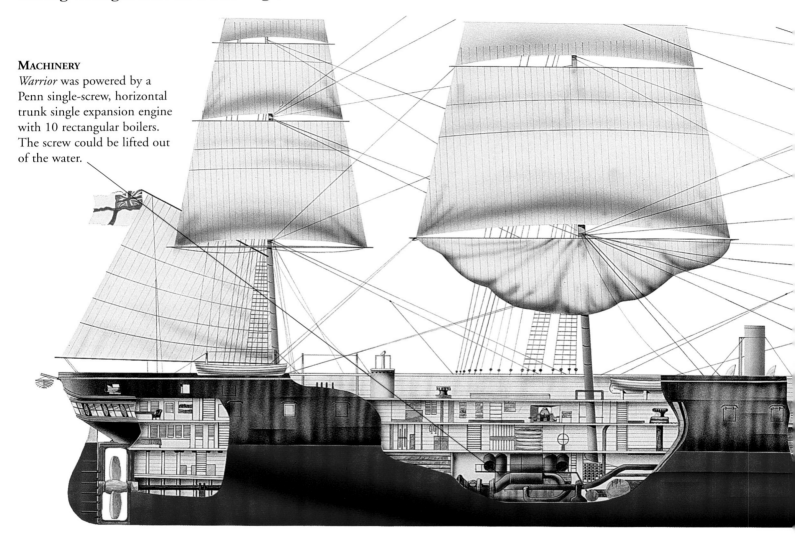

MACHINERY
Warrior was powered by a Penn single-screw, horizontal trunk single expansion engine with 10 rectangular boilers. The screw could be lifted out of the water.

WARRIOR – SPECIFICATION

Country of origin: United Kingdom
Type: Armoured battleship
Laid down: 25 May, 1859
Builder: Thames Ironworks and Shipbuilding Co. Ltd
Launched: 29 December, 1860
Commissioned: 1 August, 1861
Decommissioned: 31 May, 1883
Status: Museum ship
Complement: 705 officers and men

Dimensions:
Displacement: 8489 tonnes (9358 tons)
Length: 127 m (418 ft);

Beam: 17.8 m (58.4 ft);
Draught: 7.9 m (26 ft)

Powerplant:
Propulsion: Steam engine: Penn jet-condensing, horizontal trunk, single expansion; Sail: Full rigged
Speed: 13 knots (sail); 14.5 knots (steam); 17 knots (combined)

Armour & Armament:
Armament: 26 muzzle-loading 31-kg (68-lb) guns; 10 x RBL 178-mm (7-in) Armstrong guns; 4 x RBL 18-kg (40-lb) Armstrong guns
Armour: 114-mm (4.5-in) belt, as protection along the hull

SAILS

Warrior was a full rigged ship. She had a similar area of sail to contemporary line-of-battle ships, but her larger size meant that she was slower in ordinary weather and had to use steam to keep up.

ARMAMENT

Warrior was constructed on the traditional pattern of a broadside ship. She started her career with an armament of muzzle-loading and breech-loading guns of various calibres, but the breech mechanism was prone to failure. In 1867 the armament was changed to 32 muzzle-loaders.

F A C T S

- Launched on 29 December, 1860, completed 24 October, 1861.

- Damaged in collision with ironclad *Royal Oak,* 1868.

- Refitted in 1893.

- Torpedo depot ship, Portsmouth, 1902.

- Oil Hulk, 1929, renamed C77 in 1945.

- Acquired by the Maritime Trust for restoration as a museum ship in 1979.

ARMOUR

The belt and bulkheads were protected by 114 mm (4.5 in) of armour. The armour belt over the midships section consisted of iron plates weighing 3.6 tonnes (4 tons) each.

HULL

All the main guns, engines, and boilers were housed within her armoured iron hull. The hull was constructed with a partial double bottom, 73 m (240 ft) long, below the machinery and the midships magazine, and was subdivided into 92 watertight compartments, 57 of which were in the double bottom.

CREW

Warrior carried a complement of 705, of which 42 were officers. The remainder included 455 seamen and boys, 10 engineers, and 66 stokers and trimmers. Also on board were 118 Royal Marines, commanded by three officers and six NCOs.

Warrior's construction, although far from radical, started a race to develop better guns and armour that lasted until air power made the battleship obsolete in World War II. She, too, became quickly outdated, and was withdrawn as a fighting unit in May 1883.

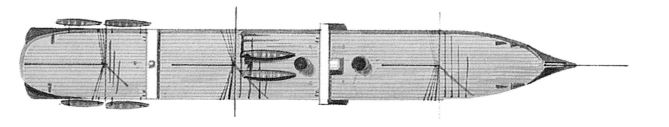

WARRIOR

Warrior and her sister ship, *Black Prince*, were classed as frigates at the time of their construction because of their single gun deck, despite being the most powerful warships in the world. The ships were re-classified as armoured cruisers in 1880, when both had been placed in reserve. *Black Prince* became a training ship in 1899, being renamed *Emerald* in 1903 and *Impregnable III* in 1910. *Warrior* was converted to a depot ship in 1902, renamed *Vernon III* in 1904, hulked in 1923, and spent decades as an oil pipeline pier at Pembroke Dock before being rescued for restoration.

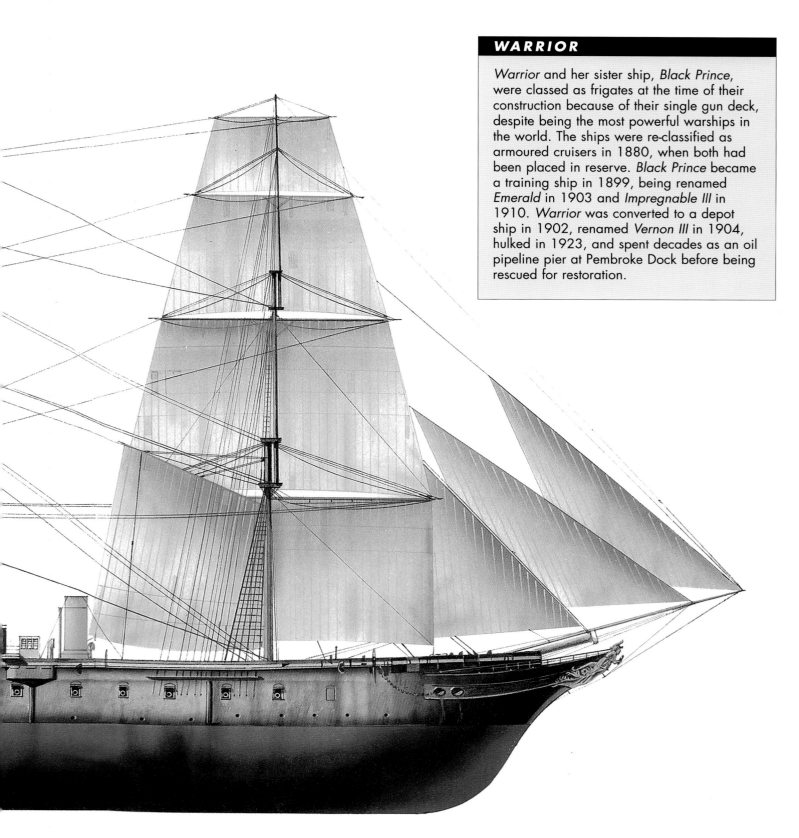

Warrior and her sister ship *Black Prince* *were handsome vessels. In this painting, one is pictured under full sail while the other proceeds under steam power alone, providing an interesting contrast.*

The conservative British Admiralty remained unconvinced that ironclads like *Warrior* and *Black Prince* had any real value, and were concerned about the relative strength in "wooden walls" between Britain and France. The result was that the ironclad programme was only slightly expanded, while construction of wooden vessels continued.

In 1858, the British government learnt that France had been secretly building a new battle fleet, spearheaded by revolutionary vessels like the battleship *Gloire*. Unless drastic measures were taken the French would soon match the Royal Navy in terms of steam-powered ships and utterly outclass the British service in terms of ironclads. In response, the Admiralty called for a new wooden-hulled, armour-plated warships with dimensions similar to those of *Gloire*.

The problem was that timber was in short supply, and the new ship needed to be built quickly. Iron construction was the answer, and the design that evolved envisaged a single-deck broadside ship, as armour plating precluded a design with several gun decks. To provide adequate firepower, this meant that the new ship would need to be 116 m (380 ft) long, 30 m (100 ft) longer than any warship built previously.

The contract to build the new warship was awarded to the Thames Ironworks and Shipbuilding Company in London. On 29 December, 1860, *Warrior* was ready to be launched. That winter was the coldest there had been for half a century. The ship froze to the slipway, and six tugs were needed to haul her into the river.

HANDLING AND MANOEUVRING FAULTS
Warrior was completed on 24 October, 1861, some three years since the requirement had been defined that led to her construction. During her sea trials in 1862, she recorded a speed of 13 knots under full sail, and on one occasion made 17 knots with combined steam and sail. The trials revealed one particular fault; her high length-to-beam ratio of 6.5:1 and fine lines forwards, designed for high speed, resulted in poor handling and manoeuvrability.

Although *Warrior* never saw action during her career, she sailed on a number of prestigious voyages, one of which was to escort Princess Alexandra of Denmark, who was sailing to England to marry the Prince of Wales in 1863.

OIL JETTY DUTY

Withdrawn from service in 1883, she was used as a storage hulk and depot ship. In the 1920s, all efforts to sell her for scrap having failed, she was towed to Pembroke Dock in Milford Haven, Wales, where she was transformed into a floating oil jetty. During the next 50 years she refuelled some 5000 ships. She was now the last surviving British ironclad, all the others having been scrapped. She might have gone the same way, had not the Duke of Edinburgh convened a meeting in 1968 to discuss rescuing her. A year later the Maritime Trust was founded, gaining control of the ship after a decade of negotiations and feasibility studies.

On 3 September, 1979, *Warrior* was towed to the Coal Dock at Hartlepool, where she was painstakingly restored over an eight-year period. On 16 June, 1987, she berthed at Portsmouth as a museum ship, a fitting tribute to the ingenuity of British shipbuilders.

Inside *Warrior*

Warrior and *Black Prince* rendered all other warships obsolete. Unlike the French *Gloire*, they were true ocean-going vessels, and set a pattern that would make the Royal Navy supreme.

① **Single Gun Deck:** *Warrior* and *Black Prince* were classified as frigates on their completion because of their single gun deck.

② **Hull:** Constructed with a partial double bottom below the machinery and the midships compartments, it was subdivided into 92 watertight compartments.

③ **Armament:** *Warrior* and *Black Prince* were armed with 10 50-kg (110-lb) breech-loading guns, with a further 26 31-kg (68-lb) and four 32-kg (70-lb) guns.

④ **Stowage:** On Royal Navy warships cleanliness and good order were important, and there was plenty of space for stowage.

⑤ **Rifle Racks:** Every warship carried its complement of Royal Marines and their weapons were kept in rifle racks such as this one.

⑥ **Ropes and Pulleys:** *Warrior*'s guns had a fearsome recoil, and ropes and pulleys were needed to prevent them careering across the gun deck on being fired.

Virginia 1861

The *Virginia* began life as the Union screw frigate *Merrimack*, which was raised and reconstructed by the Confederates after she had been burned at Norfolk to prevent capture. She was rebuilt as a casemate ironclad.

RAM
Concerned by reports that the Union navy was planning to build an ironclad warship, and worried that *Virginia's* guns would not have sufficient penetrating power to take on such a vessel, *Virginia's* designers fitted her with a ram.

HULL
During reconstruction, the burnt hull timbers were cut down to the waterline, and a new deck and armoured casemate were added. The *Virginia* set the pattern for all Confederate armoured ships, with the forward and after parts of the hull awash except for a low coaming at the bows.

VIRGINIA – SPECIFICATION

Country of origin: Confederate States of America
Type: Ironclad ram
Laid down: 1862 (overlay USS *Merrimack*)
Launched: 8 March, 1862
Commissioned: 1862
Decommissioned: n/a
Fate: Scuttled by crew, 11 May, 1862
Complement: 320 officers and men

Dimensions:
Displacement: 4082 tonnes (4500 tons)
Length: 84 m (275 ft); **Beam:** 11.8 m (38.6 ft);
  Draught: 6.7 m (22 ft)

Powerplant:
Propulsion: steam
Speed: 9 knots

Armament & Armour:
Armament: 2 x 5-kg (12-lb) howitzers; 2 x 178-mm (7-in) rifles;
  2 x 152-mm (6-in) rifles; 6 x 229-mm (9-in) smoothbores
Armour: Double iron plating, 51-mm (2-in) thick

ARMAMENT

The battery consisted of four single-banded Brooke rifles and six 229-mm (9-in) Dahlgren smoothbore shell guns. Two of the rifles, bow and stern pivots, were 178-mm (7-in) weapons; the other two were 152-mm (6-in) rifles, one on each broadside.

FACTS

- Launched as the U.S. screw frigate *Merrimack* at Boston, 14 June, 1855.

- Burnt to prevent capture at Norfolk in 1861.

- Refloated by Confederate Navy and rebuilt as ironclad named *Virginia*; completed in February 1862.

- Engaged *Monitor* at Battle of Hampton Roads, 9 March, 1862; first engagement between ironclad warships.

- Run ashore and burnt by crew to prevent capture, James River, 11 May, 1862.

MACHINERY

The Confederates discovered that *Merrimack*'s single-shaft returning rod connecting engine was still intact and no plans were made to fit a new powerplant. However, *Merrimack*'s engine had not been very efficient to begin with, and struggled to cope with the *Virginia*, made much heavier by the addition of tons of armour and ballast.

ARMOUR

The deck was protected by iron plate 102-mm (4-in) thick. The casemate was a laminate of oak and pine, topped with two 51-mm (2-in) layers of iron plating laid perpendicular to each other, and angled to deflect shot hits.

The success of the *Merrimack/Virginia*, or at least the promise of it, blinded the Confederates to any type of warship other than the casemate ironclad, and many vessels of this type were placed under construction.

MERRIMACK

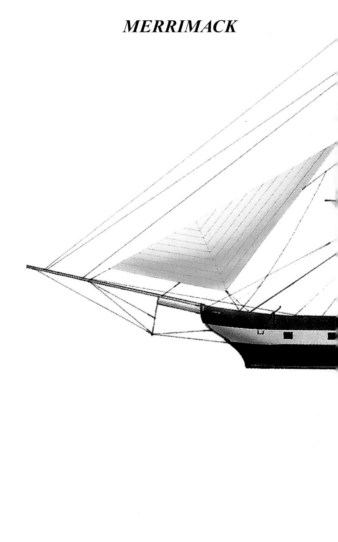

MERRIMACK

RIVAL: *MONITOR*

MERRIMACK

The rebuilding of the *Merrimack* gave the Confederate Navy a new type of fighting ship that promised to cancel out the Union's great superiority in conventional warships. Commissioned as *Virginia* in mid-February 1862, the ship's iron armour made her virtually invulnerable to contemporary gunfire. She carried 10 guns of her own, a 178-mm (7-in) pivot-mounted rifle at each end and a broadside battery of two 152-mm (6-in) rifles, and six 229-mm (9-in) smoothbores. Affixed to her bow was an iron ram, allowing the ship herself to be employed as a deadly weapon.

All the Confederate Navy's casemate ironclads were built in the southern ports, where they remained isolated. They were slow and non-seagoing. Many were never completed, while others lacked armour or were built with inefficient engines.

Virginia made her first combat sortie on 8 March, 1862, steaming down the Elizabeth River from Norfolk and into Hampton Roads. Accompanied by other warships, her mission was to break the blockade imposed by the Union Navy, which had deployed the large sloop-of-war *Cumberland* and the smaller *Congress*. In an historic action that dramatically demonstrated the superiority of armoured steam-powered warships over their wooden sailing counterparts, she rammed and sank the *Cumberland*, which broke off the *Virginia's* ram as she went down. The captain of the *Congress* ordered his ship to be beached in shallow water

Close-up

The Battle of Hampton Roads took place at a roadstead in Virginia where the Elizabeth and Nansemond rivers meet the James River just before it flows into Chesapeake Bay.

(1) **Flag:** The Confederate flag flies proudly from the *Virginia* at the Battle of Hampton Roads.

(2) **Virginia:** In action at Hampton Roads, which was arguably the most important naval engagement of the American Civil War in terms of future warship development.

(3) **Battle:** Amid the smoke of battle, *Monitor* and *Virginia* fought an inconclusive battle that lasted for approximately three hours.

(4) **Beached:** *Virginia* badly damaged the Union warship *Congress*, which was beached at the command of her captain.

(5) **Damage:** Shot from the grounded *Congress* and other warships riddled the *Virginia's* smokestack with holes and caused damage in other areas.

(6) **Turret:** *Monitor's* turret was steam trained, which meant that control was not highly precise.

In the aftermath of the Battle of Hampton Roads, the names Virginia *and* Merrimack *were used equally by both sides, as attested by the newspapers and correspondence of the day. This caused much confusion among later historians.*

and traded gunfire with *Virginia*, being eventually shelled into submission. In Washington, D.C., many of the Union Government's senior officials panicked, convinced that *Virginia* posed a grave threat to Union seapower and coastal cities. They were unaware that her serious operational limitations, caused by her deep draught, weak powerplant, and extremely poor seakeeping, essentially restricted her use to deep channels in calm, inland waterways.

Virginia did not emerge from the battle unscathed. As she was being shot at from *Cumberland* and *Congress*, shore-based Union troops riddled her smokestack. All of this combined to reduce her already low speed. Two of her guns were out of order, and a number of armour plates had been loosened. Nevertheless, she returned to Hampton Roads the next day to attack the grounded steam frigate *Minnesota*, which had run aground on a sandbank while trying to get away during the earlier action.

THREE-HOUR BATTLE

During the night, however, the ironclad Union ship *Monitor* had arrived and had taken a position to defend *Minnesota*. When *Virginia* approached, *Monitor* intercepted her. The two ironclads confronted each other in combat for about three hours, with neither able to inflict significant damage

on the other. The duel ended indecisively, *Virginia* returning to her home at the Gosport Navy Yard for repairs and strengthening, and *Monitor* turning back to her station defending *Minnesota*.

Over the next two months, the two ironclads kept each other in check. *Virginia*, having been repaired and strengthened at the Norfolk Navy Yard, re-entered the Hampton Roads area on 11 April and 8 May, but no further combat with the *Monitor* resulted. As the Confederates abandoned their positions in the Norfolk area, *Virginia* was threatened with the loss of her base. After a futile effort to lighten the ship enough to allow her to move up the James River, on 11 May the *Virginia* was destroyed by her crew off Craney Island, some 10 km (6 miles) from where she had fought her engagements of 8 and 9 March. *Virginia*'s wreck was largely removed between 1866 and 1876.

A TURNING POINT

There is no doubt this engagement – the first between two ironclad warships – inspired the world's navies to abandon the traditional pattern of wooden warship construction and concentrate instead on ironclad vessels. The *Virginia*'s success in sinking the *Cumberland* with her ram also persuaded navies to retain this feature as a viable weapon.

Alabama 1862

The naval engagements of the American Civil War were generally confined to the great rivers of the North American continent, but one Confederate ship achieved fame as a commerce raider. She was the *Alabama*, and she wrought havoc among the merchant shipping of the Union.

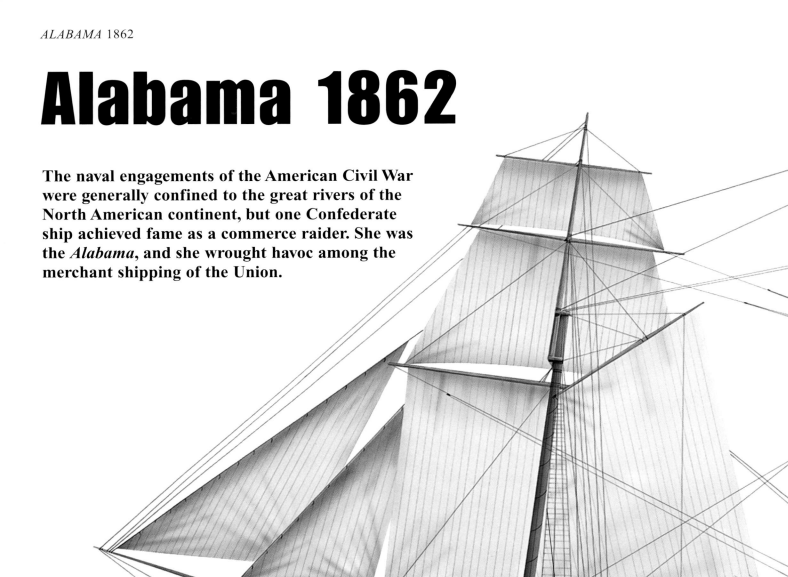

CREW
Alabama carried a complement of 145 officers and men. Eighty-three men originally signed on, many of them British, while others were recruited from friendly ports of call or from captured merchant vessels.

RIGGING
The ship was fitted with three masts, the foremast and mainmast being square-rigged and the mizzenmast rigged fore-and-aft.

MACHINERY
The *Alabama* was powered by both sail and a John Laird Sons and Company 224-kW (300-hp) steam engine, driving a single Griffiths-type, twin-bladed brass screw. With the screw retracted using the stern's brass lifting gear mechanism, *Alabama* could make up to 10 knots under sail alone and 13.25 knots when her sail and steam power were used together.

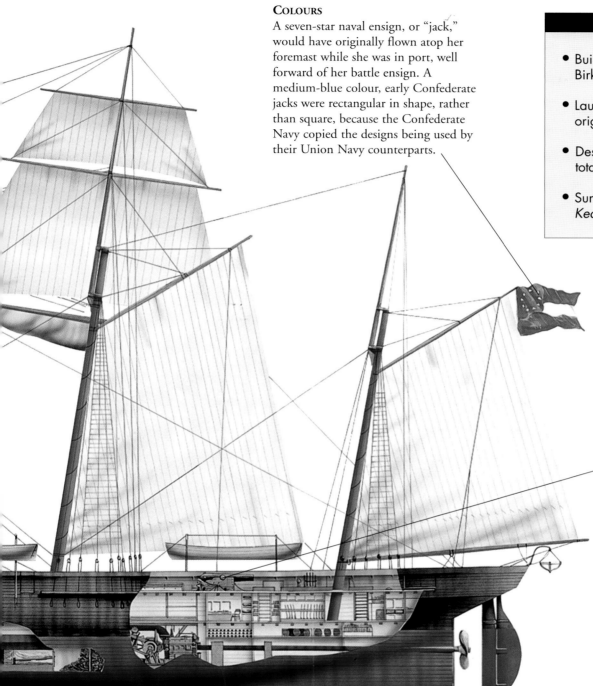

COLOURS
A seven-star naval ensign, or "jack," would have originally flown atop her foremast while she was in port, well forward of her battle ensign. A medium-blue colour, early Confederate jacks were rectangular in shape, rather than square, because the Confederate Navy copied the designs being used by their Union Navy counterparts.

F A C T S
• Built by John Laird and Sons of Birkenhead, England, 1862.
• Launched on 29 July, 1862, and originally named *Enrica*.
• Destroyed 69 Union vessels in total, mostly merchant ships.
• Sunk by the Union sloop *Kearsarge*, 19 June, 1864.

ARMAMENT
The British-made ordinance comprised six broadside 15-kg (32-lb) naval smoothbores and two larger and more powerful pivot cannons. Both pivot cannons were positioned roughly amidships along the deck's centreline, fore and aft of the main mast.

ALABAMA – SPECIFICATION

Country of origin: Confederate States of America
Type: Propeller sloop-of-war, commerce raider
Laid down: 1862
Builder: John Laird Sons and Company, Birkenhead, England
Launched: 29 July, 1862
Commissioned: 24 August, 1862
Decommissioned: 19 June, 1864
Fate: Sunk in battle

Complement: 145 officers and men

Dimensions:
Displacement: 952.5 tonnes (1050 tons)

Length: 67 m (220 ft)
Beam: 9.65 m (31 ft 8 in)
Draught: 5.38 m (17 ft 8 in)

Powerplant:
Propulsion: Steam engine
Installed power: 223.7 kW (300 hp)
Speed: 10 knots under sail alone and 13.25 knots with sail and steam power

Armament:
Armament: 6 x 15-kg (32-lb) cannons; 1 x 50-kg (110-lb) cannon; 1 x 31-kg (68-lb) cannon

The ship that sank the *Alabama* was the *Kearsarge*, a sloop of war built at Portsmouth Navy Yard in Kittery, Maine, under the 1861 American Civil War emergency shipbuilding programme. Commissioned in January 1862, she set about hunting Confederate commerce raiders in European waters. *Atlanta* and *Baltic* were other ironclads used by the Confederate States.

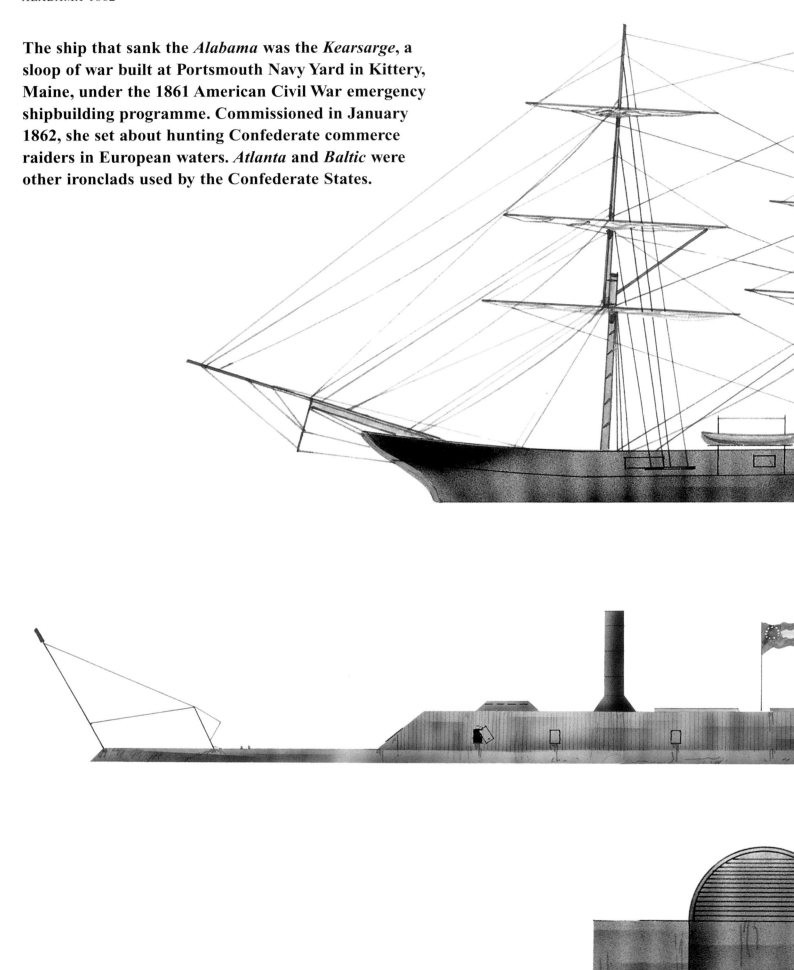

RIVAL: *KEARSARGE*

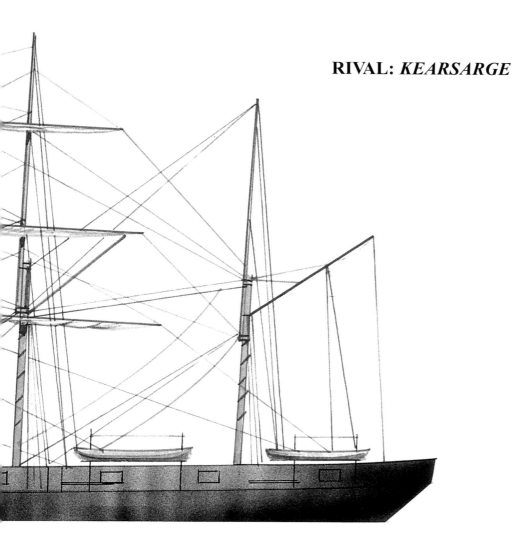

CONFEDERATE IRONCLAD: *ATLANTA*

CONFEDERATE IRONCLAD: *BALTIC*

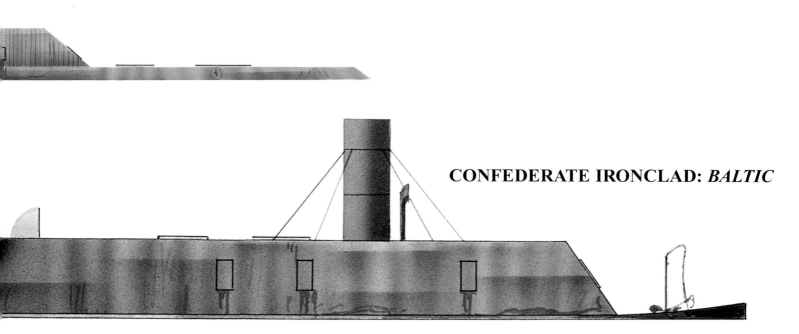

Alabama *was a well-proportioned ship, demonstrating the very best qualities of British shipbuilding. Few commerce raiders in naval history have proved so successful. She never laid anchor in a Confederate port during her two-year rampage.*

At *Alabama*'s commissioning ceremony on 24 August, 1862, Captain Raphael Semmes stood on a gun carriage and read out his orders from President Jefferson Davis, authorizing him to take command. The British colours were struck, and those of the Confederacy hoisted.

Under Captain Raphael Semmes, *Alabama* spent the next two months capturing and burning ships in the North Atlantic and intercepting American grain ships bound for Europe. Her second expedition took her to the eastern seaboard of North America, where she operated off Newfoundland and New England, ranging as far as Bermuda before heading for the Gulf of Mexico, where she made a much-needed rendezvous with her supply ship, *Agrippina*. After that she sailed for Texas in support of Confederate land forces near Galveston, where she began the year of 1863 by engaging and sinking the Union side-wheeler *Hatteras*.

Her most successful raiding venture took place between February and July, 1863, when she took 29 prizes off the coast of Brazil before crossing the Atlantic to Cape Town.

From South Africa she sailed for the East Indies, spending the next six months cruising for enemy shipping. While there, the formidable commerce raider destroyed seven more ships before redoubling the Cape of Good Hope and returning to Europe. After so much time at sea she was in a very shabby state, and badly in need of a refit. Apart from that, her crew needed a rest. Both were to be denied by events that were about to overtake her.

KEARSAGE CATCHES UP

On 11 June, 1864, *Alabama* arrived at Cherbourg, France, and Captain Semmes requested the permission of city officials to dock and overhaul his ship. Three days later, the sloop-of-war *Kearsarge*, which was commanded by Captain John Winslow and had been pursuing the raider, arrived off Cherbourg and began patrolling just outside of the harbour. On 19 June, *Alabama* sailed out of Cherbourg to engage *Kearsarge*. As *Kearsarge* turned to meet its opponent, *Alabama* opened fire. *Kearsarge*'s crew waited until the distance between both vessels closed to less than 900 m (1000 yards) before returning fire. According to survivors of the battle, the two ships steamed on opposite circular courses as each commander tried to cross the bow of his opponent to deliver a heavy raking fire. The battle quickly turned against *Alabama* owing to the poor quality of her powder and shells. By contrast, *Kearsarge* enjoyed the advantage of additional protection provided by chain cables along her sides.

SURRENDER AND ESCAPE

Approximately one hour after firing the first shot, *Alabama* had been reduced to a rapidly sinking hulk. According to witnesses, *Alabama* fired 150 rounds to the *Kearsarge*'s 100. When a shell fired by *Kearsarge* tore open a section of *Alabama*'s hull at the waterline, seawater quickly rushed into the cruiser and she began to sink. Semmes subsequently struck his colours and sent a boat to surrender to his opponent. Even though *Kearsarge*'s crew rescued most of the raider's survivors, the British yacht *Deerhound* picked up Semmes and 41 others who escaped to England. During her two-year career as a commerce raider, *Alabama* inflicted considerable disorder and devastation on United States merchant shipping all around the globe.

The wreck of the *Alabama* was located in 1984 by a French minehunter, and in 2002 a diving expedition recovered the ship's bell, along with some 300 other artefacts.

Close-up

Alabama was built in great secrecy by John Laird of Birkenhead, Merseyside. The deal was arranged between James Dunwoody Bulloch, a Confederate agent, and the Fraser Trenholm Company, cotton brokers with strong Confederate ties.

(1) **Officer:** *Alabama*'s officers donned full dress uniform and stood on the quarterdeck to take part in the commissioning ceremony.

(2) **Unarmoured:** A major contributory factor in *Alabama*'s downfall was that she was unarmoured, unlike the *Kearsarge*, which had chain cables strung along her sides.

(3) **Gun carriage:** Raphael Semmes mounted this gun carriage to read out his commission from Confederate President Jefferson Davis, authorizing him to take command of the ship.

(4) **Crew:** Semmes signed on 83 seamen, many of them British, for service in the Confederate Navy.

(5) **Arms:** *Alabama*'s British-made guns included six 15-kg (32-lb) smoothbore naval cannon and two larger pivot guns, one a 50-kg (100-lb) example with a rifled barrel.

(6) **Power:** *Alabama* was powered by both sail and a John Laird Sons and Company 224-kW (300-hp) steam engine, driving a single twin-bladed brass screw.

Victoria 1887

Victoria **was the first battleship to be fitted with vertical triple-expansion engines. She was originally named** *Renown***, but was renamed** *Victoria* **just before her launch in April 1887.**

DESIGN
The ship was nicknamed "the slipper" (or, when she was with her sister ship *Sans Pareil*, also attached to the Mediterranean squadron, "the pair of slippers") because of a tendency for her low forecastle to disappear from view in even a slightly rough sea.

SECONDARY ARMAMENT
Victoria's secondary armament comprised a single 254-mm (10-in) gun mounted close to the stern. Six 356-mm (14-in) torpedo tubes were also fitted.

VICTORIA – SPECIFICATION

Country of origin: United Kingdom
Type: Battleship
Laid down: 13 June, 1885
Builder: Armstrong Whitworth Elswick yard
Launched: 9 April, 1887
Commissioned: March 1890
Fate: Accidentally rammed and sunk, 22 June, 1893
Complement: 430, as flagship 583

Dimensions:
Displacement: 10,160 tonnes (11,200 tons)
Length: 100 m (340 ft)
Beam: 21 m (70 ft)

Draught: 8.15 m (26 ft 9 in)

Powerplant:
Installed power: 6000 kW (8000 ihp) (natural draught);
10,799 kW (14,482 ihp) (foced draught)
Propulsion: 2 x Humphreys & Tennant triple-expansion engines;
Speed: 16 knots (natural draught); 17.3 knots (forced draught)

Armament & Armour:
Armament: 2 x 413-mm (16.25-in) guns; 1 x 250-mm (10-in) gun; 12 x 150-mm (6-in) BL guns; 12 x 2.7-kg (6-lb) guns; 6 x 356-mm (14-in) torpedo tubes
Armour: 5.1–46 cm (2–18 in)

FUNNELS
Victoria and her sister ship, *Sans Pareil*, had tall twin funnels set side by side, creating a distinctive recognition feature.

ARMAMENT
The barrels of the 413-mm (16.25-in) main guns were so heavy that they drooped when installed on their mountings and could only fire 75 rounds before the barrels became excessively worn. If the guns were fired forwards, the blast buckled the deck.

FACTS

- Laid down by Armstrong as *Renown*, April 1885.

- Renamed *Victoria*, 18 March, 1887.

- Launched 9 April, 1887; completed March 1890.

- Went aground at Snipe Point, Platea, Greece, 29 January, 1892; refloated 4 February.

- Sunk in collision when rammed by battleship *Camperdown* off the coast of Syria, 22 June, 1893; 358 dead.

- Wreck located, 22 August, 2004.

ARMOUR
The main armour belt extended only along some 49.5 m (162 ft) of her total length of 104 m (340 ft) and varied in thickness from 406–457 mm (16–18 in). Contemporary French battleships had heavier armour, but *Victoria*'s guns could outrange them and she was faster.

MACHINERY
The triple-expansion steam engines were constructed by Humphrys, Tennant and Company of Deptford and had cylinders of 76 mm (3 in), 155 cm (61 in) and 240 cm (94 in).

Victoria was constructed at a time of innovation and development in ship design. The reason for changing her name from *Renown* to *Victoria* was to celebrate Queen Victoria's Golden Jubilee, which occurred in the year the battleship was launched.

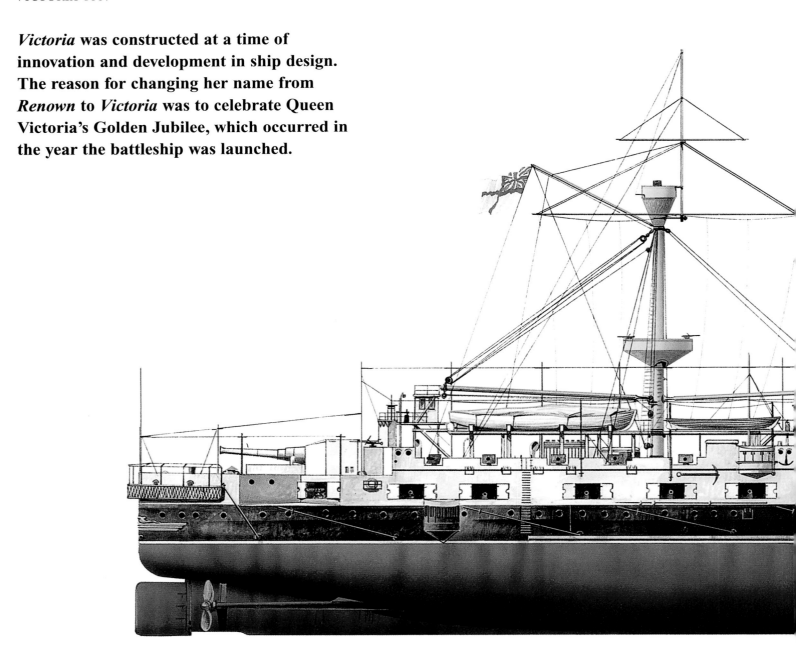

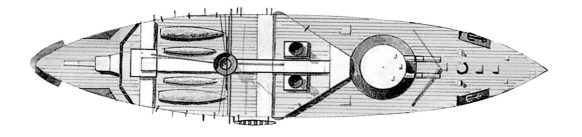

ENGINE

The installation of triple-expansion engines in *Victoria* and *Sans Pareil* was a bold step, and a sign that the British Admiralty was at last accepting innovation. A triple expansion engine works on the principle that if the steam does not fully expand in one cylinder, it can be exhausted into a second, larger cylinder to expand further and give up a greater part of its initial energy. In this way, an engine can be compounded for double or triple expansion, producing a great deal of power. Apart from her VTE engines, *Victoria* was the first Royal Navy vessel to have a steam turbine, which was used to power a dynamo.

In the late nineteenth century, the British Admiralty was concerned by the growing strength of the French and Italian navies, and so maintained a very strong naval presence in the Mediterranean.

The importance of the Mediterranean as a theatre of naval operations increased enormously after the opening of the Suez Canal in 1869, providing British commerce with a much faster passage to India than had been possible with the long haul around southern Africa. *Victoria* joined the Mediterranean Squadron in 1890, and in the following year became the flagship of Vice-Admiral Sir George Tryon.

On 29 January, 1892, *Victoria* ran aground at Snipe Point near Platea on the Greek coast while practicing torpedo attacks in relatively shallow water. The ship's bottom was damaged, and three compartments were flooded. After being

Close-up

Victoria was intended to be a great asset to the Royal Navy's Mediterranean Squadron, and her launch – in the year of Queen Victoria's Jubilee – was attended by considerable publicity.

1. **Funnel:** A distinctive feature of *Victoria* was her twin side-by-side funnel arrangement. This was abandoned in future warships.

2. **Armour:** *Victoria*'s main armour extended only along some 49 m (162 ft) of her total 103-m (340-ft) length, but the weight saving gave her greater range and speed.

3. **Forecastle:** She had a very low forecastle, which was usually awash in a high sea. This meant the main gun turret had to be fitted low down to improve stability.

4. **Gun Turret:** The huge main gun turret, with its 413-mm (16.25-in) guns, was chosen because guns of a similar caliber were being mounted in foreign warships.

5. **Bow:** *Victoria*'s bow had a traditional design. The whole vessel closely followed the design of her predecessor *Conqueror*.

6. **Model:** A detailed model of the ship was exhibited at the Royal Navy exhibition in 1892 and another, fashioned in silver, was given to Queen Victoria as a Jubilee gift.

Victoria's sister ship Sans Pareil, *seen here nearing completion, also served with the Mediterranean Squadron. She was paid off in 1904 and scrapped in 1907. She too was involved in a collision, sinking a schooner off Land's End in 1898.*

lightened, the ship was refloated on 4 February and sailed to Malta, where repair work was completed by May.

On 22 June, 1893, *Victoria* was on manoeuvres with eight battleships and three large cruisers off Tripoli, Syria. Admiral Tryon, in *Victoria*, led one column of six ships, and his deputy, Rear-Admiral Hastings Markham, led the other column of five ships in the battleship *Camperdown*. The plan was to execute a series of turning manoeuvres before the ships dropped anchor for the night, the whole process being watched by a large crowd onshore. The afternoon was fine and sunny, with excellent visibility.

STRATEGIC PLACING

The two lines of warships were 1100 m (1200 yards) apart, heading out to sea. Admiral Tyron's intention was to turn each pair of ships through 180 degrees, creating a stunning spectacle as they came to within 366 m (400 yards) of each other and proceeded towards the land. They would then turn 90 degrees to form one column, and anchor in unison.

The gap between the two columns was less than double the ships' minimum radius of turn, and the distance should have been widened in order to increase the safety margin, but Tryon gave no such order. Instead, he sent separate signals to each of the two columns: They were: "Second division alter course in succession 16 points to starboard preserving the order of the fleet," and "First division alter course in succession 16 points to port preserving the order of the fleet."

The columns turned towards each other, placing *Victoria* and *Camperdown* on a collision course. *Camperdown*'s ram sliced through the bow of *Victoria*. The ships locked together for a few minutes, and as *Camperdown* reversed and pulled clear, the water rushed into her. She capsized and went down in 12 minutes, taking 358 of her 715 crew with her. Admiral Tryon was not among the survivors.

WRECK DISCOVERY

Victoria went down vertically, her screws still turning. On 22 August, 2004, her wreck was located by a diving expedition after a search of eight years. The weight of her massive forward gun turret, and the fact that her screws were still turning as she entered her final plunge, had embedded her vertically, her nose deep in the mud, in 150 m (490 ft) of water.

Maine 1890

Legislation authorizing the foundation of a new U.S. Navy was only passed in 1883, and progress was slow. The first two American battleships, the *Texas* and *Maine* of 1888, were little more than armoured cruisers. Both were based on foreign designs.

MACHINERY
Power was provided by two Quintard vertical triple-expansion engines, with eight cylindrical boilers. These gave her a maximum speed of 17 knots.

BUNKERS
The coal bunkers were placed around the perimeter of the hull in the belief that this would afford extra protection, the magazines being positioned inboard of the bunkers.

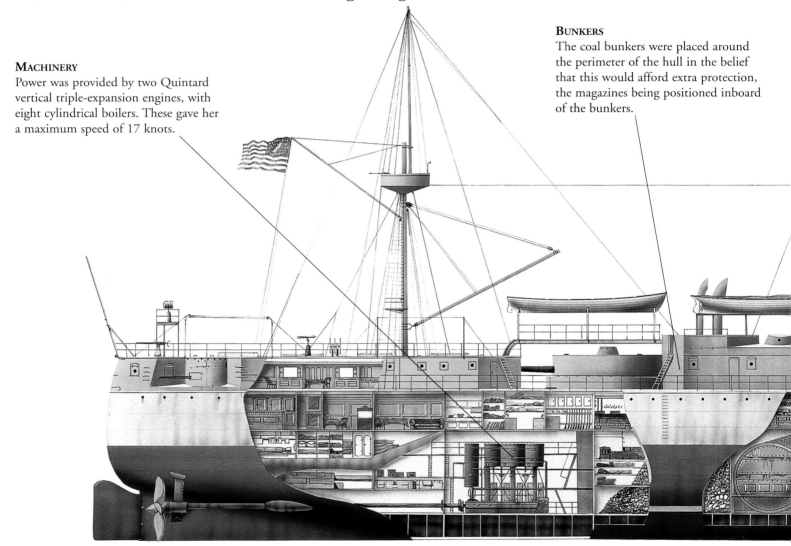

MAINE – SPECIFICATION

Country of origin: USA
Type: Pre-dreadnought battleship
Laid down: 17 October, 1888
Builder: New York Naval Shipyard, Brooklyn, New York
Launched: 18 November, 1890
Commissioned: 17 September, 1895
Status: Remains scuttled in the Strait of Florida, 16 March, 1912
Complement: 374 officers and men

Dimensions:
Displacement: 6159 tonnes (6789 tons)
Length: 98.86 m (324 ft 4 in)
Beam: 17 m (57 ft)

Draught: 6.86 m (22 ft 6 in)

Powerplant:
Installed power: 6930 kW (9293 hp)
Propulsion: 2 shafts, 2 x vertical triple-expansion steam engines, 8 boilers
Speed: 17 knots
Range: 6670 km (3600 nm) at 10 knots

Armament & Armour:
Armament: 4 x 254-mm (10-in) guns; 6 x 152-mm (6-in) guns
Armour: 51–305 mm (2–12 in)

ARMAMENT

Maine and *Texas* were unusual in that their main armament was mounted *en echelon*, which meant it projected off to either side, severely limiting their ability to fire a broadside.

ARMOUR

Maine's armour belt was 55 m (180 ft) long and 152–279 mm (6–11 in) thick. The turrets were protected by 203 mm (8 in) and the barbettes by 305 mm (12 in). The deck carried 51–102 mm (2–4 in) of armour plating.

FACTS

- Launched 18 November, 1890; completed 1895.

- North Atlantic, 1895–98.

- Destroyed by gas explosion in Havana harbour, 260 dead, 1898.

- Hulk refloated and sunk at sea, February 1912.

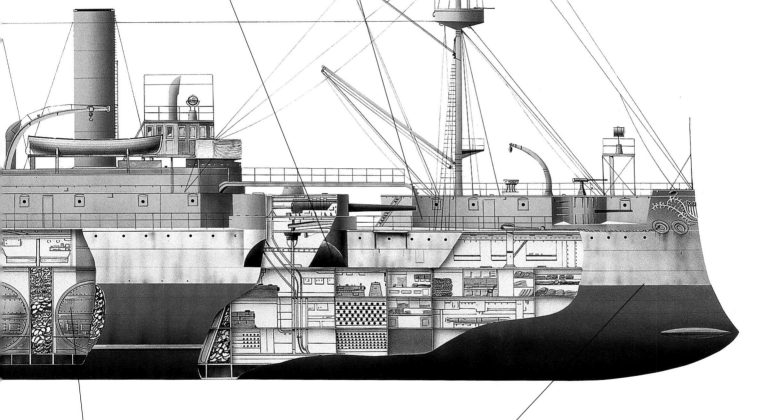

ENDURANCE

Maine's coal capacity was 895 tons, which meant that she could not spend lengthy periods at sea. It also meant that she could not operate at high speed for any length of time, as coal consumption increased dramatically in these circumstances.

HULL

When *Maine* was completed and fully fitted out, it was found that the bow section had a draft 1 m (3 ft) deeper than the stern. This was caused not by a fault in the design, but a mistake in the loading plan. As a result, 43.5 tonnes (48 tons) of ballast had to be loaded near the stern, resulting in unplanned extra weight.

There have been four major investigations into the sinking of the *Maine* since 1898. Even today, experts cannot agree whether the explosion was caused by a mine or by spontaneous combustion in a coal bunker.

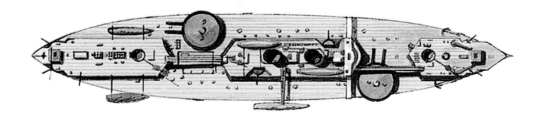

MAINE

The *Maine* arrived at Havana on 25 January, 1898. The Spanish authorities in Havana were wary of American intentions, but they afforded Captain Charles Sigsbee and the officers of *Maine* every courtesy. In order to avoid the possibility of trouble, *Maine*'s commanding officer did not allow his enlisted men to go on shore. Sigsbee and the consul at Havana, Fitzhugh Lee, reported that the Navy's presence appeared to have a calming effect on the situation, and both recommended that the Navy Department send another battleship to Havana when it came time to relieve the *Maine*. Events were to take a very different turn.

Maine *was the U.S. Navy's first battleship. Following her destruction, a second* Maine, *designated BB-10, was laid down in 1899, and served until 1920. A third* Maine *was ordered in 1940, but was cancelled.*

The *Maine* and the *Texas* were the U.S. Navy's first true battleships. However, they were second-class vessels that would not have been a match for any capital ships built by any other major maritime power during this period.

In the United States, support for the building of new, modern warships was rather feeble in the latter half of the nineteenth century. Despite the success of the Union's ironclad warships in the Civil War, after the conflict ended interest in the navy waned, and monitors for coastal defence were thought to be the only necessary warships. No money was made available for building new ships, and new vessels, including five monitors, were surreptitiously built using funds provided for repairing old ones. It was not until 1883 that legislation was

passed for the building of a "New Navy," its first vessels to be based on foreign designs. What may be described as the "monitor mentality" was still strong, however, and the first of the new vessels, the *Indiana* class, were completed as coast defence battleships with low freeboard.

MAINE'S CAREER
The *Maine* spent her active career operating along the East Coast of the United States and the Caribbean. In January 1898, she deployed from Key West, Florida, to Havana, Cuba, to protect U.S. interests during a local insurrection and civil disturbances. Three weeks later, on 15 February at 2140, an explosion on board the warship occurred in the Havana Harbour. Later investigations revealed that more than 5 tonnes (5.1 tons) of powder charges for the vessel's 152- and 254-mm (6- and 10-in) guns had detonated, virtually obliterating the forward third of the ship.

The remaining wreckage rapidly settled to the bottom of the harbour. Most of the crew of the *Maine* were sleeping or resting in the enlisted quarters in the forwards part of the ship when the explosion occurred. As a result of the explosion, or shortly thereafter, 236 men lost their lives, and eight more died later from injuries. Captain Charles Sigsbee and most of the officers survived because their quarters were in the aft portion of the ship. Altogether, there were only 89 survivors, 18 of whom were officers. On 28 March, the U.S. Naval Court of Inquiry in Key West declared that a naval mine had been the cause of the explosion.

The destruction of the *Maine* was a major contributory factor in the outbreak of the Spanish-American War in April 1898. The belief that a mine had caused the disaster was seen as provocation to go to war. A subsequent investigation of the wreck in 1911, when bottom hull plates around the forwards reserve magazine were found to have been bent inwards and back, seemed to confirm the theory that a mine had been responsible, and it was not until decades later that this explanation was seriously challenged. Another theory was advanced in 1976, suggesting that the fatal explosion had been caused by the spontaneous explosion of coal dust.

Interior view

The captain's cabin on the *Maine* was spacious. Access to it was through a door leading from a kind of lobby, which was called the "Captain's Flat."

1. **Personal possessions:** The captain's possessions were confined to a few books, manuals, and personal photographs.

2. **Furniture:** The cabin was made a little brighter by a chintz-covered table and an armchair or two. This was the captain's office when the ship was in harbour.

3. **Air:** Two or three scuttles – portholes – provided light and air. The captain was able to enjoy the benefit of these as his cabin was clear of the armour belt.

4. **Enamel:** The cabin had lots of white enamel. The deckhead above was of rough, white-painted cork to prevent sweating.

5. **Corticene:** The deck of the cabin was gleaming with shellacked corticene, a cork-like material that prevented slipping.

6. On active duty the captain would use his sea cabin, up on the bridge, ready at hand if his presence there was necessary.

Shikishima 1898

The *Shikishima* class pre-dreadnought battleships were built in the United Kingdom for the Imperial Japanese Navy and were based on the British *Majestic* class. There were two vessels, the other being the *Hatsuse*.

ARMAMENT
The main armament of 305-mm (12-in) guns was mounted in twin gun turrets fore and aft. The secondary armament of 14 quick-firing 152-mm (6-in) guns was mainly intended to counter torpedo-boat attacks.

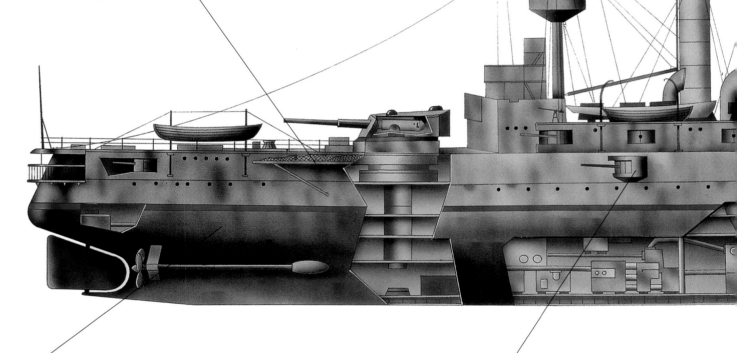

HULL
The ship was built on the bracket frame system, with the wing passages being used for extra bunkerage. There was a double bottom amidships and the vessel had a total of 261 underwater compartments.

ARMOUR
Shikishima was fitted with a new type of armoured deck. Instead of resting flat on top of the armoured belt, it sloped up from the bottom of the belt, increasing vertical protection. Any shell penetrating the main belt would also have to pass through the slope of the deck before reaching the machinery spaces.

FUNNELS
Unlike the side-by-side funnel arrangement of the
Royal Navy's *Majestic*-class battleships, on which she
was based, *Shikishima* had three funnels arranged in
more orthodox fashion along the centreline.

MACHINERY
The engines in the *Shikishima*-class vessels were
triple-expansion steam engines with 25 Belleville
water tube boilers and two screws. The engines
produced 10,810 kW (14,500 shp), yielding a
design speed of 17 knots. In trials *Shikishima*
achieved 18.7 knots.

TORPEDOES
The *Shikishima* class was fitted
with five Whitehead torpedo
tubes, four tubes being below
the waterline and the fifth
mounted on deck.

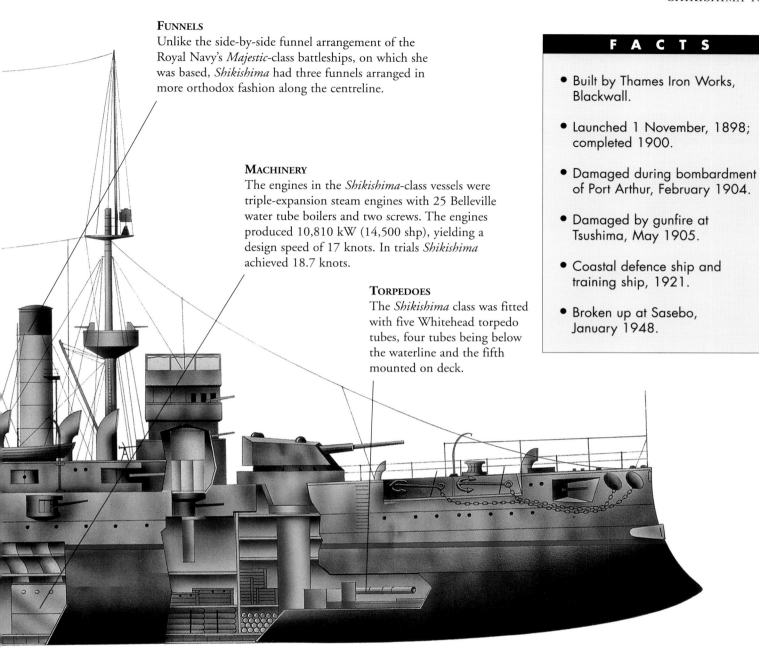

FACTS

- Built by Thames Iron Works, Blackwall.

- Launched 1 November, 1898; completed 1900.

- Damaged during bombardment of Port Arthur, February 1904.

- Damaged by gunfire at Tsushima, May 1905.

- Coastal defence ship and training ship, 1921.

- Broken up at Sasebo, January 1948.

SHIKISHIMA – SPECIFICATION

Country of origin: Japan
Type: Pre-dreadnought battleship
Laid down: 29 March, 1897
Builder: Thames Iron Works, Leamouth, London
Launched: 1 November, 1898
Commissioned: 26 January, 1900
Decommissioned: 1923
Fate: Scrapped 1948
Complement: 836

Dimensions:
Displacement: 14,018 tonnes (15,453 tons)
Length: 126.5 m (415 ft)
Length (overall): 135 m (442.9 ft)
Beam: 135 m (442.9 ft)
Draught: 8.29 m (27.2 ft)

Powerplant:
Propulsion: Two shaft Reciprocating VTE steam engine;
  25 Belleville boilers; 10,810 kW (14,500 shp)
Speed: 17 knots
Range: 13,000 km (7000 nm) @ 10 knots

Armament & Armour:
Armament: 4 x 305-mm (12-in) guns;
14 x 152-mm (6-in) QF guns;
20 x 1.3-kg (3-lb) guns;
12 x 1.13-kg (2.5-lb) guns;
5 x 457-mm (18-in) torpedo tubes;
2 x 76-mm (3-in) anti-aircraft guns added 1917
Armour: 50–360 mm (1.97–14.17 in)

The name *Shikishima* means "the outspread isles," which was an ancient name for Japan. The name of the second vessel in the class, *Hatsuse*, means "new tide." They were the first modern battleships of the Imperial Japanese Navy. *Asahi*, *Fuji* and *Mikasa* are other Japanese battleships of the same era.

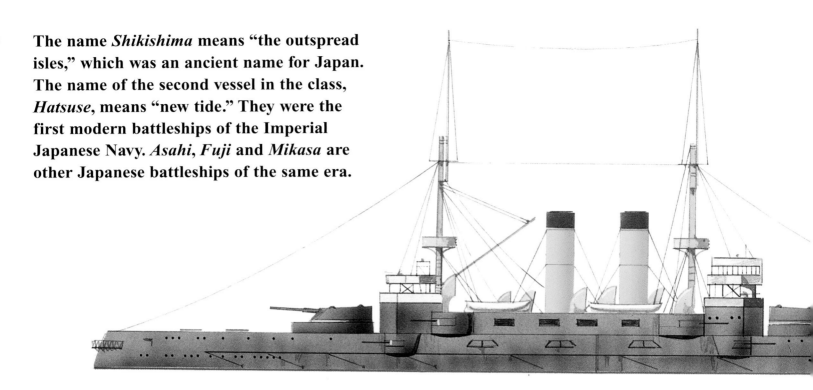

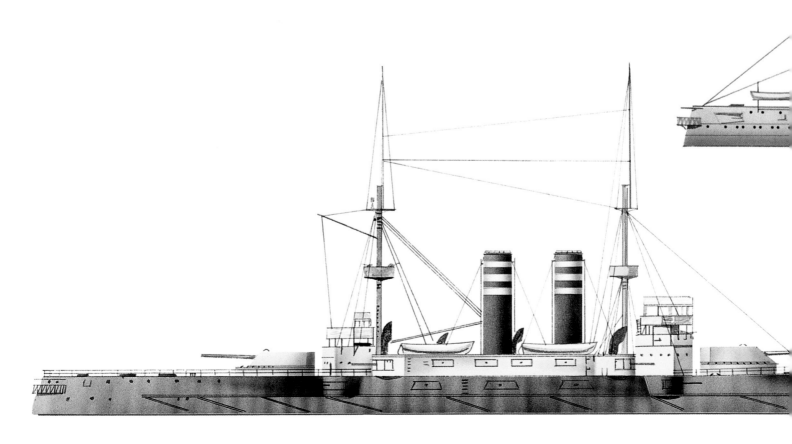

JAPANESE BATTLESHIP: *ASAHI*

JAPANESE BATTLESHIP: *FUJI*

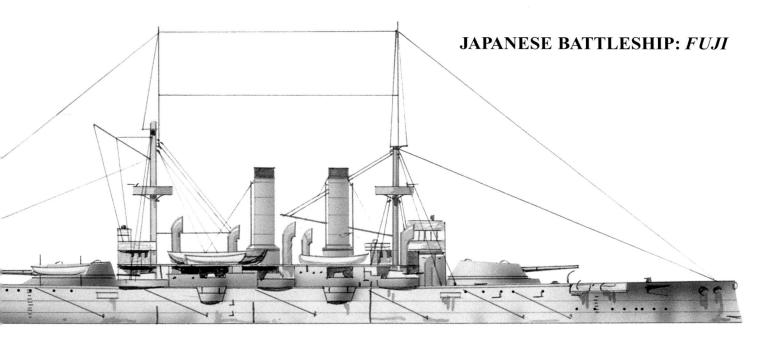

JAPANESE BATTLESHIP: *MIKASA*

MODERNIZING THE JAPANESE NAVY

The modern Japanese Navy began with the construction of the ironclad *Fuso* and two armoured corvettes in 1875. They joined the Confederate ironclad ram *Stonewall*, acquired after the American Civil War. These ships, and the acquisition of some modern cruisers, enabled Japan to inflict a decisive defeat on China's obsolete warships in the Battle of the Yalu River, which took place in 1894. In a bid to modernize the navy still further, Japan turned to British shipyards for the construction of *Shikishima* and *Hatsuse*, and British naval influence would remain strong for the next two decades.

Commissioned in January 1900, *Shikishima* went on to serve with distinction in Japan's naval battles of the early twentieth century. Unlike most other Japanese warships, she was still intact at the end of World War II. Her sister *Hatsuse*, however, suffered an early demise.

When the Japanese fleet was reorganized in 1903 *Hatsuse* became the flagship of the 1st Squadron, 1st Division of the Imperial Japanese Navy's First Fleet, under Rear Admiral Nashiba Tokioki. On 14 May, 1904, Admiral Nashiba put to sea with the battleships *Hatsuse* (flag), *Shikishima* and *Yashima*, the cruiser *Kasagi*, and the dispatch-vessel *Tatsuta* to relieve the Japanese blockading force that had held the Russian Far Eastern Squadron penned up inside Port Arthur since the beginning of the Russo-Japanese War. On the morning of 15 May he reached Encounter Rock and continued northwest until he was about 24 km (15 miles)

Close-up

Designed along the lines of the Royal Navy's *Majestic*-class pre-dreadnoughts, *Shikishima* was one of six battleships that formed the main Japanese line of battle in the Russo-Japanese War of 1904–05.

1 Compartments: *Shikishima* had a total of 261 watertight compartments.

2 Armament: The ship had a heavy armament of four 305-mm (12-in) guns mounted in twin turrets fore and aft, backed up by 14 152-mm (6-in) guns.

3 Flag: The flag flown is the national flag of Japan, known as the *Hinomaru* (sun disc), with the addition of sunrays. This was the ensign of the Imperial Navy.

4 Bridge: *Shikishima*'s capacious bridge gave the captain and his executive officers a commanding view of the surrounding area.

5 Deck: Instead of resting flat on top of the armoured belt, *Shikishima*'s deck sloped up from the bottom of the belt, increasing vertical protection.

6 Launch: Japanese capital ships were equipped with a motorized launch, an "Admiral's Barge" used to transfer key personnel to the flagship for conferences.

The Japanese pre-dreadnought battleship Shikishima *as she was depicted on a postcard of 1905. In 1920* Shikishima *was used as a support vessel to cover the landings of Japanese troops in Russia during Japan's intervention in Siberia during the Russian Civil War.*

off Port Arthur. From there the Japanese squadron set a north-easterly course on a patrol line across the mouth of the port. Unknown to Admiral Nashiba, he was sailing straight into a minefield sown previously by the Russian minelayer *Amur*. At 1050, *Hatsuse* struck a mine and began to heel over with her steering engine compartment flooded and her port main engines useless. Only minutes later, *Yashima* also struck a mine and began to sink. By 1130, *Kasagi* came alongside *Hatsuse* but the battleship's stern was mostly under water, and she was listing four degrees. A hawser passed from *Kasagi* was just being hauled in when *Hatsuse* struck another mine. Her funnels toppled, her mainmast broke off, her upper deck disintegrated, and within 90 seconds she had gone down. *Tatsuta* and *Kasagi* managed to save the admiral and Captain Nakao with 21 other officers and 313 men. However, 38 officers and 458 men went down with the ship.

DAMAGED AT TSUSHIMA

Hatsuse's sister ship, *Shikishima*, was damaged by fire from Russian shore batteries during operations at Port Arthur, but survived to take part in the great Russo-Japanese naval battle of Tsushima in 1905. *Shikishima* was an early casualty there,

however, and was hit several times by the opening Russian salvoes at a range of 8230 m (9000 yards).

After being repaired, she was withdrawn from first-line service, having been rendered obsolete by the new dreadnought battleships that Japan was bringing into service. Based on Sasebo, she was assigned the secondary duty of patrolling the East China Sea. *Shikishima* served in Japanese home waters during World War I, and was damaged by a boiler explosion in July 1916, suffering further damage in a similar incident almost exactly a year later.

REFITTED AND DISARMED

In 1919 *Shikishima* was used as a support vessel, covering the landing of Japanese troops in Siberia as an intervention force during the Russian Civil War. In 1921 she underwent a refit, after which she was de-rated to Coastal Defence ship and training vessel. After 1923, disarmed under the terms of the Washington Naval Treaty, she was used as a depot and training ship for submarine crews. She was stricken in 1926, but remained at her moorings in Sasebo as a training vessel and floating barracks. *Shikishima* was still there at the end of World War II, and was broken up at the Sasebo Naval Arsenal in 1948.

Dreadnought 1906

Dreadnought was the first battleship to feature a main armament of a single calibre. Her appearance initiated a naval arms race that was to reach global proportions by the onset of World War I in 1914.

COMPARTMENTS

Another major innovation was the elimination of longitudinal passageways between compartments below the main deck level. Connected compartments had been found to be a cause of weakness.

MACHINERY

Dreadnought was the first capital ship to be powered by steam turbines instead of the old triple-expansion engines, making her the fastest battleship in the world at the time of her completion.

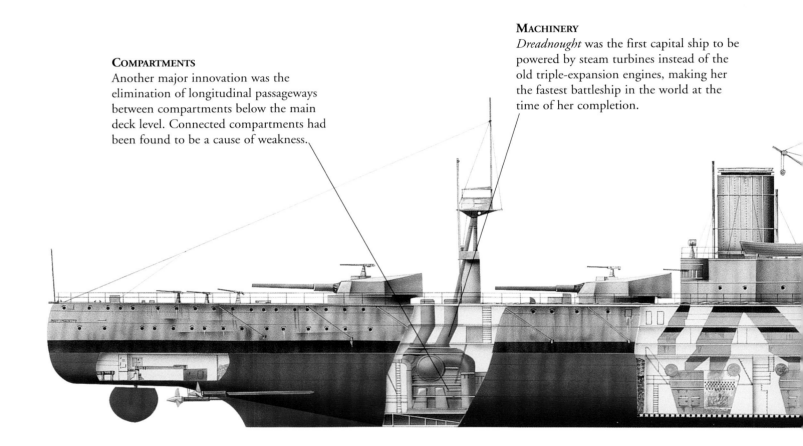

DREADNOUGHT – SPECIFICATION

Country of origin: United Kingdom
Type: Dreadnought
Laid down: 2 October, 1905
Builder: HM Dockyard, Portsmouth
Launched: 10 February, 1906
Commissioned: 2 December, 1906
Decommissioned: 1919
Fate: Scrapped 1923
Complement: 695–773

Dimensions:
Displacement: 16,710 tonnes (18,420 tons)
Length: 161 m (527 ft)
Beam: 25 m (82 ft)
Draught: 7.9 m (26 ft)

Powerplant:
Propulsion: 18 Babcock & Wilcox 3-drum water-tube boilers;

Parsons direct drive steam turbines; 17 MW (22,500 shp) on four shafts
Speed: 21 knots
Range: 816/2630 tonnes (900/2900 tons) coal, 1016 tonnes (1120 tons) oil
12,260 km (6620 nmi) at 10 knots
9090 km (4910 nmi) at 18.4 knots

Armour & Armament:
Armament: 10 x BL 305-mm (12-in) Mk X guns, 5 twin B Mk.VIII turrets (one forwards, two aft, two wing);
27 x 5.4-kg (12-lb) 18 cwt L/50 Mk.I guns, single mountings P Mk.IV;
5 x 457-mm (18-in) torpedo tubes (submerged);
Armour: 65–280 mm (2.5–11 in)

MAST
The tripod mast, which carried the fire control platform, was situated immediately behind the forward funnel so that the platform became very hot and filled with smoke when the ship was travelling at speed, making it virtually useless. This and other design flaws were later corrected.

GUNNERY CONTROL
Instead of relying on voice pipes to transmit commands to the gun turrets, *Dreadnought* was fitted with electronic instruments for transmitting range and other data.

FACTS

- Launched 10 February, 1906; completed 3 October, same year.

- Served with the Grand Fleet, 1914–16.

- Rammed and sank U29 in North Sea, 18 March, 1915.

- Sold in 1921 and broken up at Inverkeithing, 1923.

ACCOMMODATION
Sailing ships were controlled from the aft part of the ship, and officers were customarily housed aft. *Dreadnought* reversed the old arrangement, housing officers in the forward part of the ship and enlisted men aft, so that both were closer to their action stations.

ARMAMENT
The use of guns of a uniform calibre made it much easier to adjust the fall of shot in action. All the shells had the same ballistic characteristics, so they would fall simultaneously in a cluster around the point of aim, whereas shells fired by mixed batteries had different flight times and tended to arrive sporadically.

Once the concept of the dreadnought had been proven, construction of this revolutionary type of battleship proceeded rapidly, at the rate of three or four a year. As a result, by 1913, 31 more were either in service or due to be commissioned.

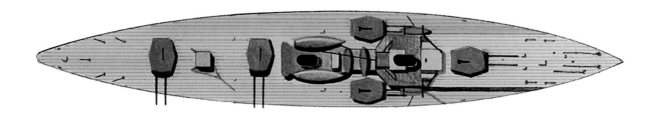

DREADNOUGHT

Critics claimed that the introduction of the dreadnoughts made the great mass of British battleships obsolete and vulnerable, but supporters of the concept had come to realize that secondary armament was now of minor importance. The increasing range of torpedoes was making close-in actions dangerous. Gunnery experts understood that at the immense ranges – 12,810 m (14,000 yards) or more – now possible for 305-mm (12-in) guns – only the biggest guns would count. Effective ranging depended on the firing of salvoes of shells and of a greater number in the salvo, and a full salvo from a dreadnought meant that 3.85 tonnes (3.79 tons) of high explosive was on its way to the enemy almost 15 km (8 nm) away.

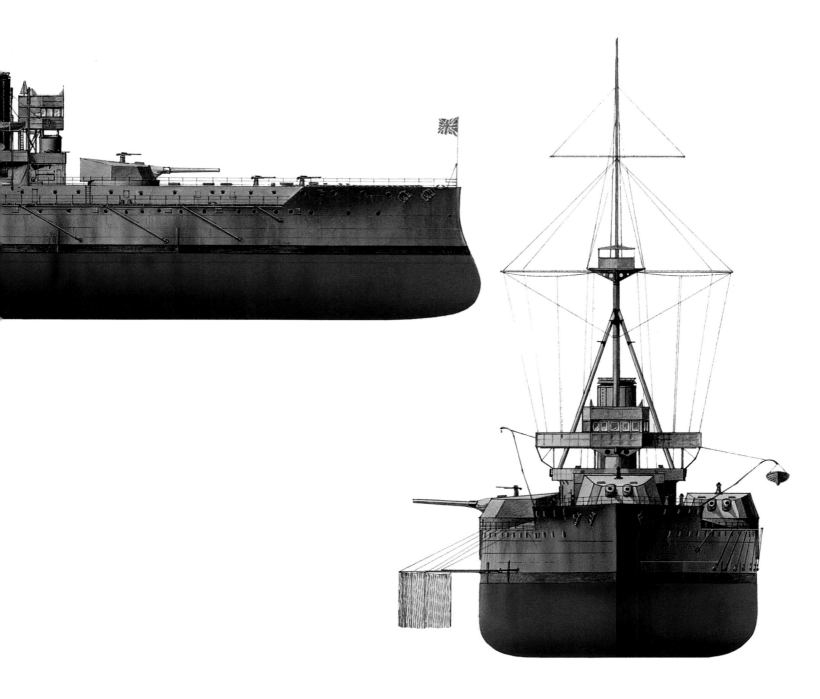

Dreadnought, *seen here in harbour, is readily distinguished by her massive tripod foremast. By 1916, however, she was considered too slow, and consequently did not see action in the Battle of Jutland.*

In the last two decades of the nineteenth century, supremacy on the high seas unquestionably rested with Great Britain. Unprecedented ideas and inventions were emerging so quickly that a new vessel could be rendered obsolete before it could even be launched.

Much of this problem was created by Britain's own naval policy, described as a "two-power standard," which kept the Royal Navy equal in numbers to any two foreign navies. In simple terms, warships were being built at too fast a rate to incorporate the latest technological advances.

In 1889, the two-power standard was modified somewhat when the Naval Defence Act came into force, decreeing that the Royal navy must be capable of matching the world's second- and third-largest navies. The result was a new phase of shipbuilding, and at its forefront was the *Royal Sovereign* class of battleship. A highly successful design, they were faster than any contemporary battleships.

In the 1890s the Royal Navy, closely followed by other major naval powers, developed a new standard type of battleship later known as the "pre-dreadnought." The first was the 12,548-tonne (13,831-ton) *Renown* of 1892, but it was the *Majestic* class of 1893–94 that served as the pattern for battleship design for the next decade. Displacing 15,129 tonnes (13,724 tons), they were armed with four 305-mm (12-in) guns, 16 76-mm (3-in) guns and 12 47-mm (1.85-in) guns, as well as five 457-mm (18-in) torpedo tubes. In all, 42 pre-dreadnoughts were built for the Royal Navy up to 1904.

BATTLESHIPS REVOLUTION

The true revolution in battleship design began with the appointment of Admiral Sir John Fisher as First Sea Lord in 1904. "Jackie" Fisher, as he was known throughout the Service, was a comparative rarity in the Royal Navy of the day in that he was a senior officer with a firm grasp of scientific and technological principles. By the time he took over as First Sea Lord at the age of 58, Fisher had already put a lot of consideration into the concept of a battleship armed with a maximum number of 254-mm (10-in) guns at the expense of secondary armament. Within weeks of his appointment in 1904, Fisher convened a committee to design a battleship armed with the maximum number of 305-mm (12-in) guns, which was the calibre that the Admiralty preferred. The committee was also meant to study a second type of warship, which would carry a battery of 305-mm (12-in) guns but which would have a speed of 24 knots or thereabouts. This vessel would be somewhat of a hybrid, in that it would be a cross between a heavy cruiser and a battleship. In other words, it was to be a battlecruiser.

"SUPER BATTLESHIP"

The concept of a "super battleship" took shape rapidly, its development spurred on by the acceleration of the international naval arms race, and a prototype was laid down by Portsmouth Dockyard in October 1905. It was constructed in great secrecy and in record time, the vessel being ready for initial sea trials a year and a day later. The name given to the formidable new ship was *Dreadnought*. At one stroke, she swept away all previous concepts of battleship design, and launched naval strategy into an entirely new era.

Close-up

Dreadnought brought about a revolution in naval warship design, altering almost every aspect of the battleships of her day. She also initiated a naval arms race that would endure for decades.

(1) **Rear Mast: The rearmost of *Dreadnought*'s two masts supported communications and other essential equipment.**

(2) **Main Turret: *Dreadnought*'s massive main turrets were protected by 279 mm (11 in) of armour plating. Her design rendered all other battleships obsolete overnight.**

(3) **Armour: *Dreadnought*'s decks carried varying thicknesses of armour, ranging from 26–102 mm (1–4 in). Her armoured bulkheads were 203 mm (8 in) thick.**

(4) **Heavy Guns: From 1906 onwards a first-class battleship was defined as one capable of firing 10 heavy guns on either side.**

(5) **Secondary Armament: This was now of reduced importance, the development of the torpedo having made close-in engagements too dangerous.**

(6) **Turret guns: *Dreadnought* was revolutionary in that she was armed with 10 305-mm (12-in) guns, two in each of five turrets placed on the centreline.**

U9 1910

U9 was the lead boat of a class of four German submarines laid down in 1910, and the only one to survive World War I. She achieved some spectacular successes during her career under the command of Germany's first U-boat ace, Kapitänleutnant Otto Weddigen.

MACHINERY
U9 was powered by four Körting kerosene engines plus two electric motors. Range was 3334 km (1800 nm) at 14 knots on the surface, or 148 km (80 nm) at 5 knots submerged.

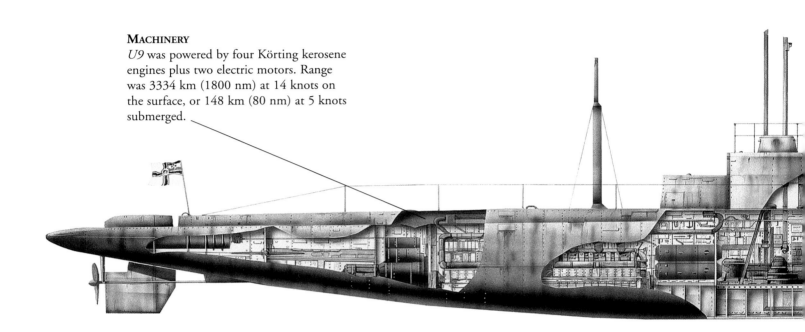

U9 – SPECIFICATION

Country of origin: Germany
Type: Submarine
Builder: Kaiserliche Werft, Danzig
Launched: 22 February, 1910
Commissioned: 18 April, 1910
Decommissioned: N/A
Fate: Surrendered 26 November, 1918;
    Broken up at Morecambe, UK, in 1919
Complement: 29

Dimensions:
Displacement (surfaced): 385.5 tonnes (425 tons)
Displacement (submerged): 545 tonnes (601 tons)
Length: 57.3 m (188 ft)
Beam: 6 m (19.7 ft)
Draught: 3.5 m (11.5 ft)

Powerplant:
Propulsion: Two-shaft kerosene engines/electric motors

Speed (surfaced): 14.2 knots
Speed (submerged): 8 knots
Range: 3334 km (1800 nm)

Armament:
4 x 457-mm (18-in) torpedo tubes (two bow, two stern; six torpedoes); 1 x 37-mm (1.45-in) deck gun

Service record
Part of: Kaiserliche Marine: I Flottille
Commanders:
    1 August, 1914–11 January, 1915: Otto Weddigen
    12 January, 1915–19 April, 1916: Johannes Spiess
Operations: 7
    1 August, 1914–7 July, 1915: I Flotilla
    7 July, 1915–19 April, 1916: Baltic Flotilla
    20 April, 1916–11 November, 1918: Training Flotilla
Victories: 14 ships sunk for a total of 8813 tonnes (9715 tons)
4 warships sunk for a total of 39,326 tonnes (43,350 tons)

BRIDGE
A small bridge was set on top of the conning tower, and a detachable rubber strip was mounted on stanchions along the deck to give crew protection when the boat was travelling on the surface.

TORPEDOES
The torpedo room was at the forward part of the cylindrical pressure hull. It contained two torpedo tubes and two reserve torpedoes. There were two further torpedo tubes in the stern.

FACTS

- Launched 1910 at Danzig.

- Sank the British cruisers *Hogue*, *Cressy*, and *Aboukir* off the Netherlands, 22 September, 1914.

- Sank the British cruiser *Hawke* in the North Sea, 15 October, 1914.

- Relegated to training duties, 1916.

- Surrendered 1918 and scrapped at Morecambe, UK, 1919.

CONNING TOWER
The conning tower was fitted with two periscopes, and also contained 24 levers for releasing air from the ballast tanks, electrical control gear for depth steering, a depth indicator, voice pipes, and the electrical torpedo-firing switches.

VENTILATION
The storage battery cells, which were located under the living spaces and filled with acid and distilled water, generated hydrogen gas on charge and discharge. This was drawn off through the ventilation system.

ACCOMMODATION
The officers' and warrant officers' accommodation was immediately aft of the torpedo room. This was separated from the main crew accommodation by a watertight bulkhead. Most of the crew slept in hammocks.

In 1914 Germany had not yet fully realized the potential of the submarine. However, as the war progressed so did the importance of the submarine arm, until in 1916 and later years it was the main offensive arm of the German Navy.

DEADLY SUBMARINES

Germany's submarines struck the first blow in the conflict that was to come, and proved how deadly submarines could be to unprotected surface shipping. Strangely enough, the German Naval Staff at the turn of the century failed to appreciate the potential of the submarine, and the first submarines built in Germany were three "Karp" class vessels ordered by the Imperial Russian Navy in 1904. Germany's first practical submarine, *U1*, was not completed until 1906. She was, however, one of the most successful and reliable of the time.

REPLACEMENT: *DEUTSCHLAND*

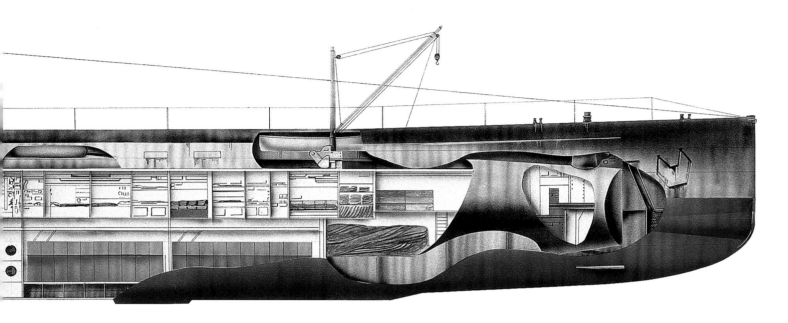

U9

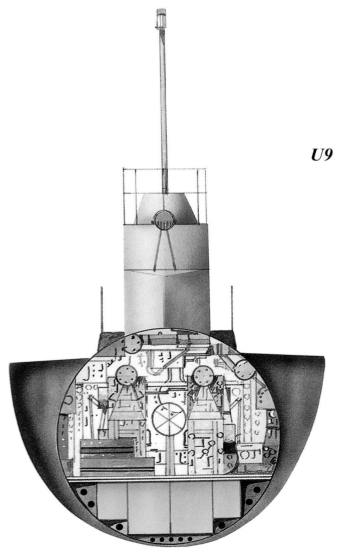

Although the Germans got away to a slow start in their submarine construction programme before World War I, from the start, the vessels were well engineered and used double hulls and twin screws. German engineers refused to install petrol engines in the early boats, preferring to use smellier but safer kerosene fuel. Diesel engines were used later on.

The *U9* was one of the first U-boats to set out on a war patrol on the outbreak of World War I, and it was not long before success came her way. On 22 September, 1914, she was patrolling south of the Dogger Bank when Otto Weddigen sighted three elderly cruisers of the British 7th Cruiser Squadron. They were the *Aboukir*, *Hogue*, and *Cressy*. A fourth cruiser had returned to port two days earlier for refuelling, while a force of destroyers, which should have been accompanying the cruisers, had become separated in heavy weather.

Close-up

In this German propaganda photograph, Captain Otto Weddigen and his officers are preparing to provide survivors of a sunken merchant ship with food and drink.

1. **Conning Tower:** This was the nerve centre of the boat, as its name implies, and was very difficult to spot because of its small size.

2. **Footholds:** Access to the U-boat's bridge could be gained from the deck by these footholds let into the side of the conning tower casing.

3. **Boathook:** The German sailor is using a boathook to pull the merchant vessel's lifeboat alongside.

4. **Supplies:** In general, Germany's U-boats were far better stocked with food and drink than their British counterparts

5. **Survivors:** Because there was no room for prisoners aboard a submarine, survivors were generally given food and drink, and then offered directions to the nearest land.

6. **Surface Warfare:** Most submarine actions in World War I were fought on the surface with gunfire.

The U9 *returns home after a successful war patrol. With the United States already on the side of the Allies, Germany announced on 31 January, 1917, that its U-boats would engage in unrestricted submarine warfare.*

The stormy weather had also forced Weddigen to take *U9* below the surface. His original mission had been to attack British transports at Ostend, but when he broke surface again and sighted the three cruisers he realized that this was too good a target to ignore.

THE SINKING OF *ABOUKIR*

At 0620 the *U9* fired a single torpedo at the nearest cruiser, *Aboukir*, hitting her on the starboard side, flooding the engine room, and forcing her to stop immediately. No submarines had been sighted, so *Aboukir*'s captain assumed that the warship had struck a mine and therefore ordered the other two cruisers to close in and help. Because of damage caused by the explosion and the failure of the steam winches needed to launch the lifeboats, only one got away. *Aboukir* capsized, and sank five minutes later.

Weddigen fired two more torpedoes at his next target, *Hogue*, from a range of only 270 m (886 ft). As the torpedoes left the submarine, her bows rose out of the water and she was spotted by the *Hogue*, which opened fire before Weddigen was able to dive again. Then his torpedoes struck the warship, which capsized and sank after 10 minutes.

At 0720 Weddigen launched two torpedoes from her stern tubes at *Cressy*. One missed, so he turned the boat and fired his one remaining bow tube from 500 m (550 yards). The stern tube torpedo struck *Cressy*'s starboard side, the other her port beam. She capsized and floated upside-down for some time before sinking.

In improving weather, rescue vessels picked up 837 men from the three British warships, but 1,459 lost their lives. Weddigen evaded British destroyers and escaped on the surface. His reputation was enhanced when, three weeks later, he sank the old cruiser *Hawke* off Aberdeen.

U29

In 1915, Weddigen, by now highly decorated, had been appointed to command a more modern submarine, designated *U29*. On 18 March, she was rammed and sunk off the Moray Firth, Scotland, by the battleship *Dreadnought*. There were no survivors.

The *U9*, having been withdrawn from first-line service and given a training role, survived the war and was surrendered to the British in November 1918. She was broken up at Morecambe in the following year.

Of her sisters, *U11* was mined and sunk in the Dover Straits on 12 December, 1914; *U12* was rammed and sunk in the North Sea by the destroyer *Ariel* on 10 March, 1915; and *U10* was mined and sunk in the Baltic on 27 May, 1916.

Lion 1910

The two vessels that constituted the *Lion* class warships of 1909–10, *Lion* and *Princess Royal*, were the first battlecruisers to surpass battleships in size. They had a number of deficiencies, the most glaring of which was that they were provided with inadequate protection against shells of a heavy calibre.

ARMOUR
The worst error in *Lion*'s construction was that she was provided with armoured protection against only 280-mm (11-in) shells, and then only in a limited area. The hull was totally vulnerable to 305-mm (12-in) missiles.

MACHINERY
The battlecruisers were fitted with four-shaft Parsons turbines, which gave a theoretical speed of more than 30 knots. In fact, neither ship was capable of 28 knots except by putting undue strain on the machinery.

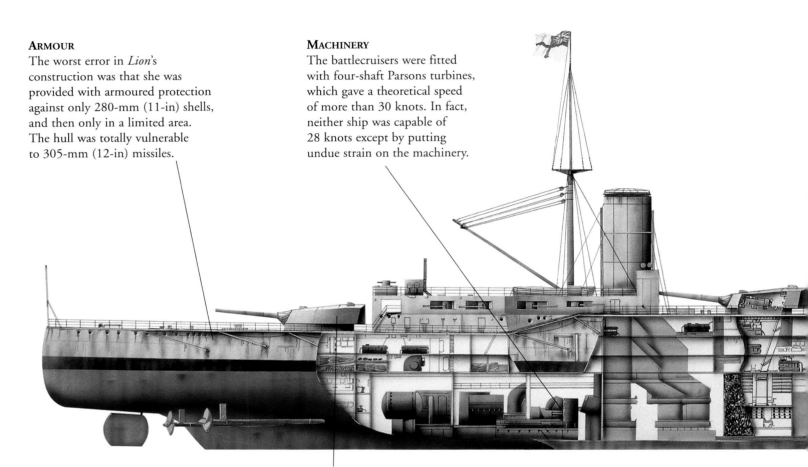

ARMAMENT
Instead of eliminating the cumbersome midships turret, the designers deleted the upper mounting of the aft superimposed guns, seriously restricting the arc of fire.

LION – SPECIFICATION

Country of origin: United Kingdom
Type: Battlecruiser
Laid down: 25 November, 1909
Builder: Devonport Dockyard
Launched: 6 August, 1910
Commissioned: 4 June, 1912
Decommissioned: 30 May, 1922
Fate: Sold for scrap 31 January, 1924
Complement: 1092

Dimensions:
Displacement (normal load):
 24,460 tonnes (26,690 tons)

Displacement (deep load):
 28,404 tonnes (31,310 tons)
Length: 210 m (700 ft); **Beam:**
 27 m (68 ft 8 in); **Draught:**
 9.9 m (32 ft 5 in) at deep load

Powerplant:
Propulsion: Four-shaft Parsons direct-drive steam turbines producing 52,199 kW (70,000 shp), 42 Yarrow boilers
Speed: 28 knots
Range: 10,390 km (5610 nm) at 10 knots

Armament & Armour:
Armament: 8 x 343-mm (13.5-in) BL Mk V guns; 16 x 102-mm (4-in) BL Mk VII guns; 2 x 530-mm (21-in) Mk II submerged torpedo tubes

Armour:
 Belt: 229–102 mm (9–4 in)
 Bulkheads: 102 mm (4 in)
 Barbettes: 229–203 mm (9–8 in)
 Turrets: 229 mm (9 in)
 Decks: 64 mm (2.5 in)
 Conning tower: 254 mm (10 in)

AIRCRAFT
By 1918, both ships had aircraft platforms on "Q" and "X" turrets.

SUPERSTRUCTURE
Lion was completed with the tripod mast aft of the fore funnel. It was moved forwards of the funnel after trials showed that the tripod became so hot personnel could not leave the fire control platform.

IMPROVEMENTS
As the war progressed the *Lion* and *Princess Royal* were improved to some degree, being fitted with – among other things – enclosed searchlight platforms and enlarged masthead platforms.

Lion was commissioned in June 1912 and joined
the 1st Cruiser Squadron, becoming its flagship
in July. In January 1913 she hoisted the flag of
Rear-Admiral Beatty, commanding the
1st Battlecruiser Squadron, and joined the
Grand Fleet in August 1914.

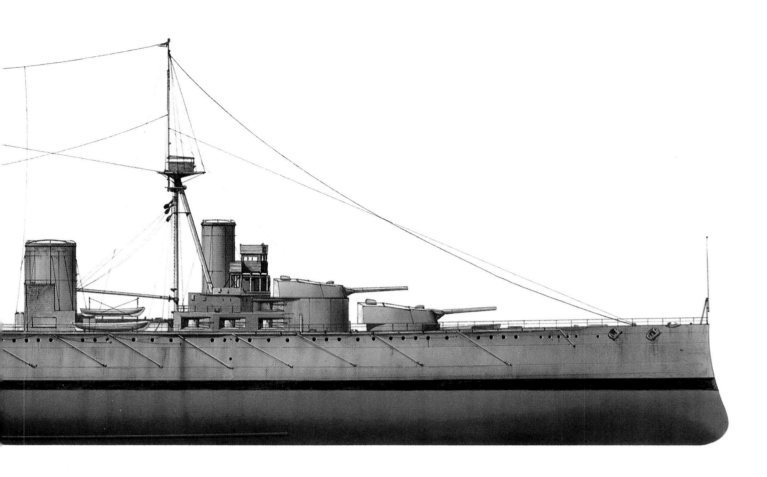

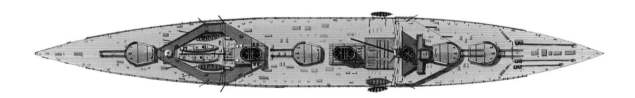

THE BATTLECRUISER

The concept of the battlecruiser arose from the simple fact that existing armoured cruisers had evolved into ships so large and expensive that they had reached the end of their development potential. The first ship of the new type was *Inflexible*, completed in 1908. Her firepower was four-fifths that of a dreadnought, but a great deal had to be sacrificed in the cause of speed. While the indicated horsepower of the *Dreadnought* was 18,000 (13422 kW), that of the *Inflexible* was 41,000 (30574 kW), so that a large hull was needed to contain the necessary 31 boilers. With a reduced armament, and protection sacrificed for speed, the battlecruisers were inevitably more vulnerable, as later events were to show.

British battlecruisers in line astern. This was a typical formation for capital ships about to engage in battle, from whence comes the term "ships of the line." The ships made an impressive sight, and blew up just as impressively at Jutland.

Lion's first major action of World War I was the Battle of the Dogger Bank, on 24 January, 1915, when the German Battlecruiser squadron put out of Wilhelmshaven to make an offensive sweep of the North Sea area.

Beatty's 1st Battlecruiser Squadron, comprising his flagship *Lion*, together with *Princess Royal*, *Tiger*, *New Zealand*, and *Indomitable*, sighted the German battlecruisers *Seydlitz*, *Moltke*, and *Derfflinger*, with the armoured cruiser *Blücher*, six light cruisers, and a number of destroyers, steering westwards. On sighting the British, the German warships turned and made for home, but were pursued at 28 knots and brought to battle at 0900 east of the Dogger Bank. *Lion* led the British line, but dropped out after she was hit, Beatty transferring his flag to *Princess Royal*. During the action *Blücher* was sunk and *Derfflinger* and *Seydlitz* seriously damaged. Great punishment might have been inflicted on the Germans but Beatty, thinking he had spotted a submarine's periscope, altered course, enabling the enemy to escape.

During the battle, *Lion* had expended 243 shells, but had scored only four hits. She herself was hit by 18 shells, suffering such serious damage that she had to be towed home by *Indomitable*. She was temporarily repaired at Rosyth, and after more permanent repair she returned to service as flagship of the newly formed Battle Cruiser Force (BCF).

THE BATTLE OF JUTLAND

On 31 May, 1916, she just escaped destruction at the Battle of Jutland. The British forces comprised the Battlecruiser Fleet (1st and 2nd Squadrons), with *Lion* (Admiral Beatty), *Princess Royal* (Admiral Brock), *Tiger*, *Queen Mary*, *New Zealand*, and *Indefatigable*, supported by the 5th Battle Squadron with the battleships *Barham*, *Warspite*, *Valiant*, and *Malaya*, in advance of the main battle fleet under Admiral Jellicoe. At 1420 British light forces scouting ahead of the Battlecruiser Fleet sighted German ships to the east–southeast and signalled the information to Admiral Beatty, who turned his ships south–southeast to intercept. Fifteen minutes later Beatty altered course again, making for heavy smoke that could be seen to the east–northeast.

Then began what was to be a very bad day indeed for the British battlecruisers. At 1548 both battlecruiser forces opened fire almost simultaneously at about 17,000 m (18,500 yards), the range being reduced to 14,600 m (16,000 yards) over the next 10 minutes or so. At 1606, *Indefatigable* was hit by a salvo from the *Von der Tann*. The battlecruiser's magazine exploded and a second salvo tore into the wreck, completing her destruction. She sank in minutes with the loss of 1017 lives. At 1630, there was a repeat of the earlier disaster when the battlecruiser *Queen Mary* took a direct hit from the German battlecruiser

Derfflinger and exploded. There were only nine survivors from her original crew of 1,266.

FATAL BLOWS

Lion herself was hit 12 times during an exchange of fire with the battlecruiser *Lützow*, one of whose shells started a fire in "Q" turret. Only an order to flood the magazine, issued by a fatally wounded Royal Marines officer, prevented a disaster. *Lion* suffered 99 dead in the action.

Lion remained on active service until 1923, being broken up at Blyth, Northumberland, in 1924.

Close-up

In this rather fanciful illustration, a British *Lion*-class battlecruiser comes under attack at Jutland. Battlecruiser losses at Jutland were heavy, leading to some design reconsiderations.

(1) **Ensign:** English naval ensigns were first used during the sixteenth century, and were often striped in green and white. Other colours were also used to show different squadrons.

(2) **Smoke Stacks:** Most capital ships of World War I had three smoke stacks, often reduced to two, or even one, during later years.

(3) **Armour:** The *Lion*-class battlecruisers carried eight 343-mm (13.5-in) guns and 16 102-mm (4-in) weapons.

(4) **Bridge:** The *Lion*-class battlecruisers were designed with state-of-the-art equipment, and that included the bridge, which featured the latest rangefinding gear.

(5) **Bow:** *Lion* had a typical "tumblehome" bow design. Later warships designs gave way to straight bows and then "clipper" bows.

(6) **Upper deck:** This was lightly armoured and was their most vulnerable aspect, being easily penetrated by plunging shot.

Derfflinger 1913

The battlecruiser *Derfflinger* and her sisters, *Hindenburg* and *Lutzöw*, were arguably the finest capital ships of their day, their design providing the basis for future German warships. *Derfflinger* was named after Field Marshal Baron Georg von Derfflinger (1606–95) of Brandenburg.

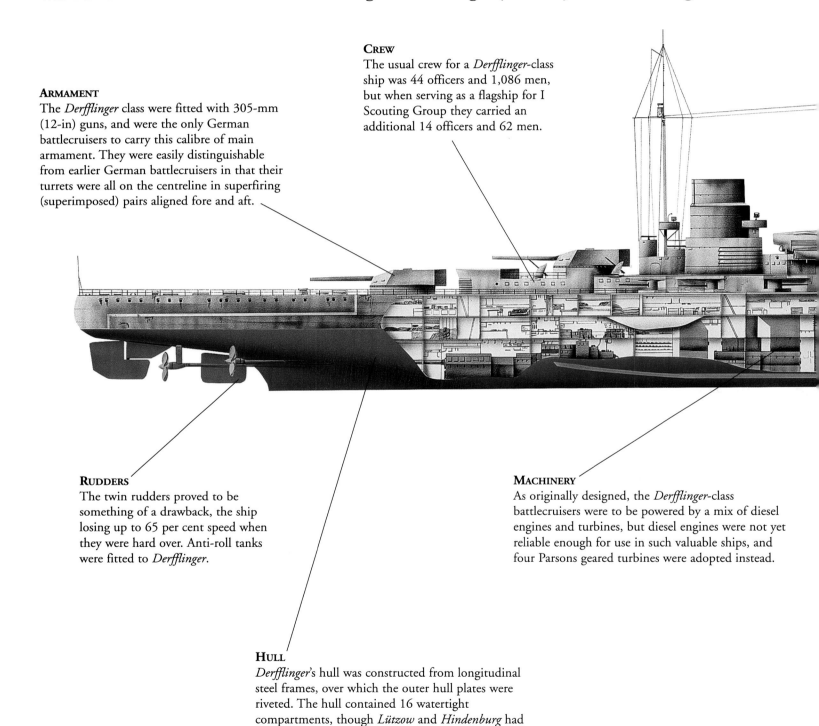

ARMAMENT
The *Derfflinger* class were fitted with 305-mm (12-in) guns, and were the only German battlecruisers to carry this calibre of main armament. They were easily distinguishable from earlier German battlecruisers in that their turrets were all on the centreline in superfiring (superimposed) pairs aligned fore and aft.

CREW
The usual crew for a *Derfflinger*-class ship was 44 officers and 1,086 men, but when serving as a flagship for I Scouting Group they carried an additional 14 officers and 62 men.

RUDDERS
The twin rudders proved to be something of a drawback, the ship losing up to 65 per cent speed when they were hard over. Anti-roll tanks were fitted to *Derfflinger*.

MACHINERY
As originally designed, the *Derfflinger*-class battlecruisers were to be powered by a mix of diesel engines and turbines, but diesel engines were not yet reliable enough for use in such valuable ships, and four Parsons geared turbines were adopted instead.

HULL
Derfflinger's hull was constructed from longitudinal steel frames, over which the outer hull plates were riveted. The hull contained 16 watertight compartments, though *Lützow* and *Hindenburg* had an additional seventeenth compartment.

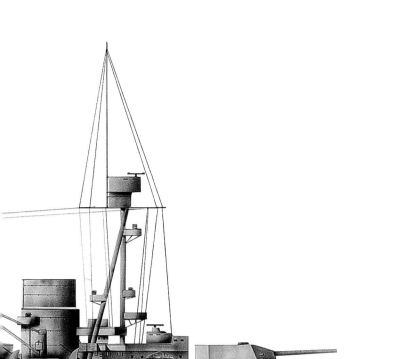

F A C T S

- Launched 12 July, 1913, completed September 1914.

- Bombarded Scarborough and Whitby, 16 December, 1914.

- Damaged in Battle of the Dogger Bank, 24 January, 1915.

- Bombarded Lowestoft and Great Yarmouth, 25 April, 1916.

- Severely damaged at Jutland, 31 May, 1916.

- Scuttled at Scapa Flow, 21 June, 1919.

- Refloated and broken up, 1934.

ARMOUR
In general, German battlecruisers were better protected than their British counterparts, but they did not sacrifice speed for armour. Their designers used lighter machinery and a lighter hull construction.

DERFFLINGER – SPECIFICATION

Country of origin: Germany
Type: Battlecruiser
Laid down: 30 March, 1912
Builder: Blohm & Voss, Hamburg
Launched: 17 July, 1913
Commissioned: 1 September, 1914
Fate: Scuttled in Scapa Flow on 21 June, 1919
Complement: 44 officers and 1,068 men

Dimensions:
Displacement (normal load): 26,180 tonnes (28,860 tons)
Displacement (full load): 31,200 tonnes (24,400 tons)
Length: 210 m (690 ft); **Beam:** 29 m (95 ft);

Draught: 9.2 m (30.2 ft)

Powerplant:
Propulsion: 4 shaft Parsons turbines; 18 boilers; 76,634 shp
Speed: 26.5 knots
Range: 10,371km (5600 nmi) at 12 knots

Armour & Armament:
Armour: 30–300 mm (1.2–12 in)
Armament: 8 x 305-mm (12-in) SK L/50 in 4 twin turrets;
12 x 150-mm (5.9-in) SK L/45 in 12 single turrets;
4 x 88-mm (3.5-in) in 4 single mounts; 4 x single 500-mm
(20-in) torpedo tubes

The Battle of Jutland, in which *Derfflinger* was
heavily engaged, marked the beginning of the
end for the German High Seas Fleet. This
formidable German force retreated to its main
base at Wilhelmshaven, and never ventured out
in strength again. The two ships shown here were
both involved in the Battle of Jutland.

GERMAN BATTLECRUISER: *MOLTKE*

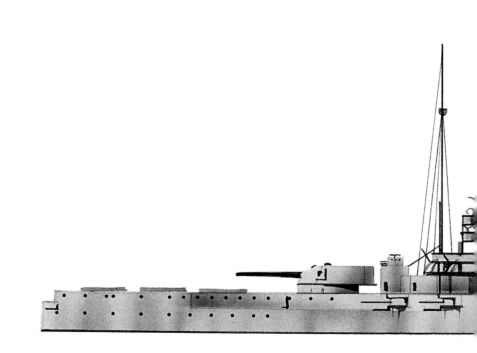

DERFFLINGER

Built by Blohm und Voss at their yard in Hamburg, *Derfflinger*'s keel was laid in January 1912. She was to have been launched on 14 June, 1913, but the wooden sledges upon which the ship rested became jammed and the ship moved only 30–40 cm (12–16 in). A second attempt was successful on 12 July, 1913. A crew composed of dockyard workers took the ship around the Skagen to Kiel. In late October, the vessel was assigned to the 1st Scouting Group, but damage to the ship's turbines during trials prevented her from joining the unit until 16 November.

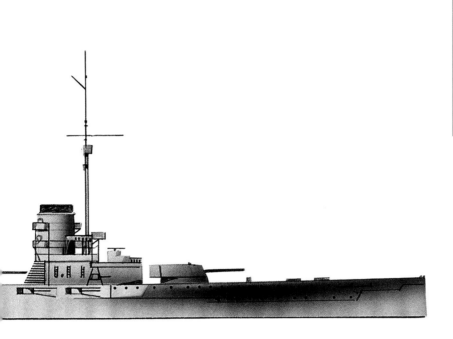

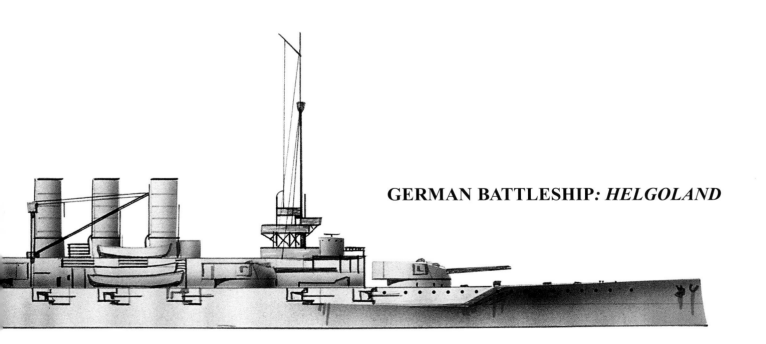

GERMAN BATTLESHIP: *HELGOLAND*

The raids on English coastal towns by *Derfflinger* and other units of the German Navy caused outrage among the British public. The attacks killed many innocent men, women, and children, giving rise to furious demands for revenge.

In the early morning of 16 December, 1914, the German battlecruisers *Seydlitz*, *Moltke*, and *Blücher* bombarded West Hartlepool, while *Derfflinger* and *Von der Tann* shelled Scarborough and Whitby, killing 127 civilians and injuring 567. *Moltke* and *Blücher* were hit by shore batteries but all the raiders escaped in the mist.

The Royal Navy's 1st Battlecruiser Squadron under Admiral Beatty and the 2nd Battle Squadron under Admiral Warrender were already at sea to intercept the attackers, which were sighted on their approach to the coast by British destroyers. At 0445 the latter were engaged by the German cruiser *Hamburg* and escorting light forces, which disabled the destroyer *Hardy* and damaged *Ambuscade* and *Lynx*. During the forenoon the German battlecruisers, returning from their attack, passed some miles astern of the 2nd Battle Squadron, which sighted the German ships and turned to close with them, only to be thwarted by bad weather and ambiguous signals from Beatty, which led to the light cruisers breaking off the chase. A golden opportunity was lost.

Close-up

Derfflinger suffered serious damage at the Battle of Jutland, but her armour enabled her to avoid the same fate as befell the British battlecruisers.

1. **Size:** *Derfflinger* was the largest and most powerful German battlecruiser of her time.

2. **Damage:** The battle scars inflicted on *Derfflinger* at Jutland are clearly visible in this photograph. Her stubborn resistance earned her the nickname "Iron Dog."

3. **Superstructure:** *Derfflinger's* superstructure was well designed, and set a trend for the construction of later battlecruisers.

4. **Derrick:** After she was repaired after the Battle of Jutland, *Derfflinger* carried out experiments with seaplanes, a derrick being mounted amidships.

5. **Hits:** *Derfflinger* took 21 shell hits at Jutland, with 157 of her crew killed. Many more were wounded, but managed to survive.

6. **Armour:** Four 88-mm (3.5-in) Flak guns were installed amidships. The ship also carried four 500-mm (20-in) submerged torpedo tubes.

Clouds of dense black smoke billow out over the sea as Derfflinger *fires a broadside. Her gunnery was extremely accurate, and reflected the high standard of training in the German Navy.*

Another opportunity was squandered on 24 January, 1915, when the Germans set out on an offensive sweep of the southeastern Dogger Bank. Decoded radio intercepts had given the British advance knowledge that a German raiding squadron was heading for Dogger Bank, so they dispatched their own naval forces to intercept it. The British found the Germans at the expected time and place; surprised, the smaller and slower German squadron fled for home. During a stern chase lasting several hours, the British slowly caught up with the Germans and engaged them with long-range gunfire. The British disabled the *Blücher*, at the rear of the German line, but the Germans put the British flagship (HMS *Lion*) out of action with heavy damage. Due to signalling errors, the remaining British ships broke off pursuit of the fleeing enemy force and returned to sink the crippled *Blücher*. By the time they had finished her off, the German squadron had escaped; all the remaining German vessels returned safely to harbour, though some, including the *Derfflinger*, had sustained heavy damage.

REPAIRED IN TIME FOR BATTLE

She was repaired in time to take part in the Battle of Jutland on 31 May, 1916, when she formed part of the German battlecruiser squadron, which also included *Lützow*, *Moltke*, *Seydlitz*, and *Von der Tann*. At 1630 that afternoon, the *Lion*-class battlecruiser *Queen Mary* took a direct hit from the *Derfflinger* and blew up with a tremendous explosion. There were only nine survivors out of her crew of 1266.

Later, *Derfflinger* was also to play a part in sinking the British battlecruiser *Invincible*, but she herself was badly damaged in the battle, sustaining 21 shell hits, with 157 of her crew dead. Her sister ship, *Lützow*, was also heavily damaged, with 116 of her crew killed. Unable to make it back to Wilhelmshaven, she was sunk by a German destroyer.

In November 1918, after the Armistice, *Derfflinger* was interned at Scapa Flow in the Orkney Islands, and on 21 June, 1919 she was scuttled there by her crew. She was raised and broken up at Rosyth in 1934.

Queen Elizabeth 1913

Laid down in 1912 as fast battleships to replace battlecruisers as the offensive element of the British battle fleet, the *Queen Elizabeth* class of dreadnoughts included the *Barham*, *Malaya*, *Valiant*, and *Warspite*. A sixth vessel, *Argonaut*, was never built.

ARMAMENT
The *Queen Elizabeth*-class were the first battleships to mount 381-mm (15-in) guns. Their firepower was designed to overwhelm any existing enemy battleship.

AIRCRAFT
A midships hangar was fitted as part of the reconstruction programme, housing a Supermarine Walrus spotter aircraft.

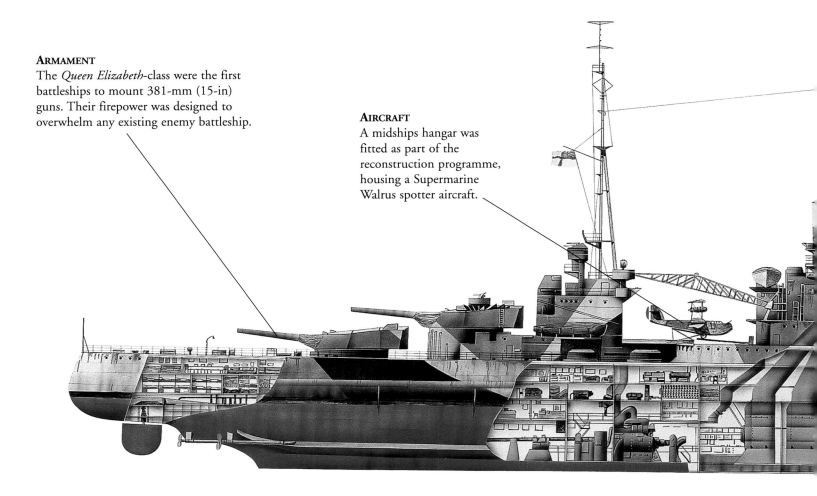

QUEEN ELIZABETH – SPECIFICATION

Country of origin: United Kingdom
Type: Dreadnought battleship
Laid down: 21 October, 1913
Builder: HM Dockyard Portsmouth
Launched: 16 October, 1913
Commissioned: 1915
Decommissioned: 1948
Fate: Scrapped
Complement: 950–1300

Dimensions:
Displacement: 33,548 tonnes (33,020 tons)
Length: (overall) 95.4 m (640 ft 10.5 in); (with stern walk fitted): 197 m (646 ft 1 in); (waterline): 183 m (601 ft 4.5 in)
Beam: 27.58 m (90 ft 6 in)

Draught (mean): 9.3–9.44 m (30 ft 6 in–30 ft 11.5 in)
Draught (deep): 10.31–10.4 m (33 ft 10 in–34 ft 2.5 in)

Powerplant:
Propulsion: Quadruple screw turbines
Speed: 27 knots
Range: 15,927 km (8600 nm) at 12.5 knots

Armament & Armour:
Armament: 8 x 381-mm (15-in) guns; 16 x 152-mm (6-in) guns (as built and before refit)
Armour: 25.4–330mm (1–13 in)

FUNNELS
Queen Elizabeth and *Valiant* were reconstructed in the 1930s and their two funnels replaced by a single large one, the forward funnel being trunked into the second.

HULL
Although they were handsome vessels, their handling was not as good as it might have been. They were seriously overweight because the designers attempted to incorporate too many innovations.

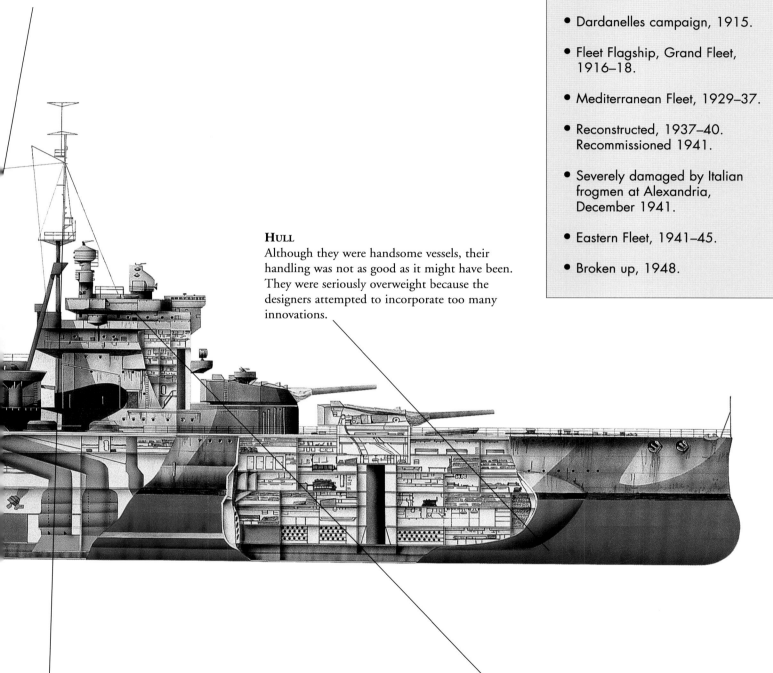

F A C T S

- Launched 16 October, 1913; completed January 1915.

- Dardanelles campaign, 1915.

- Fleet Flagship, Grand Fleet, 1916–18.

- Mediterranean Fleet, 1929–37.

- Reconstructed, 1937–40. Recommissioned 1941.

- Severely damaged by Italian frogmen at Alexandria, December 1941.

- Eastern Fleet, 1941–45.

- Broken up, 1948.

SUPERSTRUCTURE
A distinguishing feature of this class was the heavy tripod foremast and pole-type mainmast. The conning tower was redesigned and enlarged during reconstruction.

FIRE CONTROL
The *Queen Elizabeth*-class had the benefit of a very accurate fire control system, which left a profound impression on the Germans at the Battle of Jutland.

The *Queen Elizabeth*-class battleships had the
distinction of fighting in two world wars. All
were virtually rebuilt in the 1930s with the
exception of *Barham*, the planned reconstruction
of which was postponed because of World War II.
Warspite is shown here.

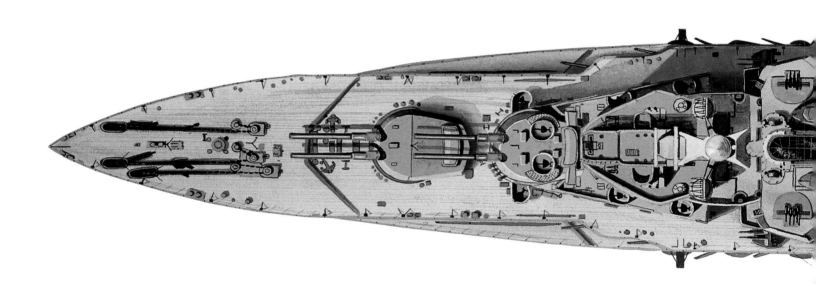

The *Queen Elizabeth*-class battleships had the
distinction of fighting in two world wars. All
were virtually rebuilt in the 1930s with the
exception of *Barham*, the planned reconstruction
of which was postponed because of World War II.
Queen Elizabeth-class battleships had the

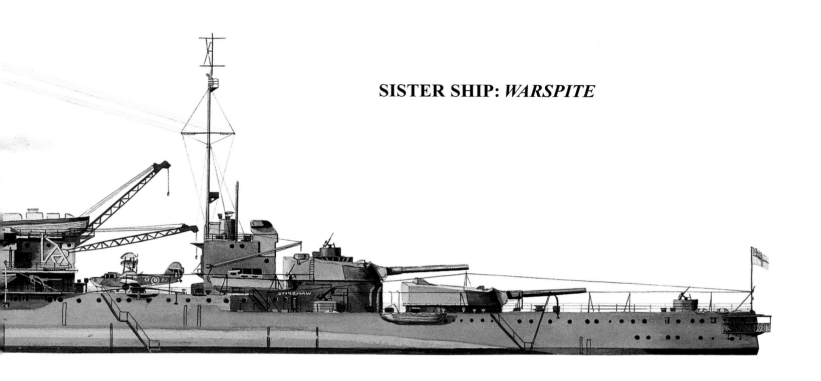

SISTER SHIP: *WARSPITE*

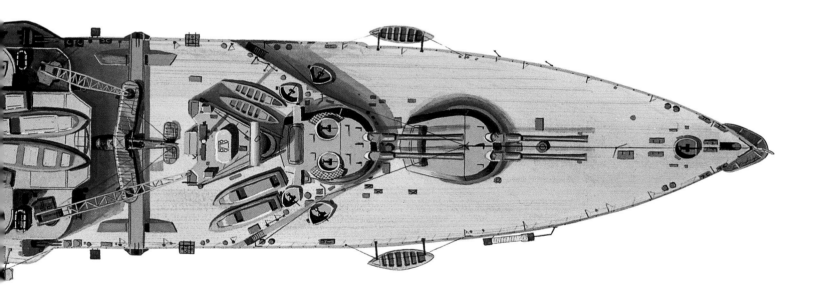

QUEEN ELIZABETH-CLASS

Although damaged in varying degrees, all the *Queen Elizabeth*-class survived World War II except *Barham*, which exploded after being hit by three torpedoes off Sollum by the *U331* on 25 November, 1941. Like *Queen Elizabeth*, *Valiant* was badly damaged by Italian frogmen and was further damaged in a series of accidents in 1944, being broken up in 1948. *Malaya* was also broken up in 1948, having survived a torpedo attack in 1941, after which she was used as a depot ship, while *Warspite*, having suffered severe damage in the Mediterranean in 1941 and again in 1943, was scrapped in 1947.

Queen Elizabeth *and her sister ship,* Valiant, *together in harbour. In December 1941, both were badly damaged at Alexandria in an audacious attack by Italian frogmen, who entered the port on "human torpedoes."*

Almost as soon as she was commissioned in January 1915, *Queen Elizabeth* deployed to the Mediterranean, where she formed part of a naval force tasked with providing fire support for Allied troops during the Dardanelles campaign.

The bombardment of the forts at the entrance to the Dardanelles began on 19 February, 1915, with aircraft from the seaplane carrier *Ark Royal* acting as spotters. The forts were shattered, enabling trawlers to sweep the first 6.5 km (4 miles) of the straits, and on 26 February the pre-dreadnoughts *Albion*, *Majestic*, and *Vengeance* proceeded to the limit of the swept area to bombard Fort Dardanus. The bombardment continued throughout March. All battleships were committed, including *Queen Elizabeth*, whose 380-mm (15-in) guns were powerful enough to hit the vulnerable reverse faces of the fortifications by shooting right across the peninsula with the help of spotting from the air.

From 1916–18 *Queen Elizabeth* was the flagship of the Grand Fleet, replacing *Iron Duke* in that capacity. She served in the Mediterranean between the two world wars,

undergoing substantial reconstruction in 1926–27 and again in 1937–40. By the time she emerged from her second period of reconstruction she was virtually a new ship, having been re-engined, re-boilered, and re-armed. She was commissioned once again in January 1941 and deployed back to the Mediterranean, where she took part in engagements with the Italian Navy.

ALEXANDRIA HARBOUR ATTACK
On 19 December, 1941, three Italian human-torpedo teams penetrated Alexandria harbour through the open boom. Launched from the submarine *Scire* (Cdr Prince Borghese) the teams were Lt Cdr Durand de la Penne and Sgt Maj Bianchi; Capt Marceglia and L/Cpl Schergat; and Capt Martellotta with Sgt Maj Marino. They succeeded in placing explosive charges under *Queen Elizabeth* and *Valiant* and the Norwegian tanker *Sagona*, all of which came to rest on the bottom, badly damaged. The destroyer *Jervis*, lying alongside the tanker, was also damaged.

Queen Elizabeth was made seaworthy and sent to Norfolk, Virginia, for repair, and was commissioned again in June 1943. After service with the Home Fleet she deployed to the Indian Ocean in January 1944, where she formed a powerful task group of the Eastern Fleet together with *Valiant*, the battlecruiser *Renown*, the carriers *Illustrious* and *Unicorn*, two cruisers, and seven destroyers, the whole force having made a fast passage through the Mediterranean after leaving Scapa Flow and the Clyde a month earlier. A little later, the fleet was strengthened still further with the arrival of the French battleship *Richelieu*.

BOMBARDMENT OPERATIONS

During subsequent operations *Queen Elizabeth* took part in several bombardment operations in the Indian Ocean.

Between 8 and 18 April 1945, for example, the Fleet carried out Operation Sunfish, which involved a sortie by *Queen Elizabeth* and *Richelieu*, the heavy cruisers *London* and *Cumberland*, and five destroyers against targets on the north coast of Sumatra, in the course of which Sabang was heavily shelled. In the following month, she was involved in the hunting down of the Japanese cruiser *Hagaro*, which was sunk in a night attack by British destroyers.

At the end of the war in the Far East, *Queen Elizabeth* returned to home water and was scrapped at Troon, her upperworks and fittings having been removed at Dalmuir.

Close-up

Queen Elizabeth was the leader of a class of five battleships. They were intended to replace battlecruisers as the offensive element of the battle fleet.

(1) **Gun:** Sailors at work around the forward gun turrets of *Queen Elizabeth*. With her eight 380-mm (15-in) guns, she was a match for any other warship.

(2) **Armour:** *Queen Elizabeth*'s main gun turrets carried armour plating measuring between 279–330 mm (11–13 in) thick.

(3) **Armament:** The *Queen Elizabeth*-class were the first battleships to be fitted with 380-mm (15-in) guns.

(4) **Sloped Armour:** The armour plating of *Queen Elizabeth*'s gun turrets was sloped, in order to deflect enemy fire. Various gun turret configurations were proposed.

(5) **Engine:** Thanks to the greater thermal efficiency of her oil-fired engines, *Queen Elizabeth* could make 27 knots.

(6) **Bridge:** The ship underwent many modifications. The bridge was remodelled and more AA guns fitted.

Hood 1918

The battlecruiser *Hood* was the very symbol of Empire, of power and majesty, underlining the fact that the *Pax Britannica* was still in force and that Britain continued to rule much of the world. At 38,000 tonnes (42,000 tons) she was the mightiest warship afloat.

ARMAMENT
Hood was fitted with the Mark I 381-mm (15-in) gun of 1912, which was at that time the standard weapon of British capital ships, and was already mounted on *Queen Elizabeth*-class, *Revenge*-class, *Renown*-class, and other classes of ships.

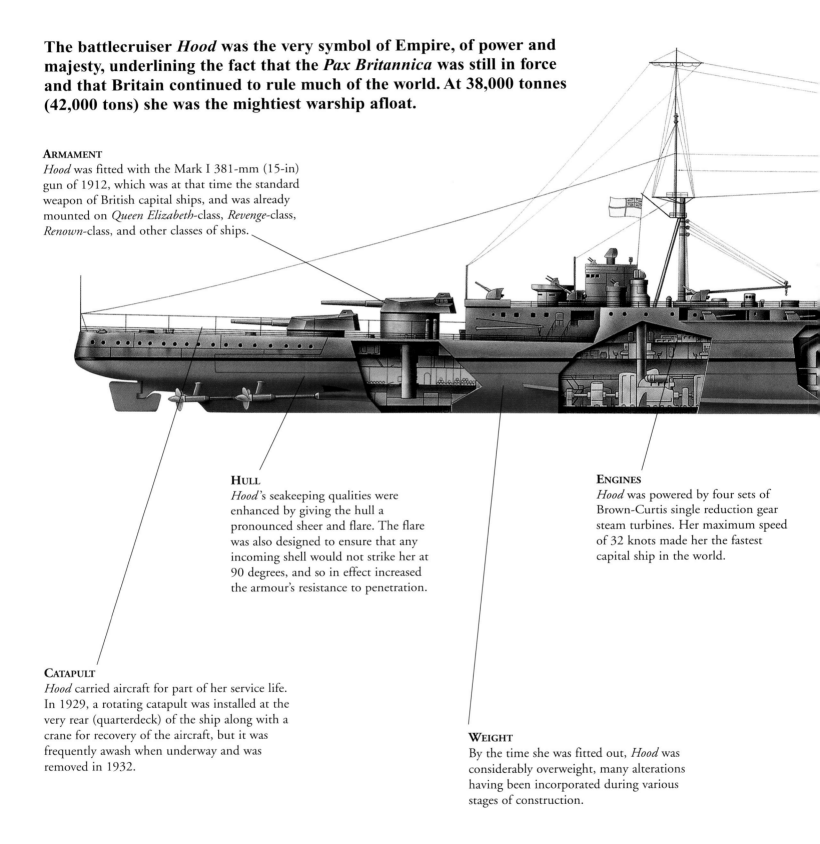

HULL
Hood's seakeeping qualities were enhanced by giving the hull a pronounced sheer and flare. The flare was also designed to ensure that any incoming shell would not strike her at 90 degrees, and so in effect increased the armour's resistance to penetration.

ENGINES
Hood was powered by four sets of Brown-Curtis single reduction gear steam turbines. Her maximum speed of 32 knots made her the fastest capital ship in the world.

CATAPULT
Hood carried aircraft for part of her service life. In 1929, a rotating catapult was installed at the very rear (quarterdeck) of the ship along with a crane for recovery of the aircraft, but it was frequently awash when underway and was removed in 1932.

WEIGHT
By the time she was fitted out, *Hood* was considerably overweight, many alterations having been incorporated during various stages of construction.

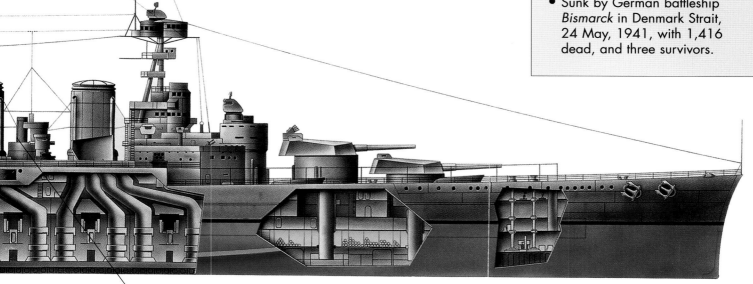

ARMOUR
Hood's biggest flaw was her armour. The deck and side armour failed to provide continuous protection against shells coming in from all angles.

HOOD – SPECIFICATION

Country of origin: United Kingdom
Type: "Admiral"-class Battlecruiser
Laid down: 1 September, 1916
Builder: John Brown & Company
Launched: 22 August, 1918
Commissioned: 15 May, 1920
Decommissioned: n/a
Fate: Sunk in combat 24 May, 1941
Complement: (1921) 1168; (1941) 1419

Dimensions:
Displacement: 38,000 tonnes (42,000 tons)
Length: 262.3 m (860 ft 7 in); **Beam:** 31.75 m (104 ft 2 in);
Draught: 9.75 m (32 ft)

Powerplant:
Propulsion: Quadruple screw Brown-Curtis geared steam turbines
Speed: 32 knots
Range: (1931) 9875 (5332 nm) at 20 knots

Armament & Armour:
Armament: (as built) 8 x BL 381-mm (15-in) Mk I guns; 12 x 140-mm (5.5-in) Mk I guns; 4 102-mm (4-in) Mark V anti-aircraft guns; 6 x 533-mm (21-in) Mark IV torpedo tubes
Armour: 19–305 mm (0.75–12 in)

Hood was an enlarged **Queen Elizabeth**-type, and was
designed in response to the planned German
Mackensen-class battlecruisers. Her original design
was modified because of lessons learnt during the
Battle of Jutland, but she remained poorly protected.

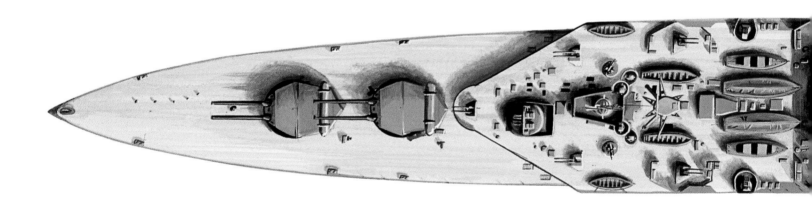

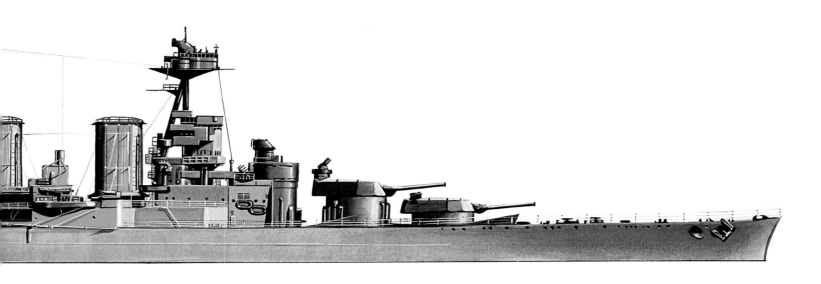

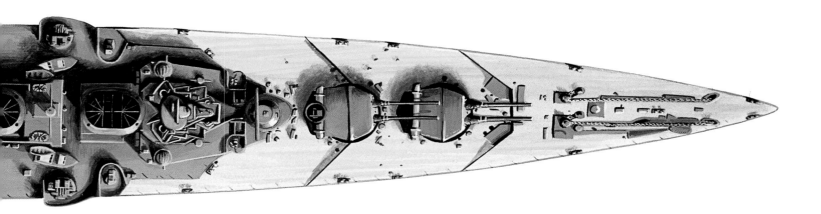

HOOD

Hood was the name of several distinguished British Admirals, the first of whom, Viscount Hood, served with distinction under Admiral Rodney during the eighteenth-century wars with France. His brother, Alexander Hood, 1st Viscount Bridport, was also an admiral, while Rear-Admiral Sir Samuel Hood, his cousin once removed, commanded the warship *Zealous* at the Battle of the Nile. The last of the line, Rear-Admiral Horace Hood, commanded the 3rd Battlecruiser Squadron at the Battle of Jutland in 1916 and was lost when his flagship, *Invincible*, exploded. It was his widow who launched the mighty *Hood* two years later.

"The mist lifted to reveal the *Hood* and her consorts coming in…. It was a wonderful sight, something I shall never forget, everyone cheering and the kids running up and down and the sirens of all the ships in the harbour going off." (Eyewitness account of *Hood*'s visit to Melbourne, Australia)

In November 1923, accompanied by the battlecruiser *Repulse* and five cruisers, *Hood* embarked on a year-long world tour. The itinerary took her and her consorts to South Africa, Zanzibar, Ceylon, Singapore, Australia, New Zealand, the Pacific Islands, San Francisco, the Panama Canal, Jamaica, and finally Newfoundland. The powerful naval squadron attracted huge crowds wherever it dropped anchor.

A LONG REFIT

But *Hood*'s true purpose was warfare, and in May 1929 she was laid up for a long refit, emerging in June 1930 with

Interior view

Like most other warships of the time, *Hood* carried an armament of torpedoes. These consisted of six 533-mm (21-in) torpedo tubes in her case mounted amidships, three on either side.

(1) Stowage: The torpedo room held stowage racks for storing, maintaining, and loading the ship's torpedoes.

(2) Torpedo Motor: The aft end of the torpedo contained the motor. Some torpedoes were powered by steam, but most had powerful electric motors.

(3) Components: Every rotating component had a matching component that turned in the opposite direction, preventing unbalanced torques (twisting forces).

(4) Usage: Naval strategy in *Hood*'s time was to use torpedoes launched from submarines or warships, as part of a fleet action on the high seas.

(5) Detonation: To avoid a warship's armoured belt, torpedoes were often set to detonate underneath a ship, where they did maximum damage to its keel.

(6) Storage Racks: Neatness was essential in the crowded space of a torpedo room, so storage racks had to be well organized.

Because of flaws in her design, it was seriously suggested that Hood *should be scrapped before she was launched, a fate that overtook her planned sister ships. However,* Hood *was too far advanced and cancellation would have cost too much.*

modifications that included the installation of a catapult for launching a spotter aircraft and a recovery crane. This was installed at the rear of the quarterdeck, but was frequently awash when the ship was travelling at speed, and it was removed in 1932.

Hood continued to serve with the Home and Atlantic Fleets until 1936, when she sailed to join the Mediterranean Fleet. In September 1938 she suffered damage when she ran aground at Gibraltar, and in the following year she went in for another refit, which involved a substantial increase in her anti-aircraft armament.

THE ROYAL NAVY'S FINEST

Her status as the Royal Navy's finest capital ship meant that she was almost constantly on active service, and by the end of the 1930s her condition was beginning to deteriorate badly. As a result her performance suffered. Among other things, she was unable to attain her maximum design speed. In 1939 she was once again serving with the Home Fleet, the flagship of the Battle Cruiser Squadron at Scapa Flow, and when war broke out in September that year she was employed principally in patrolling the vicinity of Iceland and the Faeroes to protect convoys and intercept German raiders attempting to break out into the Atlantic. In September 1939,

she was hit by a 250-kg (550-lb) aircraft bomb and sustained minor damage. As the flagship of Force H, she took part in the destruction of the French Fleet at Mers-el-Kebir in July 1940. In August, she rejoined the Battle Cruiser Squadron and resumed patrolling against German raiders.

She was due to be fully modernized in 1941, to bring her up to the standard of other capital ships built during World War I, but the outbreak of war meant that it was impossible to remove her from service. Consequently she never received the required update. That update was to have included the addition of full deck armour.

On 24 May, 1941, together with the battleship *Prince of Wales*, she engaged the German battleship *Bismarck* and the heavy cruiser *Prinz Eugen* in the Denmark Strait. The *Bismarck*'s second and third salvoes struck the battlecruiser amidships, and those from the *Prinz Eugen* started a fire among her ready-to-use AA ammunition. At 0600, as the British warships were altering course in order to bring all their guns to bear, *Hood* was hit again by a salvo that pierced her lightly armoured decks and detonated in her after magazines. She blew up with a tremendous explosion and disappeared with a speed that astounded all who witnessed the event. Only three of her crew of 1419 officers and ratings survived.

De Ruyter 1935

Much of Holland's naval strength was intended to protect her interests in the Dutch East Indies, which was rich in raw materials. *De Ruyter* **was one of three cruisers intended for deployment to the East Indies.**

AIRCRAFT
The cruiser carried two Fokker CXIW spotter aircraft, launched from a catapult built by Germany's Heinkel Company.

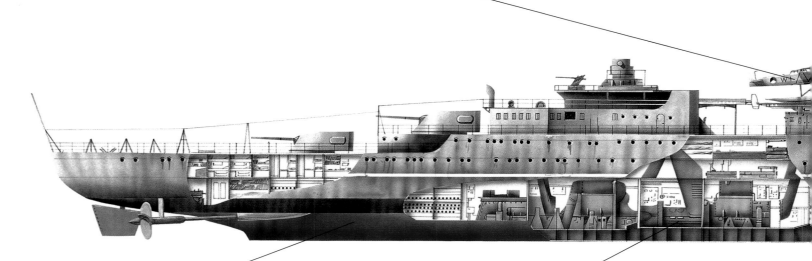

HULL
The use of electric welding and light alloy enabled *De Ruyter*'s designers to save some weight in the hull, which was subdivided into 21 watertight compartments.

MACHINERY
De Ruyter was powered by two Parsons geared turbines, producing 49.2 MW (66,000 shp) and giving her a top speed of 32 knots. The forward turbine space powered the port turbine, and was separated from the after turbine space by the gearing room.

DE RUYTER – SPECIFICATION

Country of origin: Netherlands
Type: Light cruiser
Laid down: 16 September, 1933
Builder: Wilton Fijenoord dockyard
Launched: 11 March, 1935
Commissioned: 3 October, 1936
Decommissioned: n/a
Fate: Sunk by torpedoes in the Java Sea 27 February, 1942
Complement: 435

Dimensions:
Displacement: (standard) 5937.5 tonnes (6545 tons)
  Length: 170.9 m (561 ft); **Beam:** 15.7 m (52 ft);
  Draught: 5.1 m (17 ft)

Powerplant:
Propulsion: 2 Parsons geared steam turbines, 6 Yarrow boilers, 2 screws, 49.2 MW (66,000 shp)
Speed: 32 knots
Range: 12,594 km (6800 nm) at 12 knots

Armament & Armour:
Armament: 7 x 150-mm (5.9-in); 10 x Bofors 40-mm (1.57-in) guns; 8 x Browning 12.7-mm (.50-in) machine guns
Armour: 30–50mm (1.18–1.97in)
Aircraft: 2 x Fokker CXIW spotter aircraft

FACTS

- Launched 11 May, 1935, completed October 1936.

- Deployed to the Netherlands East Indies, March 1937.

- Deployed on escort duty with convoys to Singapore, January 1942.

- Sunk in the Battle of the Java Sea, 27 February, 1942.

- Wreck located by diving expedition, 1 December, 2002.

ARMAMENT

De Ruyter's twin Mk 9 150-mm (5.9-in) gun turrets each weighed 63.5 tonnes (70 tons), while the single Mk 10 mounting weighed 23 tonnes (25 tons). The latter was equipped to fire starshell. The close-range 40-mm (1.57-in) anti-aircraft guns were grouped closely together on the aft superstructure and had a limited arc of fire.

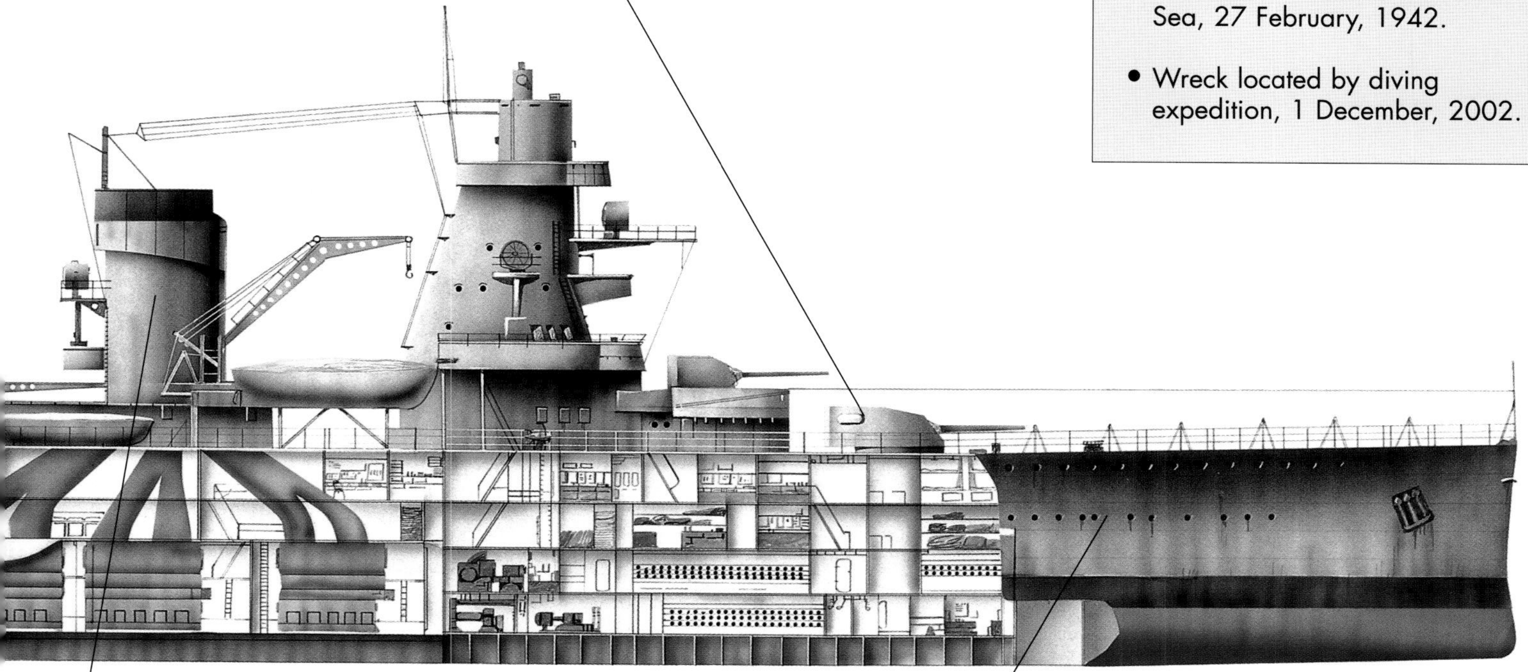

FUNNEL

The original funnel cap proved unsatisfactory and was replaced by one of a different pattern in 1936.

ARMOUR

De Ruyter's protection included a waterline belt extending from the forward end of "A" turret to the after end of the steering compartment, covered by a protective 30-mm (1.2-in) deck.

De Ruyter's original design was heavily criticized
because of its small size, a failing caused entirely
by economic constraints. The Netherlands
subsequently authorized a larger vessel.

LIGHT CRUISER: *JAVA*

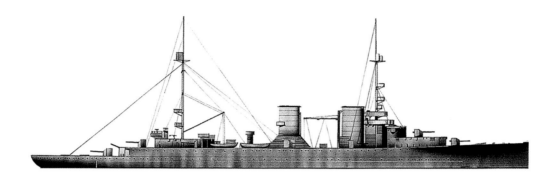

LIGHT CRUISER: *TROMP*

JAVA AND *TROMP*

The light cruiser *Java* (top left) was built as a counter to the new Japanese cruisers of the *Chikuma* class. Like *De Ruyter*, *Java* was sunk in the Battle of the Java Sea.

Originally designated as a flotilla leader and a torpedo cruiser in the Dutch Navy's Fleet Plan of 1931, *Tromp* (bottom left) was laid down by the Netherlands Shipbuilding Company, Amsterdam, in 1936 and commissioned on 18 August, 1938. She was badly damaged off Bali in February 1942, but survived the war, serving with the British Eastern Fleet in its later stages.

CRUISER: *EXETER*

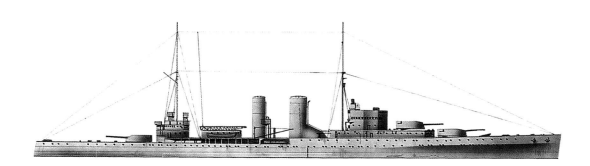

LIGHT CRUISER: *JACOB VAN HEEMSKERCK*

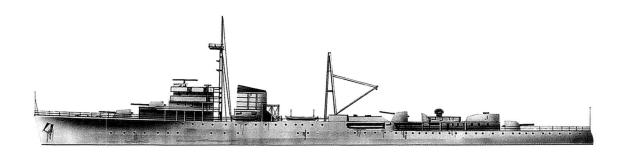

De Ruyter **was the seventh Dutch warship to bear the name of Admiral Michiel Adriaenszoon de Ruyter, who played a notable part in the Anglo-Dutch naval wars of the seventeenth century. He won a series of major victories in action against both the British and French.**

For five weeks in January and early February 1942, a motley collection of warships (mostly British and Dutch, including *De Ruyter*, flagship of the Dutch Admiral Karel Doorman) was employed in escorting troop convoys to Singapore. But by the end of January the Singapore naval base was so badly damaged it could barely function. And after the Japanese gained a foothold on Singapore island on 9 February, 1942, even the barest trickle of reinforcements was finally stopped. On the 12th, three days before the Singapore garrison surrendered, there was an exodus of every seaworthy vessel from the base, laden with civilian and military personnel.

Close-up

Due to cost-cutting policies that affected her design, *De Ruyter* was not quite up to her task. Her main battery of seven 150-mm (6-in) guns was inadequate in comparison to other light cruisers of the time.

(1) Fire Control System: *De Ruyter*'s fire control system was excellent, as was her anti-aircraft battery of Bofors guns.

(2) Waterline Belt: *De Ruyter*'s final design had a protective scheme that included a 50-mm (2-in) waterline belt, which extended from forwards to after magazines.

(3) Hull: Electric welding and some light alloy provided some weight economy in the design of the hull, which was subdivided into 21 watertight compartments.

(4) Guns: Only four pairs of 12.7-mm (0.5-in) machine guns in the bridge wings and on the top of the conning tower gave any defence against head-on air attack.

(5) Funnel: The original funnel cap proved unsatisfactory and was replaced by a new pattern in May 1936.

(6) Armament: All of *de Ruyter*'s main armament was mounted on the centreline. The single 150-mm (5.9-in) gun was also used as to fire starshell.

De Ruyter *was built as an uncluttered ship with attractive lines. Her wreck was found after the war and declared a war grave, with only the ship's bell being recovered.*

On 13 February, a Japanese invasion force was reported to be heading for Sumatra and the Allied Command despatched a naval force of five cruisers and 10 destroyers to intercept it. However, the Allied ships were heavily attacked from the air, and although none were lost to air attack, Admiral Karel Doorman, the force commander, decided to call off the operation and withdraw. The enemy blows now fell thick and fast. On 18 February Japanese forces landed on the island of Bali, isolating Java from the east, and on the following day aircraft of their main striking force, the 1st Carrier Air Fleet, launched a devastating attack on Port Darwin, sinking 11 transports and supply ships, and causing severe damage to the port installations. Darwin was the only base in North Australia from which Java could be reinforced and supplied and, as a result, this attack effectively sealed the fate of the defenders.

On 27 February, Admiral Doorman, who had meanwhile been in action against the Japanese in the Bandoeng Strait with a mixed force of Dutch and American warships, sailed from Soerabaya with five cruisers and nine destroyers to intercept Japanese invasion forces in the Java Sea. The Japanese force was escorted by four cruisers and 14 destroyers, and at 1600 the opposing cruisers began an exchange of gunfire. Shortly afterwards *Exeter* was hit by a heavy shell and compelled to withdraw to Soerabaya escorted by the Dutch destroyer *Witte de With*, another Dutch destroyer, the *Kortenaer*, having been sunk by a torpedo. *Exeter* was also sunk by Japanese naval forces on 1 March.

Admiral Doorman then reformed his force with four cruisers and six destroyers and made a sortie to the north-west, where his ships fought a brief action in the dark with the cruisers *Haguro* and *Nachi*. Soon after this, the British destroyer *Jupiter* blew up – either as the result of striking a Dutch mine, or because she was torpedoed in error by the American submarine *S38*. The Allied force suffered further losses during the night when the Dutch cruisers *Java* and *De Ruyter* were sunk by torpedoes.

De Ruyter went down with the loss of 345 perseonnel, including Admiral Doorman. Her wreck was discovered in 2002 by a diving team searching for the wreck of *Exeter*. *De Ruyter*'s bell was salvaged and now rests in the Kloosterkerk, Den Haag.

Scharnhorst 1936

The design of *Scharnhorst* and her sister, *Gneisenau*, was based on that of the uncompleted *Mackensen*-class battlecruisers of World War I, which in turn were based on the *Derfflinger* of 1913, arguably the best battlecruiser of its day. The two warships represented a powerful threat to Allied Atlantic convoys.

AIRCRAFT
Scharnhorst and *Gneisenau* were originally fitted with two catapults, but the catapult on "C" turret was deleted when a new tripod mainmast was installed. Four Arado Ar 196 floatplanes could be carried.

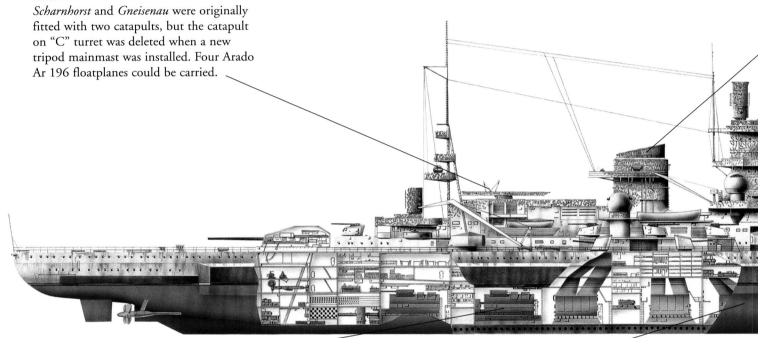

MACHINERY
Scharnhorst was powered by three Brown-Boveri geared turbines with 12 Wagner boilers, producing 123.09 MW (165,000 shp) and giving a top speed of 32 knots and a range of 16,298 km (8,800 nm) at 16 knots.

ARMOUR
The adoption of the 280-mm (11-in) armament meant that more protection could be carried without any appreciable weight penalty. The main belt was 305–330 mm (12–13 in), turrets 305 mm (12 in), and decks 152 mm (6 in).

SCHARNHORST – SPECIFICATION

Country of origin: Germany
Type: Battlecruiser
Laid down: 1935
Builder: Deutsche Werke, Kriegsmarinewerft Wilhelmshaven
Launched: Late 1936
Commissioned: Early 1939
Decommissioned: n/a
Fate: Sunk in Battle of North Cape, 26 December, 1943
Complement: 1,968 (56 officers, 1,909 enlisted)

Dimensions:
Displacement: (standard) 32,615 tonnes (35,952 tons); (full load) 34,564 tonnes (42,672 tons)

Length: (overall) 235 m (772 ft); (waterline) 226 m (741.5 ft);
Beam: 30 m (98.4 ft); **Draught:** 9.69 m (31 ft 9 in)

Powerplant:
Propulsion: 12 Wagner boilers, producing 123.09 MW (165,000 shp)
Speed: 32 knots
Range: 16,298 km (8800 nm) at 16 knots

Armament & Armour:
Armament: 9 x 280-mm (11-in) guns; 12 x 150-mm (5.9-in) guns
Armour: 95–350 mm (3.7–13.78 in)
Aircraft: 4 Arado Ar 196A-3

SUPERSTRUCTURE

The mainmast was originally immediately aft of the funnel, but was moved further back in 1939. A funnel cap was also added.

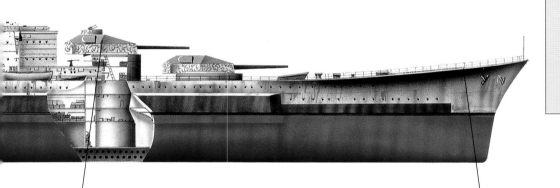

BOW

Scharnhorst's original straight stem was altered to a "clipper bow" in 1939, making her a more satisfactory seaboat.

MAIN ARMAMENT

Hitler ordered that *Scharnhorst* and *Gneisenau* were to be fitted with 380-mm (15-in) guns, but as the 280-mm (11-in) triple turret was readily available the warships were fitted with this instead. Plans to install the heavier armament at a later date were abandoned.

Scharnhorst and *Gneisenau* presented a dire threat to the vital Allied Atlantic convoys. Had they been able to form a battle group with the German battleship *Bismarck* and the heavy cruiser *Prinz Eugen* they would have been virtually invincible.

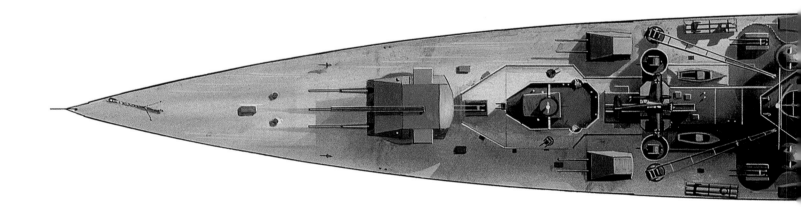

SISTER SHIP: *GNEISENAU*

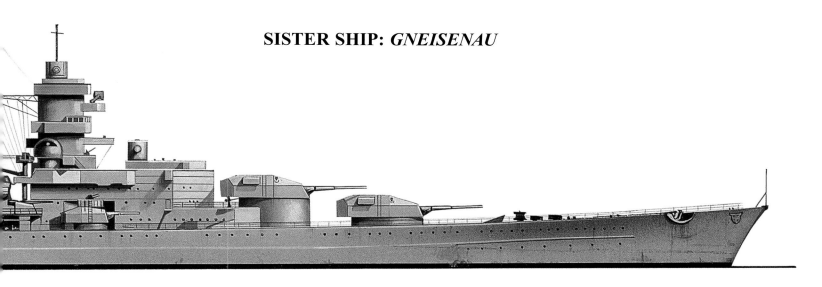

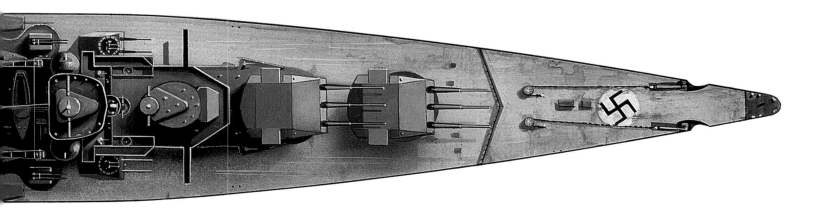

DESTROYING *SCHARNHORST* AND *GNIESENAU*

In 1941, the Royal Air Force made determined efforts to destroy *Scharnhorst* and *Gneisenau* in their bases on the French Atlantic coast. On 24 July, 15 Halifax bombers made a daylight attack on *Scharnhorst* at La Pallice; five direct hits were scored, but three bombs passed straight through the ship and the other two failed to explode. Five of the Halifaxes were shot down and all the rest damaged. However, the damage they managed to inflict on *Scharnhorst* was enough to put her out of action for four months.

"**The *Scharnhorst* must have been a hell on earth. The 14-inch from the flagship were hitting or rocketing off from a ricochet on the sea. Great flashes rent the night, and the sound of gunfire was continuous, and yet she replied, but only occasionally now with what armament she had left.**"
– Lt B. B. Ramsden.

Those words, by Lieutenant B. B. Ramsden, an officer of Royal Marines on the British battleship *Duke of York*, described the end of *Scharnhorst* on a freezing December night off Norway's North Cape. She had been a thorn in the side of the Royal Navy since 1940, when she sank the aircraft carrier *Glorious* and the destroyers *Ardent* and *Acasta* off Norway on 8 June.

Commerce raiding was her main role, and early in 1941 *Scharnhorst* and *Gneisenau* sank 22 Allied ships totalling 104,890 tonnes (115,622 tons) on a sortie into the North Atlantic, before seeking refuge in the French Atlantic ports. There they were joined by the heavy cruiser *Prinz Eugen* after the latter's consort, the battleship *Bismarck*, was sunk at the end of May. In February 1942, repaired after sustaining varying degrees of damage sustained in RAF air attacks, the three warships made an epic dash through the English Channel and reached the safety of Kiel. *Gneisenau*

Close-up

The *Scharnhorst* and her sister ship *Gneisenau* were extremely well equipped, with plenty of room below decks. This is the engine room.

1 **Machinery:** After her commerce-raiding expeditions in the Atlantic *Scharnhorst*'s machinery needed a lengthy overhaul.

2 **Main Machinery:** This was a triple-shaft steam turbine arrangement with 12 Wagner high-pressure boilers, three in each of four boiler rooms.

3 **Cruising turbines:** These were fitted initially but removed later. The after turbine room powered the centre shaft.

4 **Battlecruiser or Battleship:** Although the British referred to *Scharnhorst* and *Gneisenau* as battlecruisers, the Germans always described them as battleships.

5 **Armour:** This was equal to that of a battleship and if it had not been for her small-calibre guns she would have been classified as a battleship by the British.

6 **Gallantry:** After *Scharnhorst*'s last battle, her crew were complimented by the British Admiral Bruce Fraser, who told his officers: "I hope that if any of you are ever called upon to lead a ship into action against an opponent many times superior, you will command your ship as gallantly as *Scharnhorst* was commanded today."

The German Navy's Commander Battleships, Vice-Admiral Ciliax, inspects the crew of Scharnhorst, *accompanied by Captain Hoffman (right) and executive officers. Together,* Scharnhorst, Gneisenau, *and* Prinz Eugen *made a formidable battle group.*

was hit by Bomber Command in Kiel harbour a fortnight later and never went to sea again; her gun turrets were removed for coastal defence and she was sunk as a blockship at Gdynia, where she was seized by the Russians and broken up from 1947–51. Only *Scharnhorst* re-emerged to threaten Allied shipping on the high seas, her base now in Norway.

FINISHED OFF BY BRITAIN

At 1400 on 25 December, 1943, *Scharnhorst* (Kapt F. Hintze, flying the flag of Admiral Bey) sailed from Norway accompanied by five destroyers to intercept Convoy JW55B, which had been located by air reconnaissance on 22 December. She was intercepted by a force of British cruisers and destroyers, and damaged by their gunfire.

Her fate was sealed by the arrival of the battleship *Duke of York*, which opened fire on her and put the battlecruiser's "A" and "B" turrets out of action. Some steam pipes were also ruptured. This reduced her speed, leaving her without

the capability of outrunning her adversaries, even if the opportunity had arisen.

At 1824 the third of *Scharnhorst*'s turrets was put out of action, and British destroyers moved in to finish the job. Two of them, *Savage* and *Saumarez*, approached from the northwest under heavy fire, firing starshell, while *Scorpion* and *Stord* attacked fom the southeast, launching their torpedoes at 1849. As Hintze turned his ship to port to engage them, one of *Scorpion*'s torpedoes struck home, closely followed by three more from the first two destroyers.

A CHALLENGE THAT FAILED

By 1930 the battlecruiser was ablaze, her hull glowing red-hot in the Arctic night. Destroyers closed in to finish her off with torpedoes. At 1945 she blew up. Only 36 of her crew of 1968 were rescued from the freezing seas. So ended the Battle of North Cape, and with it the last attempt by a German capital ship to challenge the supremacy of the Royal Navy.

Enterprise (CV-6) 1936

The first U.S. carrier built from the keel up was the *Ranger* of 1930, which proved too slow to be effective as a first-line unit. She was, however, developed into the successful *Yorktown* class of 1933 (which included *Enterprise*, *Hornet*, and *Yorktown*), followed by *Wasp* of 1934.

ARMAMENT
By the end of the war, in addition to her eight 127-mm (5-in) guns, *Enterprise* had 11 quadruple 40-mm (1.57-in) guns, 8 twin 40-mm (1.79-in) guns, and 16 twin 20-mm (0.79-in) anti-aircraft weapons.

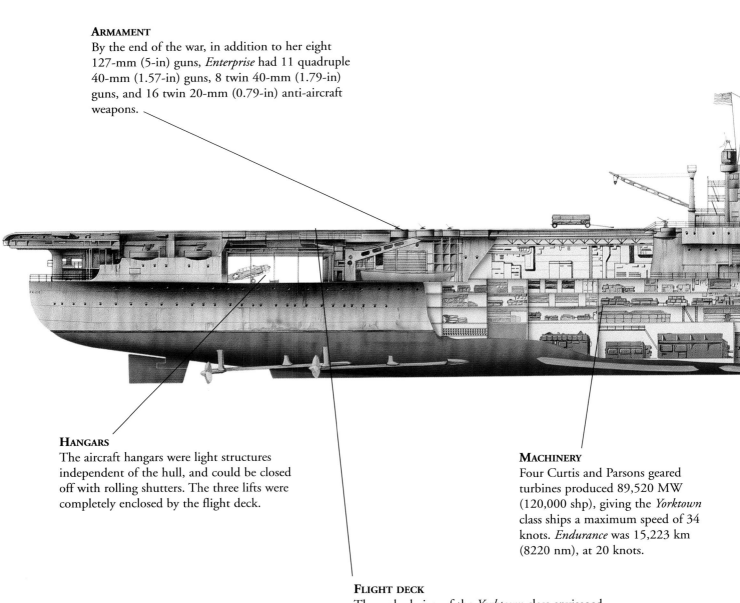

HANGARS
The aircraft hangars were light structures independent of the hull, and could be closed off with rolling shutters. The three lifts were completely enclosed by the flight deck.

MACHINERY
Four Curtis and Parsons geared turbines produced 89,520 MW (120,000 shp), giving the *Yorktown* class ships a maximum speed of 34 knots. *Endurance* was 15,223 km (8220 nm), at 20 knots.

FLIGHT DECK
The early design of the *Yorktown* class envisaged a flush flight deck with horizontal funnels, but this was thought to pose a smoke hazard to landing aircraft. Instead, the carriers were fitted with an island to carry funnel uptakes and provide space for control centres.

PROTECTION

For a time, an armoured flight deck was considered, but not enough armour could be provided for this to be useful without sacrificing speed. As a result, the deck carried only 76 mm (3 in) of armour plate.

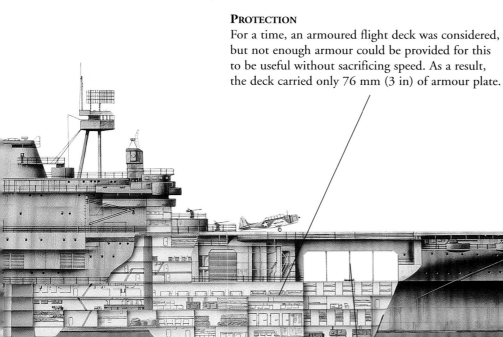

AIRCRAFT

The *Yorktown*-class carriers could carry and operate up to 80 aircraft. A hangar deck catapult was installed in all three ships, but was removed from *Enterprise* and *Hornet* in 1942.

ENTERPRISE (CV-6) – SPECIFICATION

Country of origin: USA
Type: Aircraft carrier
Laid down: 16 July, 1934
Builder: Newport News Shipbuilding
Launched: 3 October, 1936
Commissioned: 12 May, 1938
Decommissioned: 17 February, 1947
Fate: Scrapped 1958–60
Complement: 2217

Dimensions:
Displacement: (standard) 17,962 tonnes (19,800 tons), (full load) 23,133 tonnes (25,500 tons)
Length: 230 m (770 ft) (waterline); 251 m (824 ft 9 in) (overall)
Beam: 25 m (83 ft 3 in); 33.38 m (109 ft 6 in) (overall)

Draught: 7.912 m (25 ft 11.5 in)

Powerplant:
Propulsion: 4 shaft geared system turbines delivering 89.520 MW (120,000 shp)
Speed: 34 knots
Range: 15,223 km (8220 nm)

Armament & Armour:
Armament: 8 x 127-mm (5-in) guns
Armour: 63.5–101.6 mm (2.5–4 in)
Aircraft: 80

At the time of the Japanese attack on Pearl Harbor, *Enterprise* was at sea about 320 km (200 miles) west of Hawaii returning from Wake Island after delivering a Marine fighter squadron. Together with *Lexington*, *Yorktown*, and *Saratoga*, she would form the nucleus of a rebuilt Pacific Fleet.

SISTER SHIP: *YORKTOWN*

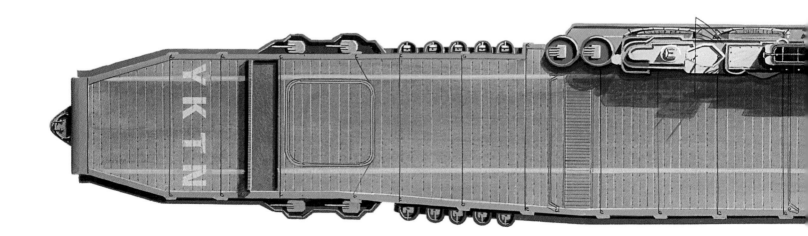

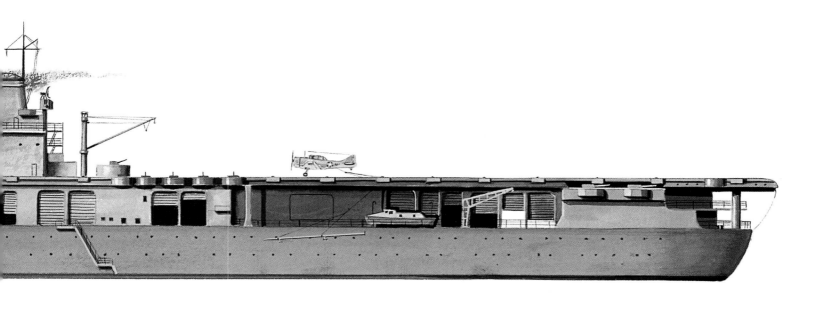

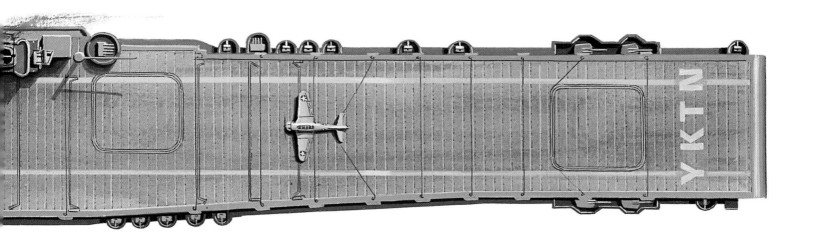

YORKTOWN CLASS

Although the four carriers of the U.S. Pacific Fleet escaped the Pearl Harbor attack, losses came more quickly than reinforcements could be redeployed from the Atlantic. The *Yorktown* was damaged by bombs in the Battle of Midway on 5 June, 1942, and was finished off by a Japanese submarine two days later. The third of the *Yorktown* class, *Hornet*, had only just been completed in December 1941; her first action, in April 1942, was to launch a force of B-25 Mitchell bombers in the famous "Doolittle Raid" on Tokyo. She was sunk at the Battle of Santa Cruz in October that year.

It would be no exaggeration to claim that *Enterprise* was the hardest-worked carrier of World War II. She fought in almost every Pacific campaign, and withstood terrible damage in enemy air attacks.

Six months after Pearl Harbor, a crushing humiliation was about to descend on the hitherto invincible Japanese Navy. Early in June 1942, the four carriers that had taken part in the Pearl Harbor attack – *Akaga, Kaga, Hiryu,* and *Soryu* – formed part of the strong naval force that was intended to bombard the island of Midway into submission prior to a Japanese landing and occupation, a crucial step in Admiral Yamamoto's plan to expand the perimeter of Japan's conquest eastwards towards the continental United States, which would then come under direct threat.

The thrust towards Midway was met by a greatly outnumbered U.S. carrier force composed of Rear Admiral Fletcher's Task Force 17, with *Yorktown*, and Rear Admiral R.A. Spruance's Task Force 16, with *Hornet* and *Enterprise*, supported by Navy, Marine Corps and Army air units based on Midway.

Close-up

Enterprise participated in more major actions of the war against Japan than any other U.S. warship. On three occasions during the Pacific War, the Japanese announced she had been sunk in action.

(1) In motion: *Enterprise* steams towards the Panama Canal on 10 October, 1945, en route to New York to participate in Navy Day celebrations.

(2) Superstructure: *Enterprise* had a traditional design for the time, with her superstructure, or "island," situated on the starboard side.

(3) Flight Deck: Three aircraft lifts provided access to the flight deck. A single hangar deck catapult was fitted with twin flight deck catapults, all three hydraulically powered.

(4) Complement: *Enterprise* had a complement of 2,217 personnel and could field 90 aircraft of various types including fighters, dive bombers and torpedo bombers.

(5) Engine: *Enterprise* was powered by nine Babcock and Wilcox boilers servicing four Parsons geared turbines, turning four shafts with an output of 89.52 MW (120,000 shp)

(6) Armour: *Enterprise*'s flight deck had 76 mm (3 in) of armour plating, about twice the thickness of other U.S. aircraft carriers. It was to save her life more than once.

Enterprise is pictured here during her early years of service with the U.S. Fleet. The aircraft on her deck are Grumman F3F biplane fighters. She went on to participate in many major actions of war.

At 0700 on 4 June *Enterprise* and *Hornet* launched their strike groups. *Enterprise*'s air group attacked *Soryu* with 12 TBDs of VT-3 and 17 SBDs of VB-3. Only five TBDs survived to make their torpedo attacks, and three of these were shot down on the way out. Of the 41 TBDs launched, only six returned to the task force, and one of these ran out of fuel and ditched.

JAPANESE SHIPS GO DOWN

The sacrifice of the three VT squadrons was not in vain. They had absorbed the bulk of the enemy fighter attacks, and the Japanese fighters were still scattered when 37 Dauntless dive-bombers from *Enterprise*'s VB-5 and the 17 from *Yorktown*'s VB-3 made their attack, sinking the *Akagi*, *Kaga*, and *Soryu*. The cost to the dive-bombers was 16 aircraft lost from *Enterprise*'s air group. A Japanese counterattack from *Hiryu* damaged *Yorktown*, but she returned to full operation after a short time. Then a second attack was made by six B5N Kate torpedo-bombers. Two were shot down, but the other four launched their torpedoes and two hit the carrier, which had to be abandoned. She was later sunk by a submarine. At 1700, *Hiryu* was

crippled in an attack by 24 SBDs from *Enterprise*. Her burnt-out hulk was sunk by a Japanese destroyer the following day. In August 1942, *Enterprise* was severely damaged by bombs during the Battle of the Eastern Solomons. Repaired at Pearl Harbor, she returned to action in October only to be damaged again. Repair work was still incomplete when she saw further action in December during the battle for Guadalcanal during the Battle of Rennell Island.

OVERHAULED AT LAST

More action in 1943 saw *Enterprise* receive a Presidential Unit Citation, the first awarded to an aircraft carrier. In July, relieved at last by the new *Essex*-class carriers, she returned to the USA for a badly needed overhaul.

Enterprise went on to gain more battle honours, her air group participating in the Battle of the Philippine Sea and striking at Palau, Leyte, Luzon, Formosa, the China coast, Iwo Jima, and Okinawa. In addition, she survived two kamikaze attacks off Okinawa.

She was scrapped in 1958, despite efforts to preserve her as a memorial.

Cossack 1937

Among the finest destroyers ever built for the Royal Navy, the 16 "Tribal"-class vessels, of which *Cossack* was one, were produced as a counter to those being built by potential enemies, rather than to fill any clearly definable role within the fleet.

HULL

By any standards the "Tribal" class were magnificent ships to look at, their pleasingly balanced profile in harmony with the high freeboard hull that was introduced to improve their fighting qualities in poor weather.

ARMAMENT

Because they were intended primarily to counter vessels like the Japanese *Fubuki*-class super destroyers, the "Tribals" carried a heavy armament of four twin 120-mm (4.7-in) guns and one quadruple 533-mm (21-in) torpedo mounting.

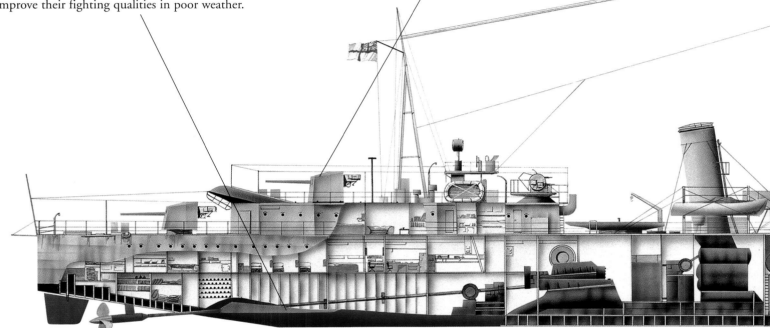

COSSACK – SPECIFICATION

Country of origin: United Kingdom
Type: Destroyer
Laid down: 9 June, 1936
Builder: Vickers-Armstrongs at Newcastle-on-Tyne, England
Launched: 8 June, 1937
Commissioned: 7 June, 1938
Fate: Sunk 27 October, 1941
Complement: 219

Dimensions:
Displacement: 1696 tonnes (1870 tons)
Length: 111.5 m (364 ft 8 in); **Beam:** 11.13 m (36 ft 6 in);
  Draught: 4 m (13 ft)

Powerplant:
Propulsion: 2 shaft Parsons geared turbines developing
  33,131 kW (44,000 shp)
Speed: 36 knots

Armament & Armour:
Armament: 8 x 120-mm (4.7-in) twin turrets; 1 x quadruple
  0.9-kg (2-lb) anti-aircraft guns; 2 x quadruple 12.7-mm (0.5in)
  calibre MGs; 1 x quadruple torpedo tubes (533-mm [21-in]
  Mk IX Torpedoes);
  2 x Depth charge throwers; 1 x Depth charge rail
Armour: Not specified

FUNNELS
A distinctive feature of the "Tribal"-class destroyers was their two raked funnels, the rearmost of which was later reduced in size to provide a better arc of fire for the ship's AA guns.

MACHINERY
The "Tribal"-class destroyers were powered by two sets of Parsons geared turbines, producing 33,131 kW (44,000 shp) and giving a maximum speed of 36 knots.

STEM
The "Tribal"-class destroyers were quite different from previous designs, featuring a sharply raked stem. This added 3 m (10 ft) to the length of the forecastle deck.

FIRE CONTROL
The "Tribal" class introduced the Fuze Keeping Clock High Angle Fire Control Computer, which was fitted in all subsequent classes of Royal Navy destroyers during World War II.

During her operations in 1939–41 *Cossack* was commanded by Captain Philip Vian, who reached high rank in the Royal Navy and eventually became commander-in-chief of the Home Fleet in the years just after the war.

RIVAL: *FUBUKI*

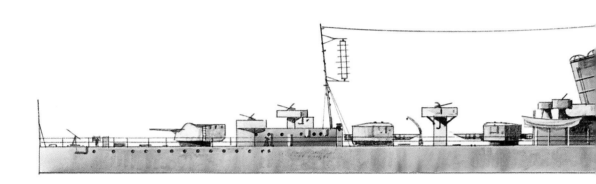

SISTER SHIP: *ESKIMO*

"TRIBAL" CLASS

Only four of the original 16 "Tribals" remained afloat by the end of 1942. Of *Cossack's* sister ships, *Afridi* and *Gurkha* were bombed off Norway; *Maori* was bombed at Malta; *Mohawk* was torpedoed by an Italian destroyer off Cape Bon; *Zulu* was bombed at Tobruk; *Bedouin* was torpedoed by Italian aircraft; *Mashona* was bombed south-west of Ireland; *Matabele* was sunk by *U454* in the Barents Sea; *Punjabi* was lost in a collision with the *King George V*; *Sikh* was sunk by shore batteries at Tobruk; *Somali* was torpedoed by *U703* south of Iceland; and *Athabaskan* was torpedoed by the German torpedo boat *T27* off the coast of Normandy.

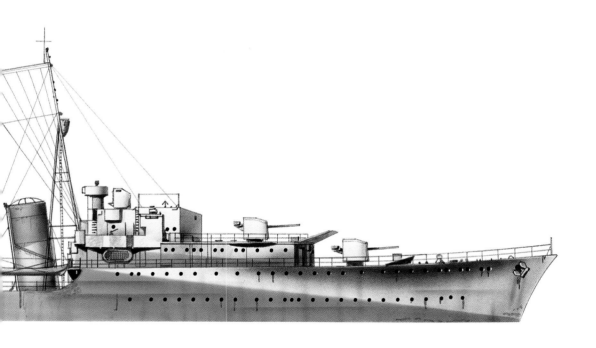

Cossack heads out into the Mediterranean from Malta's Grand Harbour in the summer of 1941. The Royal Navy succeeded in keeping Malta supplied, but only at an enormous cost in ships and men.

***Cossack*'s place in naval history was assured when, in February 1940, she carried out a dramatic rescue operation in Norwegian waters. Taking place during the so-called "Phoney War" period, the incident was to generate huge publicity worldwide.**

The use of Norwegian ports by enemy blockade runners was always a sore point. Matters in this respect came to a head when, on 14 February, 1940, the tanker *Altmark* (the supply ship of *Admiral Graf Spee*), carrying some 300 merchant seamen from vessels sunk by the pocket battleship, sought refuge in Trondheim under Norwegian protection.

Darkness on 16 February found the enemy tanker in Josing fjord, where she was followed by Captain P.L. Vian in *Cossack*. Vian informed the senior Norwegian officer that as there were British prisoners on the *Altmark*, he demanded the right to search for them. The Norwegian replied that his orders were to resist, and trained his torpedoes on *Cossack*.

Faced with this delicate situation, Vian withdrew and sought the Admiralty's instructions. Three hours later, he was instructed by Winston Churchill, then First Lord of the Admiralty, to board the *Altmark* and liberate the prisoners.

Persuading the Norwegian naval vessels to withdraw, Vian took *Cossack* into Josing fjord and went alongside the *Altmark* – evading an attempt by *Altmark*'s Captain Dau to ram him – and sent over an armed boarding party. Six German guards were killed and six wounded before the boarding party escaped ashore, leaving the British sailors free to break open the *Altmark*'s hatches. Someone asked if there were any British below, and a tremendous yell assured him that the prisoners were all British. The words that followed – "Come on up, then! The Navy's here!"– were to become enshrined in British naval tradition.

DAMAGED AT NARVIK

Only a few weeks later, on 13 April, 1940, following the German invasion of Norway, *Cossack* was badly damaged in action with German destroyers at Narvik. Returning to operational duty, she fought a night action near Egersund, attacking a group of ships in German service together with *Ashanti*, *Maori*, and *Sikh* and sinking two of them.

On 26 May, 1941, while escorting Convoy WS-8B to the Middle East, *Cossack* and four other destroyers were ordered to break away and head towards the area where the German battleship *Bismarck* had been reported. They found her and made several torpedo attacks in the evening and into the next morning. No hits were scored, but they kept her gunners from getting any sleep, making it more difficult for them to repel other British warships as they attacked her the following morning.

In the summer of 1941 *Cossack* was in Malta on convoy escort duty in the Mediterranean. At this time, she and her sister ship *Maori* shelled the Sardinian harbour of Alghero.

Back in the North Atlantic, she was escorting a convoy from Gibraltar to the United Kingdom on the night of 23/24 October, 1941, when she was sighted by the German submarine *U563*, which hit her with a single torpedo.

THE END OF *COSSACK*

On the following day, she was taken in tow by a tug from Gibraltar, but the weather worsened and she sank west of Gibraltar on 27 October, 1941, with the loss of 159 crew.

Close-up

Cossack enters harbour in February 1940, where she is greeted by jubilant crowds after rescuing the prisoners of the *Altmark* in Josing fjord.

1. **Prestige:** The "Tribals" were admired by both their crews and the public, often becoming symbols of prestige while in service.

2. **Crowds:** It was usual for crowds of dockyard workers and other personnel to gather on the quayside to greet an incoming warship, especially a successful one.

3. **Armament:** The "Tribals" were built to a concept that differed from other Royal Navy destroyers built up to the time, with more emphasis on guns than torpedoes.

4. **Technological Innovator:** The "Tribal" class introduced the Fuze Keeping Clock High Angle Fire Control Computer.

5. **Bow:** The "Tribals" were considered to be handsome ships, with their clipper bow and raked funnels and masts. The bow gave them excellent sea-keeping qualities.

6. **Corvette:** The "Tribals" were much larger and so different from other British destroyers in service that the resurrection of a corvette classification was considered for them.

Hiryu 1937

The Japanese carrier *Hiryu*, which translates as "flying dragon," was so successful a design that it became the standard for the Imperial Japanese Navy. Construction of *Hiryu* was delayed to include some improvements in her seakeeping qualities.

FLIGHT DECK
Hiryu was relatively small for a fleet carrier, which was reflected in the size of her flight deck. The position of the island on the port side proved a failure, as it created dangerous air currents and reduced deck space.

HANGARS
Hiryu's two hangars were served by three lifts. The carrier could accommodate about 70 aircraft, but her usual complement was 54 (18 Mitsubishi A6M Zeros, 18 Aichi D3A Vals, and 18 Nakajima B5N Kates).

MACHINERY
Hiryu was powered by four Kanpon geared turbines, producing 113 MW (153,000 shp) and giving a speed of just over 34 knots. Oil capacity was 3992 tonnes (4400 tons) and endurance was 19,131 km (10,330 nm) at 18 knots.

HIRYU – SPECIFICATION

Country of origin: Japan
Type: Aircraft carrier
Laid down: 8 July, 1936
Launched: 16 November, 1937
Commissioned: 5 July, 1939
Decommissioned: n/a
Fate: Sunk 5 June, 1942, Battle of Midway
Complement: 1103 + 23 officers for Carrier Division 2 Flagship

Dimensions:
Displacement: (standard) 15,694 tonnes (17,300 tons); (full load) 18,293 tonnes (20,165 tons)
Length: (waterline) 222 m (728 ft 5 in); 216.9 m (711 ft 7 in) (flight deck)
Beam: 22.3 m (73 ft 2 in)

Draught: 7.74 m (25 ft 5 in)

Powerplant:
Propulsion: 4 shaft geared steam turbines producing 113 MW (153,000 shp)
Speed: 34.5 knots (63.9 km/h)
Range: 19,131 km (10,330 nm) at 18 knots

Armament & Armour:
Armament: 12 x 127-mm (5-in) guns; 31x 25-mm (0.98-in) anti-aircraft guns
Armour: Not specified
Aircraft: 70

FACTS

- Launched 16 November, 1937; completed July 1939.

- Took part in the attack on Pearl Harbor, 7 December, 1941.

- Air strikes against Wake Island, 21–23 December, 1941.

- Air strikes on Darwin, February 1942.

- Raid on Ceylon, April 1942.

- Severely damaged by U.S. aircraft in Battle of Midway, 4 June, 1942, and sunk by escorting destroyers the following day (416 dead).

SUPERSTRUCTURE
The island was situated almost amidships and to port, where it partly balanced the two horizontally-discharging funnels to starboard. The only other Japanese carrier to share this feature was *Akagi*.

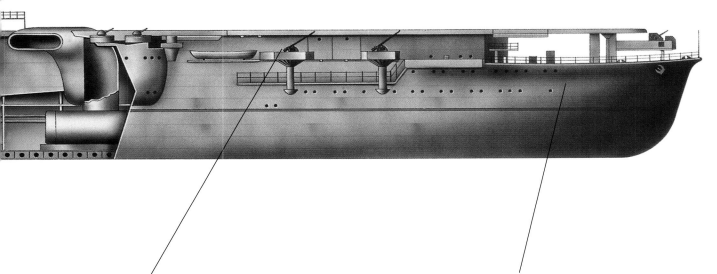

ARMAMENT
Both *Hiryu* and her sister ship *Soryu*, which translates as Blue Dragon, carried a main armament of 12 127-mm (5-in) dual-purpose guns and 31 25-mm (0.98-in) anti-aircraft guns.

HULL
The *Hiryu* was a slightly enlarged and modified *Soryu*, with the beam increased by 1 m (3 ft) to give a 20 per cent increase in oil capacity. Her protection was also strengthened and her forecastle was raised by a deck.

Naval air power was at the core of Japan's strategy. She had completed her first aircraft carrier, the *Hosho*, in 1922, and this vessel was soon to be followed by larger and more powerful fleet carriers, like the *Akagi*, seen here.

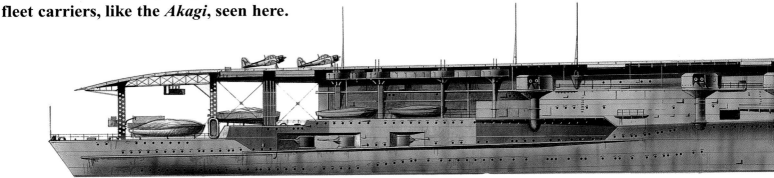

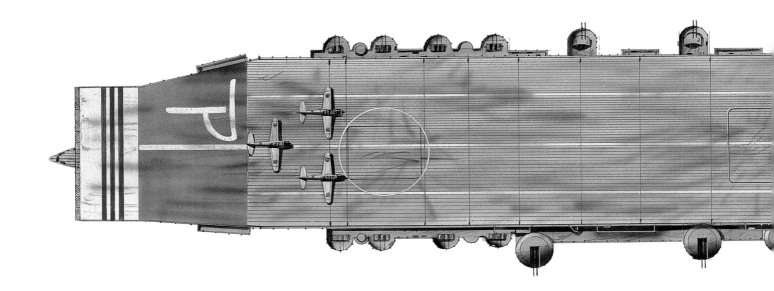

FAST-ATTACK CARRIERS

At the outset of the Pacific War in December 1941 Japan possessed the third-largest fleet in the world, with fast-attack carriers manned by highly trained crews at its core. The navy, however, had certain deficiencies that were to prove fatal. Few anti-submarine warships had been built, merchant shipping was not protected by a convoy system, and radar was not advanced enough for operational use. Moreover, the Japanese did not have the raw material resources necessary to wage a major war for any length of time. They therefore relied on rapid conquest, preceded by the neutralization of enemy assets by means of their fast-attack carriers.

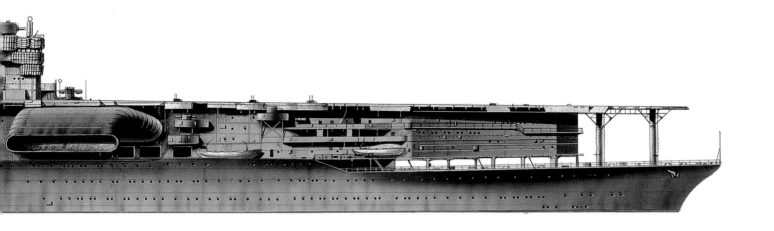

JAPANESE CARRIER: *AKAGI*

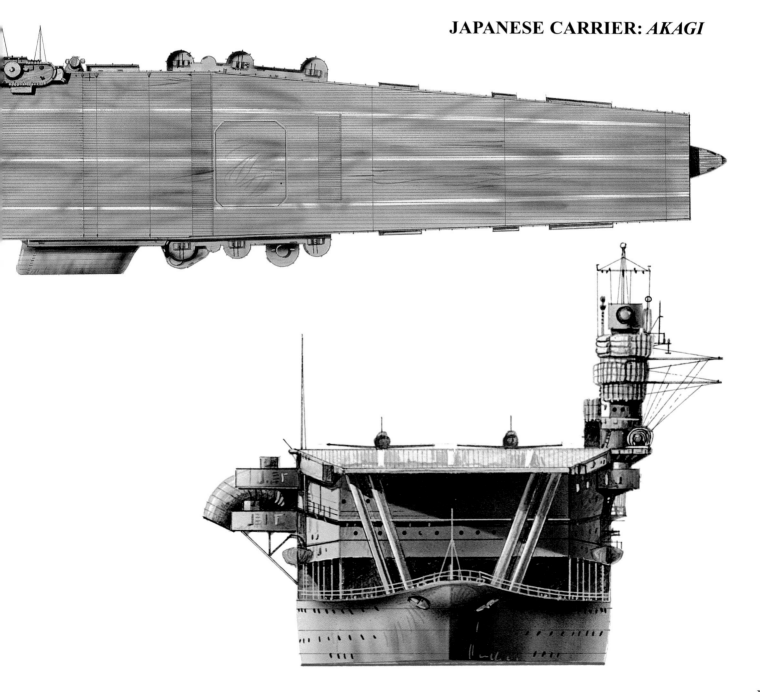

In November 1941, *Hiryu* formed part of the most formidable force assembled in Japanese waters since Tsushima, 36 years earlier. This was the battle fleet assigned by the Imperial Japanese Navy to what was known as the Hawaiian Operation, the planned surprise attack on Pearl Harbor, the principal base of the U.S. Pacific Fleet.

The Japanese Fleet sailed for Hawaii on 26 November, 1941. At its heart were the aircraft carriers of the 1st Air Fleet, the *Akagi*, *Kaga*, *Hiryu*, *Soryu*, *Zuikaku*, and *Shokaku*, under the command of Vice-Admiral Chuichi Nagumo.

The first attack on Pearl Harbor lasted 30 minutes, striking the anchorage and outlying air bases. The second

Close-up

Hiryu met her end in the open ocean, but other carriers, like the *Aso*, seen here, were scuttled or bombed to destruction in harbour.

(1) **Bridge:** The design of the *Amagi*-class carriers, of which *Aso* was one, closely followed that of the *Hiryu*, but with the bridge on the starboard side.

(2) **Power:** Due to a lack of suitable engines, *Aso* was powered by destroyer turbines. Other ships in the class used cruiser turbines.

(3) **Incomplete:** Work on *Aso* was stopped in January 1945 when she was 60 per cent complete. She was launched and left in an unfinished state.

(4) **Three completed:** Laid down in 1942–43, only three carriers of this class were completed. Others were in various stages of completion.

(5) **Hull:** This was used as a kamikaze testbed and she was half-sunk in shallow water at Kure when surrendered in August 1945.

(6) **Filling the Gap:** *Aso* was one of the carriers laid down to fill the gap left by the destruction of Japan's fleet carriers at Midway, but work began too late.

Shinano was the most modern of Japan's carriers. Adapted from a Yamato-*class battleship, she was sunk by the American submarine* Archerfish *on 29 November, 1944 while en route from Yokosuka to another naval yard for fitting out.*

strike, just over an hour later, was made by 54 Kate bombers, 78 Val dive-bombers and 35 fighters. The strike lasted 65 minutes but was hampered by dense smoke from the burning anchorage and by heavy anti-aircraft fire, as well as by small numbers of American fighters. Of the 94 warships in the harbour, 18 were sunk or suffered major damage. Eight of the losses were battleships, which had been the attackers' primary targets.

After the Pearl Harbor attack, *Hiryu* was assigned to Carrier Division 2. She participated in the launching of air strikes against Wake Island, and in January 1942 she supported the invasion of Ambon in the Moluccas. In February 1942, together with *Soryu*, she launched air attacks on Darwin, Australia, and in March she took part in the Battle of the Java Sea, her aircraft attacking Allied shipping and sinking a Dutch freighter.

ATTACKS ON CEYLON AND COLOMBO

In April 1942, Admiral Nagumo's 1st Carrier Striking Force, comprising the aircraft carriers *Akagi*, *Hiryu*, *Shokaku*, *Soryu*, and *Zuikaku*, entered the Indian Ocean to carry out an attack on Ceylon. Between them, the five carriers mustered some 300 strike aircraft and fighters.

Early on 5 April (Easter Sunday) the Japanese launched a strike of 53 Nakajima B5N Kate high-level bombers and 38 Aichi D3A Val dive-bombers, escorted by 36 Zero fighters, to attack Colombo. The Japanese raiding force was intercepted by 42 Hurricanes and Fulmars, resulting in fierce air battles developing over the city and harbour. In

the end, seven Japanese aircraft were destroyed, but 19 British fighters were shot down. The attack caused heavy damage to built-up areas. The damage to shipping and the port installations was relatively light, although the auxiliary cruiser *Hector* and the destroyer *Tenedos* were sunk.

At about noon, the cruisers *Cornwall* and *Dorsetshire* were sighted by a reconnaissance aircraft from the heavy cruiser *Tone* and 53 Val dive-bombers were immediately sent out to attack them. The bombing was devastatingly accurate and both ships were sunk.

THE TIDE OF WAR TURNS

At the beginning of June 1942, the Japanese launched a strong thrust in the central Pacific; its objective, as part of Yamamoto's eastward expansion plan, was to occupy Midway Island. The thrust was led by a four-carrier Mobile Force comprising the *Akagi*, *Kaga*, *Hiryu* and *Soryu*, supported by heavy units of the First Fleet and covered by a diversionary attack by carrier aircraft on Dutch Harbor in the Aleutians.

In the ensuing battle, which effectively turned the tide of the Pacific War, the U.S. Navy destroyed all four fleet carriers, three-quarters of the Imperial Japanese Navy's carrier striking force, for the loss of 94 aircraft and the carrier *Yorktown*. On 4 June, *Hiryu* was crippled in an attack by 24 Douglas SBD dive-bombers from *Enterprise*. Her burnt-out hulk was sunk by a Japanese destroyer the next day.

Bismarck 1939

The mighty battleship *Bismarck* was to have formed the nucleus of a powerful battle group that included the battlecruisers *Scharnhorst* and *Gneisenau* and the heavy cruiser *Prinz Eugen*. *Bismarck* was capable of engaging escorting warships single-handedly while her consorts attacked the merchant convoys.

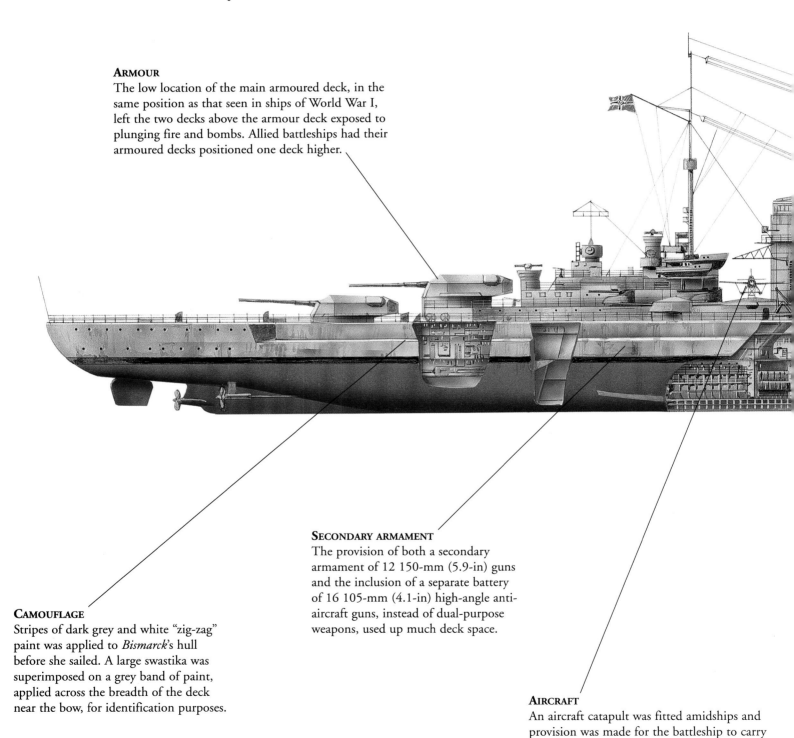

ARMOUR
The low location of the main armoured deck, in the same position as that seen in ships of World War I, left the two decks above the armour deck exposed to plunging fire and bombs. Allied battleships had their armoured decks positioned one deck higher.

CAMOUFLAGE
Stripes of dark grey and white "zig-zag" paint was applied to *Bismarck*'s hull before she sailed. A large swastika was superimposed on a grey band of paint, applied across the breadth of the deck near the bow, for identification purposes.

SECONDARY ARMAMENT
The provision of both a secondary armament of 12 150-mm (5.9-in) guns and the inclusion of a separate battery of 16 105-mm (4.1-in) high-angle anti-aircraft guns, instead of dual-purpose weapons, used up much deck space.

AIRCRAFT
An aircraft catapult was fitted amidships and provision was made for the battleship to carry six Arado Ar 196 seaplanes, although *Bismarck* carried only four. These were fast enough and sufficiently armed to intercept Allied maritime reconnaissance aircraft.

RADAR
Bismarck carried Seetakt radar. Maximum range against a ship-sized target at sea was up to 220 km (136 miles) in favourable conditions, though more typically half that.

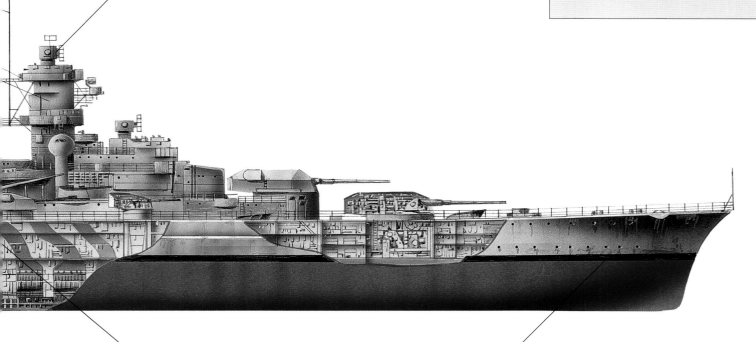

TORPEDO TUBES
Bismarck was fitted with eight 533-mm (21-in) torpedo tubes, four on either side of the main deck amidships.

BOW
Both *Bismarck* and *Tirpitz* were designed with a straight bow, but this was changed to a rakish clipper bow after launching.

BISMARCK – SPECIFICATION

Country of origin: Germany
Type: Battleship
Laid down: 1 July, 1936
Builder: Blohm & Voss, Hamburg
Launched: 14 February, 1939
Commissioned: 24 August, 1940
Fate: Sunk 27 May, 1941
Complement: 2092: 103 officers 1989 men (1941)

Dimensions:
Displacement: (standard) 47,000 tonnes (51,809 tons); (full load) 50,900 tonnes (56,108 tons)
Length: (overall) 251 m (823.5 ft); (waterline) 241.5 m (792.3 ft)
Beam: 36 m (118.1 ft) (waterline)

Draught: (Standard) 9.3 m (30.5 ft); (full load) 10.2 m (33.5 ft)

Powerplant:
Propulsion: 3 Blohm & Voss geared turbines 111.98 MW (150,170 shp)
Speed: 31.1 knots
Range: 15,788 km (8525 nm)

Armament & Armour:
Armament: 8 x 380-mm (15-in) guns; 12 x 150-mm (5.9-in) guns; 16 x 105-mm (4.1-in anti-aircraft guns)
Armour: 110–360 mm (4.3–14 in)
Aircraft: 4 x Arado Ar 196 A-3, with 1 double-ended catapult

Bismarck and *Tirpitz* were to have been followed by a class of even more powerful battleships. Six units were planned, and the first two were laid down, but the project was abandoned in the middle of 1940 when Germany seemed to be winning the war.

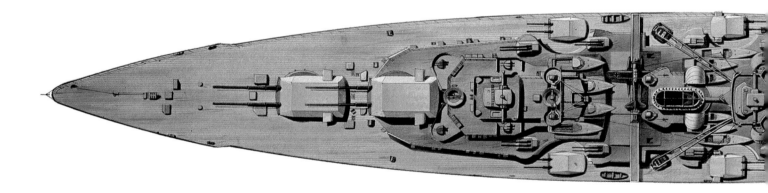

BISMARCK

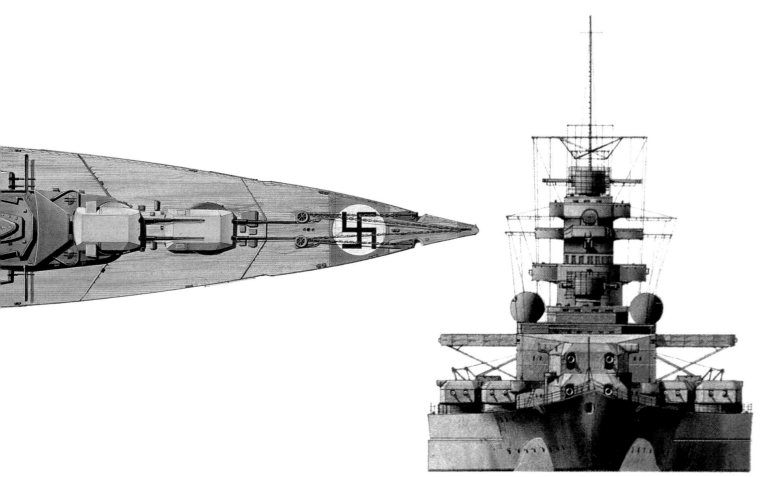

DEPLOYMENT TO THE ATLANTIC

On 2 April, 1941, the German Naval Staff issued preparatory orders for the deployment of *Bismarck* and other surface units to the Atlantic. In the next New Moon period at the end of the month *Bismarck*, *Prinz Eugen,* and the battlecruiser *Gneisenau*, which was then in the French Atlantic port of Brest together with her sister ship, *Scharnhorst*, were to rendezvous in the Atlantic to launch a combined attack on Allied shipping. Had this formidable battle group put to sea in its entirety, the result might have been disastrous for Britain. The carnage this group was capable of inflicting, as the British were well aware, would have been atrocious.

"Ship no longer manoeuvrable. We fight to the last shell. Long live the Führer." With these words, Admiral Günther Lütjens, the German Fleet Commander, signalled *Bismarck*'s impending doom to Berlin.

Bismarck had sailed only days earlier, on 19 May, 1941, in company with *Prinz Eugen*. There was to be no rendezvous. *Scharnhorst* was laid up with boiler trouble and *Gneisenau* had been torpedoed in Brest harbour by a Bristol Beaufort of RAF Coastal Command on 6 April.

Air reconnaissance revealed that the German warships were heading for Icelandic waters, and the Royal Navy rapidly deployed its forces to intercept them. On 23 May they were sighted by the cruisers *Suffolk* and *Norfolk*, which continued to shadow the ships at high speed throughout the night, *Suffolk* maintaining contact with her Type 284 radar.

Close-up

After her launch, *Bismarck* was towed to the equipping pier to be fitted out. Even though the hull was completed and the machinery was installed, months of work lay ahead before she was finished.

(1) **Armament:** The secondary armament of 12 150-mm (5.9-in) guns were installed in twin turrets, three to port and three to starboard.

(2) **Aircraft Hangar:** The large aircraft hangar was situated amidships aft of the funnel and housing up to six Arado Ar 196 floatplanes.

(3) **Seetakt radar:** Used for navigation and search purposes, this has yet to be fitted on top of the bridge.

(4) **Rangefinder:** Other equipment to be fitted includes the rangefinder, which will be installed in a cupola on the conning tower.

(5) **Mast:** The mainmast is taking shape to the rear of the funnel, with its spotting positions and signalling equipment.

(6) **Searchlight:** The ship was fitted with a very powerful searchlight, which was covered when not in use. The cover is seen here in the lowered position.

Huge crowds attended the launch of Bismarck *on 14 February, 1939. The ceremony was carried out by Dorothea von Löwenfeld, Bismarck's grand-daughter. Adolf Hitler, Hermann Göring, and Rudolf Hess were among those in attendance.*

GERMAN SHIPS DESTROY *HOOD*

The British battleship *Prince of Wales* and the battlecruiser *Hood*, meanwhile, were coming up quickly. At 0537 the opposing forces sighted each other at a range of 27 km (17 miles), and opened fire at 0553. Both German ships concentrated their fire on *Hood* and, thanks to their stereoscopic rangefinders, straddled her immediately. *Bismarck*'s second and third salvoes struck the battlecruiser amidships, and those from *Prinz Eugen* started a fire among her ready-to-use AA ammunition. At 0600, as the British warships were altering course in order to bring all their guns to bear, *Hood* was hit again by a salvo, which pierced her lightly armoured decks and detonated in her after magazines. She blew up with a tremendous explosion and disappeared with a speed that stunned all who witnessed the event. Only three of her crew of 1419 officers and ratings survived.

As *Prince of Wales* altered course sharply to avoid the wreckage she herself came under heavy fire. Within moments she sustained hits by four 380-mm (15-in) and three 203-mm (8-in) shells, one of which exploded on the bridge and killed or wounded almost everyone there except her captain, who ordered the battleship to turn away under cover of smoke. *Prince of Wales*'s gunners had obtained

three hits on *Bismarck*, causing two of her fuel tanks to leak oil and contaminating others. Because of this, Admiral Lütjens decided to abandon the sortie and to steer southwest for St. Nazaire, the only port on the Atlantic coast of France with a dry dock large enough to accommodate his flagship while repairs were carried out. He detached *Prinz Eugen* to continue on her way alone.

HUNTERS CLOSE IN

The main concern now was to reduce *Bismarck*'s speed, giving the hunters a chance to close in for the kill. At 1440 on 24 May the British commander, Admiral Tovey, ordered the carrier *Victorious* to race ahead to a flying-off point 160 km (100 miles) from the enemy ships and launch a strike against them. The first strike by Swordfish aircraft resulted in only one torpedo hit, but the second was decisive. Two torpedoes found their mark. One struck *Bismarck*'s extreme stern, damaging her propellers and jamming her rudders.

The British warships closed in during the night to finish her off. By 1020 *Bismarck* had been reduced to a blazing wreck, with all her armament out of action, but she was still afloat and it was left to the cruisers *Norfolk* and *Dorsetshire* to close in and sink her with torpedoes.

Tirpitz 1939

In the 1930s, the German Admiralty formulated a scheme designed to give Germany technological superiority on the high seas. It was based on two super-powerful battleships, *Bismarck* and *Tirpitz*. The latter was named after Alfred von Tirpitz, founder of the modern German Navy.

COMPARTMENTS
The subdivision on *Tirpitz* was extensive, with the major compartments being enlarged to allow better crew comfort, especially in the boiler rooms.

ARMOUR
Many of the design features of *Tirpitz* owed much to the *Baden* class, the last battleships designed for the Imperial German Navy. The armour arrangement followed this pattern, with thicker horizontal and somewhat thinner vertical protection.

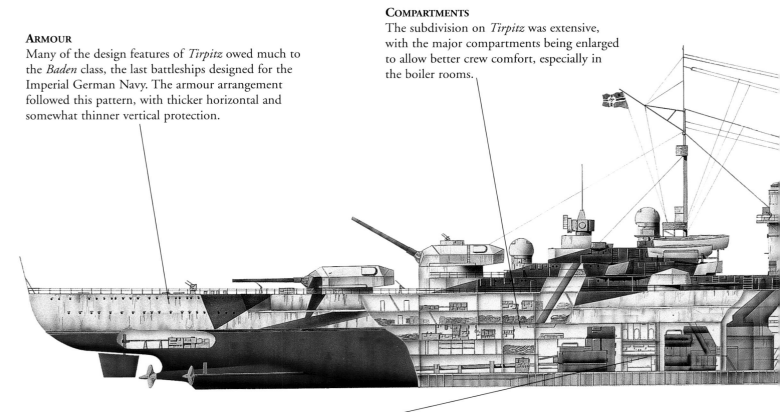

MACHINERY
Tirpitz was powered by three Brown-Boveri geared turbines, producing 102.9 MW (138,000 shp) and giving a top speed of 29 knots.

TIRPITZ – SPECIFICATION

Country of origin: Germany
Type: Battleship
Laid down: 2 November, 1936
Builder: Kriegsmarinewerft, Wilhelmshaven
Launched: 1 April, 1939
Commissioned: 25 February, 1941
Fate: Sunk 12 November, 1944
Complement: 2608

Dimensions:
Displacement: (standard) 42,900 tonnes (47,289 tons); (full load) 53,500 tonnes (58,974 tons)
Length: (overall) 251 m (823 ft); (waterline) 241.7 m (793 ft)
Beam: (waterline) 36 m (118 ft)
Draught: (standard) 9m (29 ft 5 in); (full load) 10.6 m (34 ft 8 in)

Powerplant:
Propulsion: 3 Brown-Boveri geared turbines, producing 102.9 MW (138,000 shp)
Speed: 29 knots
Range: 16,427 km (8870 nm) @ 19 knots

Armament & Armour:
Armament: 8 x 380-mm (15-in) guns; 12 x 150-mm (5.9-in) guns; 16 x 105-mm (4.1-in) guns; 16 x 37-mm (1.45-in) guns; 12 x 20-mm (0.79-in) MGs; 72 x 20-mm (0.79-in) L65 MGs C/38 (quadruple); 2 x quadruple 533-mm (21-in) G7a T1 torpedo tubes
Armour: 50–360 mm (1.97–14.7 in)
Aircraft: 4 x Arado Ar196A-3, with 1 double-ended catapult

RANGEFINDER
One of the most outstanding features was the optical rangefinder equipment, but the two original *Seetakt* radar sets on *Tirpitz* were never updated.

SECONDARY ARMAMENT
In 1942 *Tirpitz* was fitted with six 533-mm (21-in) torpedo tubes in triple mountings, removed from the cruiser *Leipzig*. Her AA armament was also steadily increased until she had 40 20-mm (0.79-in) guns in triple mountings.

HULL
Tirpitz had an extremely broad beam of 36 m (118 ft), which was adopted for reasons of stability. As a result, she was an extremely stable gun platform, even in heavy seas.

Tirpitz never engaged the Royal Navy in a surface action. However, while she was still afloat she remained a grave danger to the Allied Atlantic convoys, so the British made repeated attempts to destroy her.

TIRPITZ

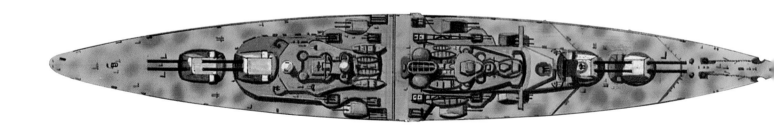

OPERATION CHARIOT

In March 1942, the Royal Navy participated in the biggest combined operation mounted so far by the British in World War II. Called Operation Chariot, it was born out of desperation. Behind it all lay the presence, in Norway, of the most powerful German naval force so far assembled, including *Admiral Scheer*, *Lützow*, and four destroyers at Narvik, and *Tirpitz*, *Hipper*, and six destroyers at Trondheim. Of these, the principal threat was *Tirpitz*, which was capable of wreaking deadly havoc on the Allied convoys should she be let loose in the North Atlantic. The goal of the combined operation was to destroy the dock facilities at St. Nazaire, which were the only ones large enough to accommodate the battleship.

The mighty Tirpitz *would have undoubtedly caused appalling destruction had she operated aggressively against the Allied Arctic convoys but, for fear of being attacked from the air, she never did. Now the Germans keenly felt the lack of an aircraft carrier to provide fighter cover.*

In September 1943 *Tirpitz* and *Scharnhorst* made one sortie to bombard installations on the island of Spitzbergen before scurrying back to their Norwegian lair. The incident was to be the only time *Tirpitz* fired her main guns in anger.

In January 1942, her trials complete, *Tirpitz* slipped out of the Baltic and arrived at Trondheim, bearing the flag of Admiral Ciliax. On 6 March, accompanied by three destroyers, she set out to intercept convoys PQ12 and QP8, the first bound for Murmansk, the second on its way home. However, no contact was made and the German force turned southwards again. Thanks to Ultra decrypts, the British knew of the Germans' intentions and ordered their forces towards the Lofoten Islands in an attempt to cut them off. At daybreak on 9 March, a reconnaissance aircraft from the carrier *Victorious* spotted *Tirpitz*, and 12 torpedo-carrying Albacores took off soon afterwards to attack the warship. The attack, unfortunately, was carried out in line astern, which gave *Tirpitz* ample room to avoid all the torpedoes, although one passed within 10 m (30 ft)

of her. Two of the Albacores were shot down. The failure of this attack was a bitter pill for the Royal Navy to swallow, but it did have one result. On Hitler's own orders, *Tirpitz* never put to sea again if carrier-based aircraft were known to be in the vicinity.

STRIKE AGAINST *TIRPITZ*

Tirpitz remained inactive at Altenfjord during most of 1942 and the early months of 1943. On 22 September, following her brief sortie to bombard Spitzbergen, she was subjected to a gallant attack by British midget submarines, which left her badly damaged.

In March 1944, in a bid to knock her out once and for all, the C-in-C Home Fleet planned a massive Fleet Air Arm strike against her while she was still immobile at Kaafjord, where she had been undergoing repair. The attack took place in the morning of 3 April, 1944, when 21 Fairey Barracudas of No 8 TBR Wing took off from *Victorious* and set course for the target. The Germans were taken by surprise and *Tirpitz*, lying virtually naked under the beginnings of a smoke screen, was hit by nine armour-piercing or semi-armour-piercing bombs. An hour later, a second attack was made by 19 Barracudas of No 52 TBR

Wing, escorted by 39 fighters, and the performance was repeated. By this time the smoke screen was fully developed, but it hindered the German gunners far more than it did the Barracuda crews, who had no difficulty in locating their target.

REPEATEDLY UNDER ATTACK

In all, the battleship was hit by 14 bombs, and 122 of her crew were killed and 316 wounded. The bombs failed to penetrate her heavy armour, but they still caused extensive damage to her superstructure and fire control systems, putting her out of action for three months. Two minor bomb hits were obtained on *Tirpitz* in an attack on 24 August, the Barracuda crews bombing blind through the smoke, and a further attack, on the 29th, was unsuccessful. Counting a mission that had to be aborted because of the weather on 20 August, the Fleet Air Arm flew 247 sorties in this series of attacks. As for *Tirpitz*, she was moved south to Tromso for repair, and it was there, on 12 November 1944, that she was finally destroyed by 5.5-tonne (6-ton) Tallboy bombs dropped by the Lancasters of Nos 9 and 617 Squadrons, RAF.

Close-up

When *Tirpitz* lay at anchor in Norway, her sailors enjoyed a life of comparative luxury. Here, a dancing troupe entertains them.

(1) **Armour: At its maximum, the ship's armour was 32 cm (12.5 in) thick.**

(2) **Anti-aircraft: The AA battery was augmented. In addition, two quadruple torpedo mounts were installed on the upper deck on each side of the ship amidships.**

(3) **Dimensions: Her overall length was 251 m (823 ft), with a beam of 118 ft (36 m), and a draught of 9 m (29.5 ft).**

(4) **Guns: Her main armament comprised eight 380-mm (15-in) guns, and she also had a formidable secondary armament.**

(5) **Protected: The inlet of Altenfjord, where *Tirpitz* spent much of her time, provided an ideal base for sorties against Allied convoys.**

(6) **Civilian Complement: Many Norwegian civilians were employed as cooks and cleaners on *Tirpitz*. About 100 lost their lives when she was sunk by the RAF.**

Yamato 1940

Although the emphasis in Japanese naval construction during the inter-war years was on aircraft carriers, the navy retained a powerful fleet of reconstructed battleships and battlecruisers. In addition, two new battleships, *Yamato* and *Musashi*, were laid down in 1937. They were the largest and most powerful battleships ever built, and were constructed in great secrecy.

AIRCRAFT
Yamato carried six or seven Mitsubishi F1M biplanes. Although designed as observation aircraft, their exceptional manoeuvrability meant that they could also be used as fighters and dive-bombers.

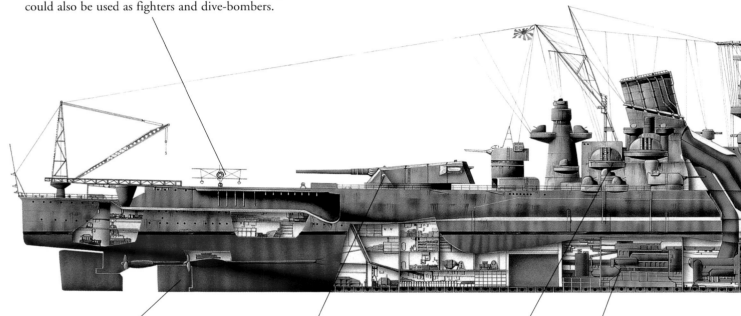

MAIN ARMAMENT
Each triple gun turret weighed 2295 tonnes (2530 tons). At an elevation of 45 degrees the guns could fire a 1458-kg (3214-lb) projectile 42,000 m (45,930 yards).

HULL
Yamato had several features that were new to Japanese warship construction. There was a bulbous bow to decrease wave resistance, and an auxiliary rudder positioned before the main rudder to assist steering under difficult conditions.

MACHINERY
Yamato was powered by four Kanpon geared turbines, producing 110 MW (150,000 shp) and giving a speed of 27 knots.

ARMOUR
Yamato's protection was designed to enable her to withstand 457-mm (18-in) shells at ranges of between 20,700–31,000 m (22,640–34,000 yards), and against a one-ton bomb dropped from 4575 m (15,000 ft). An anti-torpedo bulkhead was extended under the magazines to protect against mines.

FACTS

- Launched at Kure Naval Dockyard, 8 August, 1940; completed December 1941.

- Flagship of Combined Fleet, 1942.

- Torpedoed by U.S. submarine *Skate* south of Truk, 25 December, 1943.

- Damaged by two bomb hits during Battle of Leyte Gulf, October 1944.

- Sunk by U.S. carrier aircraft 210 km (130 miles) southwest of Kagoshima (2498 dead).

SUPERSTRUCTURE
Like most Japanese battleships, *Yamato* gave the impression of being top-heavy, with her huge tower foremast and massive funnel.

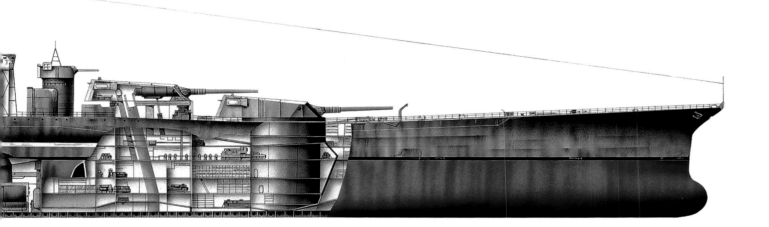

YAMATO – SPECIFICATION

Country of origin: Japan
Type: Battleship
Laid down: 4 November, 1937
Builder: Kure Naval Arsenal, Hiroshima
Launched: 8 August, 1940
Commissioned: 16 December, 1941
Fate: Sunk 7 April, 1945
Complement: 2500–2800

Dimensions:
Displacement: (standard) 65,027 tonnes (71,680 tons); (full load) 71,659 tonnes (78,990 tons)
Length: (overall) 263 m (862 ft 10 in); **Beam:** 36.9 m (121 ft);

Draught: 11 m (36 ft)

Powerplant:
Propulsion: Quadruple screw turbines producing 110 MW (150,000 shp)
Speed: 27 knots
Range: 13,334 km (7200 nm) at 16 knots

Armament & Armour:
Armament: 9 x 460-mm (18.1-in) guns; 12 x 155-mm (6.1-in), 12 x 127-mm (5-in) guns
Armour: 200–650 mm (7.87–25.6 in)
Aircraft: 7

Yamato participated in the Battle of Midway, and in the Battle of the Philippine Sea and the Battle of Leyte Gulf, where she was joined by her sister ship **Musashi**, and in the last sortie by the Imperial Japanese Navy, when she met her end.

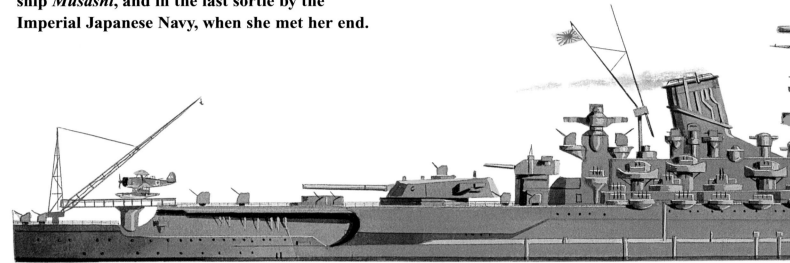

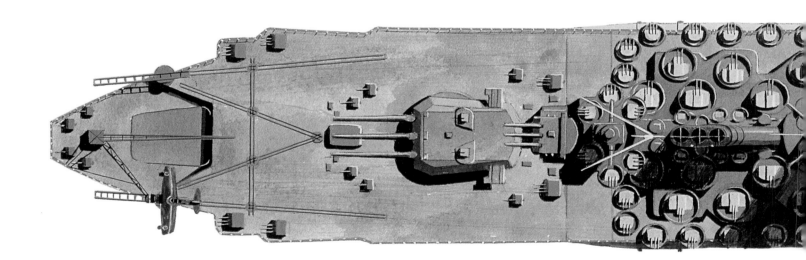

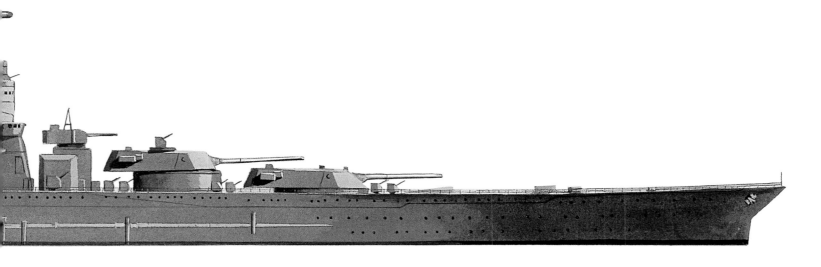

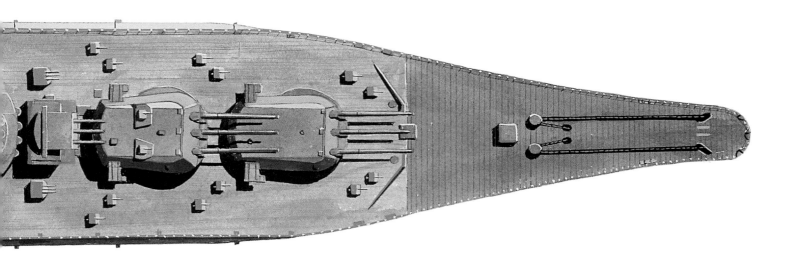

YAMATO-CLASS BATTLESHIPS

In 1937, in contravention of the various naval treaties in force at the time, Japan initiated construction of the *Yamato*-class battleships, the largest and most powerful ever built. A third vessel, the *Shinano*, was completed as an aircraft carrier and was sunk by the submarine *Archerfish* while en route to be fitted out; a fourth vessel was never completed. The ships were named after Japanese provinces, although *Yamato* is a poetic name for Japan itself.

This 1944 photo shows Yamato *steaming along at high speed. It was probably taken about the time of the Battle of Leyte, in October 1944, in which her sister ship* Musashi *was sunk.*

Yamato and Musashi were meant to be so powerful that they would cancel out America's naval superiority. Neither had a chance to justify her existence, as both were sunk by air attack after relatively brief careers.

The battleship *Yamato* was commissioned at Kure on 16 December 1941, joining the battleships *Nagato* and *Mutsu* in the 1st Battleship Division of the Imperial Japanese Navy. On 12 February 1942 she became the flagship of Admiral Isoroku Yamamoto, commander of the Combined Fleet, and it was from her bridge that he directed the Japanese naval deployments during the crucial Battle of Midway on 31 May. Following the Japanese defeat, with the loss of four fleet carriers and 332 aircraft, Yamamoto and the main battleship force withdrew to Hashirajima in Japan's Inland Sea.

In August 1942 *Yamato* left Kure for Truk. On 30 August, just as she was approaching Truk, she was sighted by the U.S. submarine *Flying Fish*, which launched a spread of four torpedoes at her. They all missed.

In November 1943 the Japanese decided to use *Yamato* and *Musashi* as transport vessels, and in the following month, while transporting troops and equipment to the Admiralty Islands, she was attacked by the submarine *Skate*, two torpedoes striking her starboard side. Her armoured belt failed and, with the upper magazine of the rear turret flooded, she limped back to Truk for emergency repairs, after which she sailed for Kure.

LANDINGS AT LEYTE

In October 1944 the reconquest of the Philippines began with the American landings at Leyte. On 22 October the battleships *Yamato*, *Musashi*, *Nagato*, *Kongo*, and *Haruna*, two cruisers, and 15 destroyers sailed from Brunei, Borneo, in an operation designed to disrupt the landings. On 24 October, the force was attacked by four waves of American aircraft from the Fast Carrier Force. During these attacks the *Musashi* was hit by 10 bombs and six torpedoes and sank in about eight hours with the loss of 1039 of her crew. *Yamato* was attacked by aircraft from the *Essex* and hit by three armour-piercing bombs, but they did little damage.

On 6 April, 1945, a Japanese task force sailed from Tokuyama on Japan's Inland Sea. At its heart was the

Yamato, accompanied by the cruiser *Yahagi* and eight destroyers. The battle group's destination was Okinawa, and its purpose was to inflict as much damage as possible on the U.S. invasion fleet. It would be a one-way mission; a critical shortage of fuel ensured that there could be no return to port.

AMERICAN AIRCRAFT STRIKES

Early on 7 April, the warships were sighted by two U.S. submarines, and at 1000 hours the American carriers off Okinawa launched a strike of 280 aircraft. In the first attack, the cruiser *Yahagi* and the destroyer *Hamakaze* were sunk;

the *Yamato* was hit by two bombs and a torpedo. A second strike of 100 aircraft was launched at 1400 hours. After taking nine more torpedo and three bomb hits, the *Yamato* began to flood uncontrollably and develop a serious list. Finally, after the order to abandon ship had been given, she rolled over and blew up with a tremendous explosion as her magazines detonated, her end marked by a huge column of smoke that could be seen 160 km (100 miles) away on Honshu. The loss of life was enormous. On that day 3,665 Japanese sailors perished, 2498 of them on the *Yamato* herself. Only 10 American aircraft were lost in the two attacks.

Close-up

The Japanese battleship *Yamato*, the mightiest to serve in World War II, is pictured here as she was nearing completion in 1941, only a few months before the attack on Pearl Harbor.

(1) **Superstructure:** Like all Japanese battleships, *Yamato* had a tall and crowded superstructure, which tended to give her a top-heavy appearance.

(2) **Firepower:** The *Yamato* class were designed to engage multiple enemy battleships at once. It was hoped their firepower would offset the U.S. Navy's numerical superiority.

(3) **Armament:** Each of *Yamato*'s main guns was 21.13 m (69 ft) long, and weighed 147 tonnes (162 tons).

(4) **Kure:** With war looming, priority was given to accelerating construction, and *Yamato* was commissioned at Kure on 16 December, 1941, months ahead of schedule.

(5) **Dockyard:** The dockyard at Kure was adapted to contain *Yamato*'s enormous hull. The dock was deepened by 1 m (3 ft) and upgraded cranes were installed.

(6) **Security risk:** *Yamato* was built in strictest secrecy. Canvas awnings were erected around the ship to shield her from view.

Iowa 1942

Although the U.S. Navy laid much emphasis on the construction of aircraft carriers between the wars, they did not neglect battleships. In the late 1930s three new classes of fast battleship emerged: *North Carolina* of 1937; *South Dakota* of 1938; and the *Iowa*-class of 1939. The basis was being laid for the task forces that would one day dominate the Pacific.

AIRCRAFT
Iowa originally carried three floatplanes for scouting and gunfire spotting. She had two quarterdeck catapults but, during her Korean War deployment, they were removed and *Iowa* carried helicopters instead.

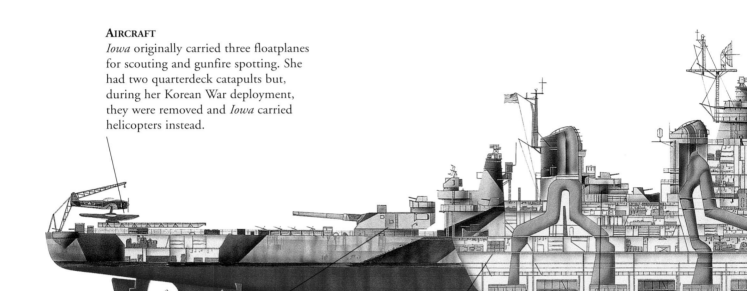

ARMOUR
The *Iowa* class were the most heavily armoured U.S. warships ever constructed, being designed to survive ship-to-ship combat with enemy ships armed with 406-mm (16-in) guns. The armour belt was inside the hull.

SUPERSTRUCTURE
The *Iowa*s were handsome vessels with two large funnels and a tall tower foremast. All were fitted with a tripod foremast after World War II.

FUEL
On average, during deployment in World War II, *Iowa* consumed fuel at the rate of about 565 litres per km (200 gallons per mile) at a mean speed of just under 18 knots.

DESIGN

Iowa's design included a clipper bow and long foredeck, with graceful sheer. They were the fastest battleships ever built, with a high length-to-beam ratio.

ARMAMENT

The Mk VII 406-mm (16-in) main armament fired projectiles weighing up to 1225 kg (2700 lb) over a maximum distance of 39 km (23 miles).

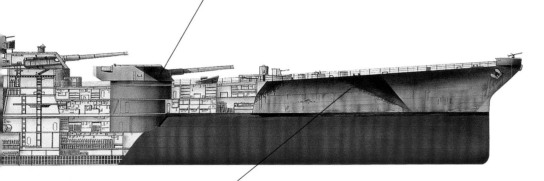

FACTS

- Launched 27 August, 1942; completed February 1943.

- Damaged by grounding off Maine, 16 July, 1943.

- Carried President Roosevelt to Casablanca Conference, October 1943.

- Bombardments of Luzon and Formosa, Leyte, and Okinawa, 1944–45.

- Refit 1951.

- Recommissioned for service in Korean War, 1952.

- Atlantic Fleet, 1952–58.

- Decommissioned 1958.

- Reactivated 1984.

- Gun turret wrecked by explosion, 1989; 47 dead.

- Decommissioned 1990.

MACHINERY

Iowa was powered by four General Electric geared turbines, producing 158.09 MW (212,000 shp). The design maximum speed was 33 knots, but all the *Iowa*-class ships reached 35 knots in service.

IOWA – SPECIFICATION

Country of origin: USA
Type: Battleship
Laid down: 27 June, 1940
Builder: New York Naval Yard
Launched: 27 August, 1942
Commissioned: 22 February, 1943
Decommissioned: 26 October, 1990
Fate: Struck 17 March, 2006
Complement: 151 officers, 2637 enlisted

Dimensions:
Displacement: 40,823 tonnes (45,000 tons)
Length: 270.43 m (887 ft 3 in)
Beam: 32.9 m (108 ft 2 in)
Draught: 11.33 m (37 ft 2 in)

Powerplant:
Propulsion: Quadruple screw turbines delivering 158.09 MW (212,000 shp)
Speed: 33 knots
Range: 27,780 km (15,000 nm) @ 12 knots

Armament & Armour:
Armament: 9 x 406-mm (16-in) guns; 20 x 127-mm (5-in) guns
Armour:
Belt: 307.3 mm (12.1 in)
Turrets: 500 mm (19.7 in)
Decks: 190.50 mm (7.5 in)
Aircraft: Floatplanes and helicopters

Designs for the *Iowa* class of battleship were
started in 1936 in response to reports that the
Japanese were laying down battleships of 41,730
tonnes (46,000 tons). *Iowa* was laid down in 1940
and commissioned in 1943.

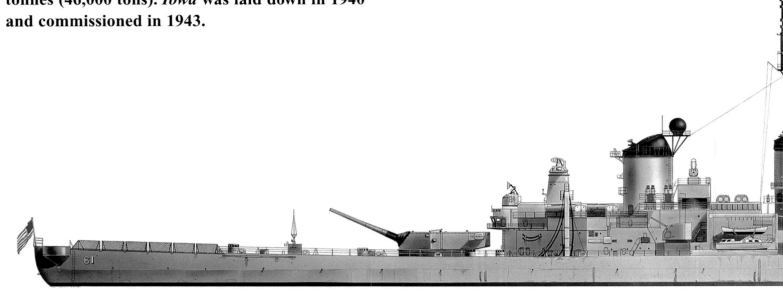

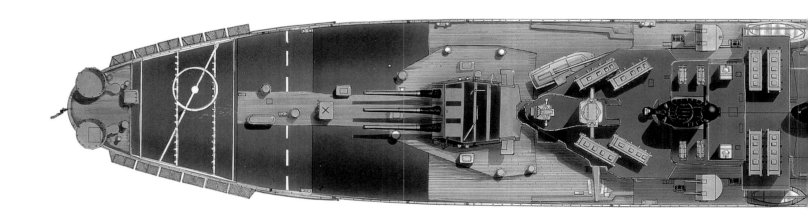

IOWA (POST WAR REFIT)

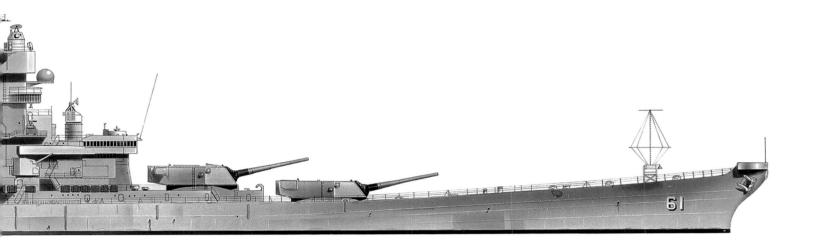

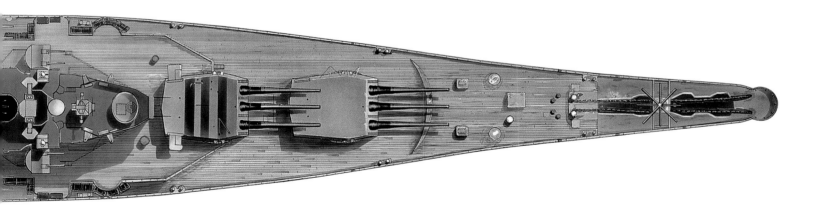

IOWA CLASS

The *Iowa* class, which included the *Missouri*, *New Jersey*, and *Wisconsin*, had a greater displacement than the previous *South Dakota* class, and had more power and protection. They served mainly as escorts for carrier task groups during World War II, being the only battleships fast enough to keep up with them. *Iowa* was recommissioned for service in the Korean War, being used to bombard shore targets in North Korea. Two more *Iowa*-class ships were laid down; the *Illinois* was cancelled when construction was 22 per cent complete, and *Kentucky* was launched in 1950 to clear the slip while still incomplete. Her bow section was subsequently used to repair damage to the *Wisconsin*.

The *Iowa*-class battleships were the largest and fastest battleships ever constructed for the U.S. Navy. They were also the last.

Iowa's designers set out to create the finest battleship possible. The fact that all the *Iowa*s that were commissioned were still on active service half a century later bears witness to their success. The ships had to be able to pass through the Panama

Close-up

The role of the new fast battleships like *Iowa* was not merely to ward off possible surface attacks on the all-important aircraft carriers, but also to provide additional anti-aircraft firepower.

(1) **Armament:** The *Iowa* firing her 406-mm (16-in) guns in a broadside. Her main turrets were protected by 241–432mm (9.5-17in) of armour plating.

(2) **Armour:** The *Iowa* class carried the same armament as earlier U.S. battleships, but their length was increased because of the increased armour protection.

(3) **Length to Beam:** These were the fastest battleships ever built, with a high length-to-beam ratio.

(4) **Mast:** All the *Iowa* class were fitted with a high tripod mainmast after World War II and their aircraft catapults were removed.

(5) **Electronics:** After *Iowa* was reactivated in 1983, it was found that the shock of firing her main armament caused problems with newly installed electronic equipment.

(6) **Designation:** *Iowa* was the fourth battleship in the U.S. Navy to be named in honour of the 29th state, and the last lead ship of any class of U.S. battleships.

Iowa's sleek lines are easy to see in this photograph, which reveals her long, narrow bow section to good advantage. The Iowas were arguably the most aesthetically pleasing of the modern battleships.

Canal, which meant that the beam could be no wider than 33.55 m (116 ft). The *Iowa*s displaced close to 54,431 tonnes (60,000 tons) at extra-deep load, yet they were still capable of making well over 30 knots. Such impressive performance was possible because she had 60 per cent more power and the fact that she was longer by almost 30 per cent than the preceding *South Dakota* class.

The long, narrow bow in particular, with its considerable sheer, was an outstanding feature of the *Iowa*s. They had the same protection as the earlier class and the same main armament, but the barrels were lengthened by five calibres. This development increased their effective range to a maximum of 38.8 km (21 nm) for a shell that weighed about the same as a small car. The battleships also carried enormous numbers of light AA guns, though most of these were removed at the end of World War II.

Iowa was built at the New York Navy Yard and commissioned on 22 February, 1943. She operated out of Atlantic ports for almost a year, her operational career being interrupted briefly when she ran aground off Maine in July 1943, and then deployed to the Pacific, where she spent the rest of the war. During the Battle of Leyte Gulf, on 25 October, 1944, Task Force 34 was formed from the battleships *Iowa, New Jersey, Washington, Alabama,*

Massachusetts, and *Indiana,* four cruisers and 10 destroyers, with the intent to eradicate a Japanese diversionary force, approaching from the north under Vice-Admiral Ozawa. Instead, Admiral Halsey, flying his flag on *New Jersey,* took his ships south to hunt down what remained of the main enemy force, leaving carrier aircraft to deal with Ozawa. This tactic succeeded, and the carriers *Chitose, Zuikaku, Zuiho,* and *Chiyoda,* as well as a destroyer, were all sunk.

RETURN TO THE ATLANTIC

In 1953, after Korean War service, she returned to the Atlantic. On one occasion, together with *Wisconsin,* she exercised with Britain's last battleship, *Vanguard,* the last time an Anglo-American battleship force put to sea together.

Iowa was reactivated twice, first in 1951–58 and then in 1983–90. She received new fire control and multi-functional radar systems, Tomahawk and Harpoon cruise missiles, and upgraded communications equipment. In 1989, an explosion in one of *Iowa*'s 406-mm (16-in) gun turrets killed 47 officers and men; plans for repairs were deferred when it was decided that *Iowa* and *New Jersey* would be mothballed in 1991. In fact, *Iowa* was paid off in October 1990 and *New Jersey* in February 1991. In 2009, *Iowa* was waiting to be officially allocated as a museum ship in Vallejo, California.

Lexington 1942

The *Lexington* (CV-16) was one of the famous *Essex*-class aircraft carriers that conveyed the war to the Japanese in the Pacific. She was originally named *Cabot*, but was renamed *Lexington* shortly before her launch in September 1942.

HANGAR
The entire hull structure protected the hangar against non-armour-piercing bombs. The deck, flight deck, and hangar were built on as a superstructure.

AIRCRAFT
The 1942 aircraft complement comprised 36 fighters, 37 dive-bombers, and 18 torpedo-bombers. Aviation fuel capacity was 908,500 l (240,000 gal).

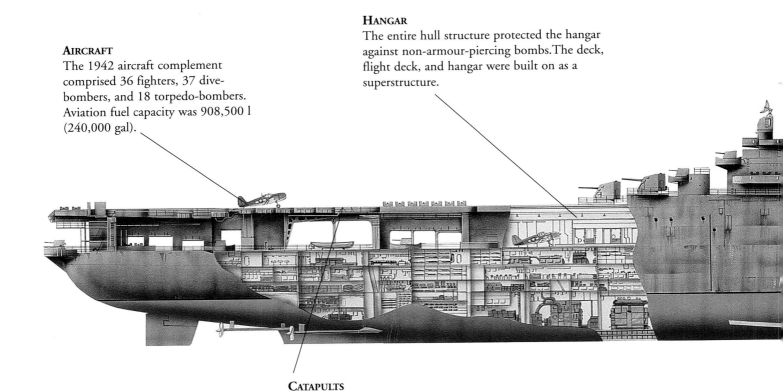

CATAPULTS
The original design called for three catapults – two on the flight deck and one athwartships on the hangar deck – but the third one was not very useful and later deleted.

LEXINGTON – SPECIFICATION

Country of origin: USA
Type: Aircraft carrier
Laid down: 15 July, 1941
Builder: Bethlehem Steel Company, Quincy, Massachusetts
Launched: 23 September, 1942
Commissioned: 17 February, 1943
Decommissioned: 8 November, 1991
Fate: Museum ship
Complement: 2,600 officers and men

Dimensions:
Displacement: as built standard: 24,585 tonnes (27,100 tons); as built full load: 33,003 tonnes (36,380 tons); 1991 full load: 16,579 tonnes (18,275 tons)
Length: (waterline) 250 m (820 ft); overall 266 m (872 ft)

Beam: (waterline) 28 m (93 ft); (overall) 45 m (147 ft 6 in);
Draught: (light) 8.66 m (28 ft 5 in); (full) 10.41 m (34 ft 2 in)

Powerplant:
Propulsion: Geared steam turbines delivering 110 MW (150,000 shp) to four shafts
Speed: 33 knots
Range: 37,040 km (20,000 nm) at 15 knots

Armament & Armour:
Armament: 12 x 127-mm (5-in) 38-calibre guns; 8 x 40-mm (1.57-in) quadruple 56-calibre guns; 46 x 20 mm (0.79-in) single 78 calibre guns
Armour: 40–100 mm (1.5–4 in)
Aircraft: 110 aircraft

FACTS

- Completed February 1943.

- Raids in Japanese-occupied islands, 1943–44; Battle of Leyte, 1944; Iwo Jima, 1945.

- Twice damaged by Japanese air attacks, 1943–44.

- Decommissioned 1947.

- Recommissioned as CVA-16, 1952 for service with Pacific Fleet.

- Decommissioned 1991.

ARMAMENT
In their final armament fit, the *Essex*-class mounted 18 127-mm (5-in) and 68 40-mm (1.57-in) guns.

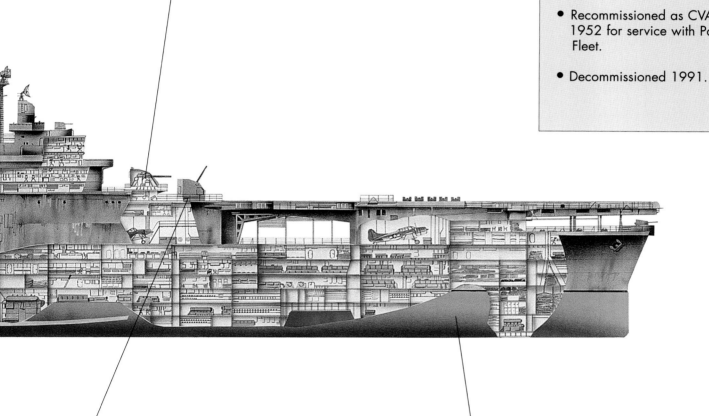

MACHINERY
Lexington and the other *Essex*-class carriers were powered by four Westinghouse geared turbines sustained by eight Babcock and Wilcox boilers, producing 110 MW (150,000 shp) and a maximum speed of nearly 33 knots.

HULL
By the end of the 1930s, the increased air-cover needs of the U.S. Navy led to an explosion in the size of aircraft carriers. As a result, a larger hull was introduced to stow the aviation fuel required for the complement of 91 aircraft carried by the *Essex* class.

In all, 26 *Essex*-class carriers were laid down, including *Intrepid*, seen here. Two more, *Reprisal* and *Iwo Jima*, were cancelled in August 1945, when it became apparent that the Pacific War was at an end.

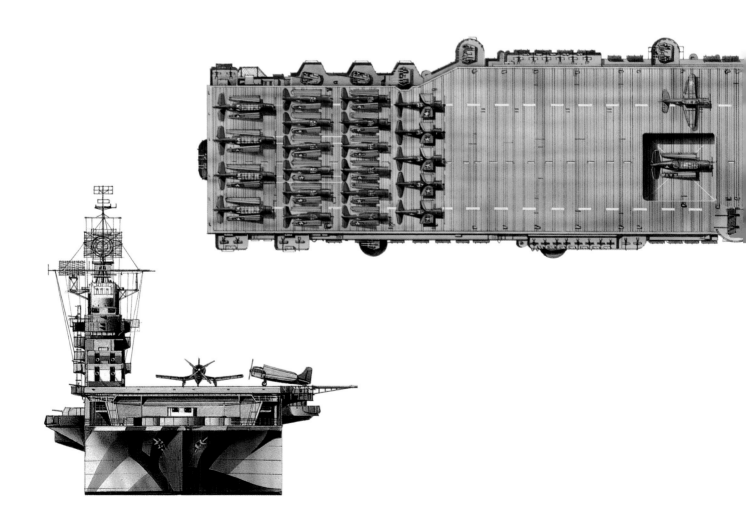

SISTER SHIP: *INTREPID*

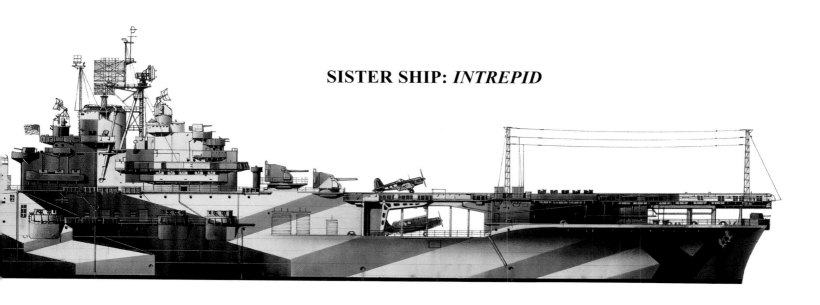

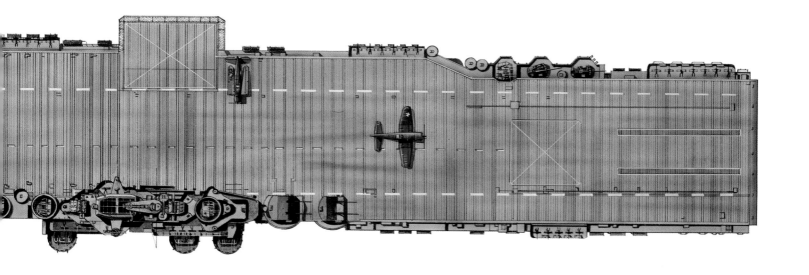

LEXINGTON

CV-16 was the second carrier to bear the name *Lexington*. The first, launched in 1925, was lost in the Battle of the Coral Sea in May 1942. Japanese carrier aircraft hit the *Lexington* with two torpedoes and also damaged the carrier *Yorktown* with a bomb hit below decks, although she remained operational. Later, fuel vapour in *Lexington* exploded, causing uncontrollable fires; the carrier was abandoned and sunk by a U.S. destroyer. Although a tactical victory for the Japanese, the Battle of the Coral Sea left them with no option but to call off their planned invasion of Port Moresby, New Guinea. The result was a clear strategic victory for the Allies.

Lexington is pictured here after she had been fitted with an angled flight-deck. The latter was a British invention, as was the steam catapult; both revolutionized carrier operations.

Lexington was to have the longest career of any of the *Essex* class, being finally decommissioned in December 1991 for preservation as a museum ship at Corpus Christi, Texas.

By 1937, with the lapse of the Washington Naval Treaty, the only restriction on the size of the warships that the U.S. Navy could build was imposed by Congress. In May that year, it voted funds to construct carriers up to 36,290 tonnes (40,000 tons) in total; *Hornet* and *Yorktown* took up less than half of that, and designers began drawing up plans for a slightly improved version based on a requirement to carry 10 per cent more aircraft and offer improved protection. The result was a design for a ship some 30 per cent bigger than the *Yorktown* class which, when it came to fruition, would set the standard for a new generation of fleet carriers, the *Essex* class. The designers had one major factor working in their favour; advances in steam machinery since *Yorktown* was built meant they could make considerable weight savings in that area, while actually

increasing the installed power by 25 per cent. The new ships were to be 15 m (50 ft) longer on the waterline than the *Yorktown*s, and 3 m (10 ft) broader abeam, still allowing them to pass through the Panama Canal easily. They were almost 50 per cent heavier at standard displacement, and much of the disproportionate increase came about as a result of their protection being increased by the addition of a second, thicker, armoured deck.

Lexington was laid down by Bethlehem Steel at Quincy, Massachusetts, on 15 July, 1941, her sister ship *Bunker Hill* also being laid down alongside her that day. She was originally designated *Cabot*, but her name was changed after the original *Lexington* was scuttled after the Battle of the Coral Sea in May 1942. She entered service just 73 weeks later, on 17 February, 1943.

EVER PRESENT IN BATTLE

During the Pacific War *Lexington* served as the flagship of Task Force 58, and was present at every major engagement from Tarawa to Tokyo. During the Battle of Leyte Gulf in October 1944, her aircraft were solely responsible for sinking the carrier *Zuikako* and the cruiser *Nachi*, and shared in the destruction of the battleship *Musashi* and the carriers *Chitose* and *Zuiho*.

She was placed in reserve in April 1947 until September 1953, when she was transferred to Puget Sound Navy Yard for major reconstruction. This involved reconfiguring her flight deck to incorporate an angled landing area and steam catapults, provision of an enclosed foredeck, strengthening of the arrester gear, and the enlarging of her forward lift.

In August 1955 *Lexington* was recommissioned as CVA-16. She rejoined the Pacific Fleet and was again reclassified, this time as an anti-submarine carrier (CVS-16). During this second career, she operated in the Atlantic, the Mediterranean, and the Pacific, but spent most of her time, nearly 30 years, on the East Coast as a training carrier (CVT) until her decommissioning in 1991.

Lexington was the final *Essex*-class carrier in commission and the last wooden-decked aircraft carrier to serve with the U.S. Navy.

Close-up

Lexington was constantly busy as a training carrier, qualifying student aviators and maintaining the high state of training of both active duty and reserve naval aviators.

1 **Film set:** In 1975 and 1987 *Lexington* served as a filming location at sea for the films *Midway* and *War and Remembrance*.

2 **CVT-16:** *Lexington* marked her 200,000th arrested landing on 17 October, 1967, and was redesignated CVT-16 on 1 January, 1969.

3 **Preservation:** *Lexington*'s World War II-era gun battery is also being partially restored using guns salvaged from scrapped ships.

4 **Catapult room:** Areas of the ship previously off limits are becoming open to the public, including such areas as the catapult room.

5 **Aircraft:** The aircraft seen here on *Lexington*'s deck during her training days are Vought A7 Crusader IIs.

6 **Capacity:** *Lexington* had hangar deck capacity for 103 aircraft, including F6F-3 Hellcats, SBD-5 Dauntless dive-bombers, and TBF-1 Avenger torpedo bombers.

The Sullivans 1943

The *Fletcher*-class destroyer *The Sullivans* was named in honour of the five Sullivan brothers, who lost their lives when *Juneau* was sunk by a Japanese submarine in the Battle of Guadalcanal in November 1942. It was the greatest combat loss suffered by any one American family in World War II.

ANTI-AIRCRAFT ARMAMENT
The destroyer's AA weaponry was progressively increased as the Pacific war went on, additional firepower being added in 1945 following serious losses sustained in kamikaze attacks.

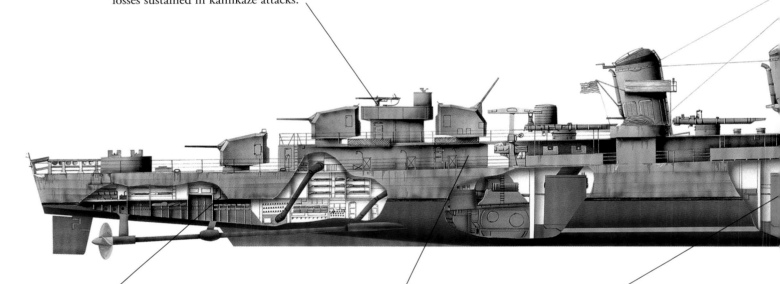

HULL
The flush deck hull of the *Fletcher* class added strength, but reduced internal hull volume, so that conditions on board were somewhat cramped.

SUPERSTRUCTURE
The U.S. Navy ordered the *Fletcher* class to be built with a simplified superstructure to hasten production. A new bridge design also increased the overhead view available to the captain.

MACHINERY
The *Fletcher*-class boats were powered by two General Electric turbines, producing 45 MW (60,000 shp) and giving maximum speed of 38 knots. Range was 12,038 km (6500 nm) at 15 knots, much greater than the overweight *Sumner* class, which followed them.

F A C T S

- Laid down as the *Putnam*; renamed *The Sullivans* and launched on 4 April, 1943.

- Operations in the Pacific, 1944, supporting carrier task force strikes.

- Operations in support of the Leyte landings, October 1944.

- Operations off Okinawa, 1945.

- Reserve Fleet, 1946.

- Reactivated for operations off Korea, 1951–53.

- Operated as part of U.S. naval forces imposing blockade of Cuba, October 1962.

- Donated as memorial museum ship to the Buffalo and Erie County Naval and Military Park, New York State, 1977.

TORPEDO TUBES
The *Fletcher* class originally carried 10 533-mm (21-in) torpedo tubes, but as the threat from Japanese warships lessened and air attack became the main danger, some of these were removed to make way for AA weapons.

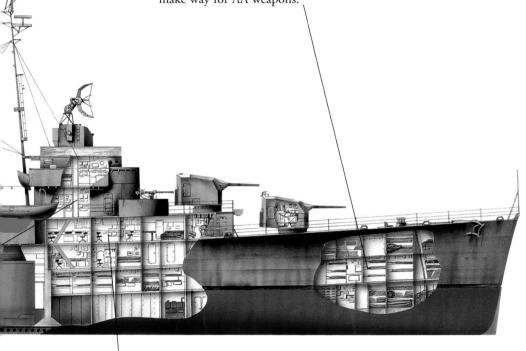

COMPLEMENT
The usual complement of the *Fletcher* class was 208, and despite the rather congested conditions below decks veteran U.S. Navy destroyer men claimed that the boats were the best of their era.

THE SULLIVANS – SPECIFICATION

Country of origin: USA
Type: Destroyer
Laid down: 10 October, 1942
Builder: Bethlehem Steel Corporation, California
Launched: 4 April, 1943
Commissioned: 30 September, 1943
Decommissioned: 7 January, 1965
Fate: Struck 1 December, 1974
Complement: 208

Dimensions:
Displacement: 1859.7 tonnes (2050 tons)
Length: 114.7 m (376 ft 6 in); **Beam:** 12.1 m (39 ft 8 in);

Draught: 5.4 m (17 ft 9 in)

Powerplant:
Propulsion: 2 General Electric steam turbines driving 2 screws developing 45 MW (60,000 shp)
Speed: 38 knots
Range: 6500 nm @ 15 knots

Armament & Armour:
Armament: 5 x 127-mm (5-in) guns; 10 x 40-mm (1.57-in) AA guns; 7 x 20-mm (0.79-in) AA guns; 10 x 533-mm (21-in) torpedo tubes; 6 x depth charge projectors and tracks
Armour: Not available

Though the extensive *Benson* class achieved the aim of putting the U.S. destroyer-building industry onto a war footing, the design had limitations for a Pacific war, both in terms of endurance and in its curtailed weapons fit. The *Fletcher* class would remedy these deficiencies. *Johnston* of the *Fletcher* class is shown here.

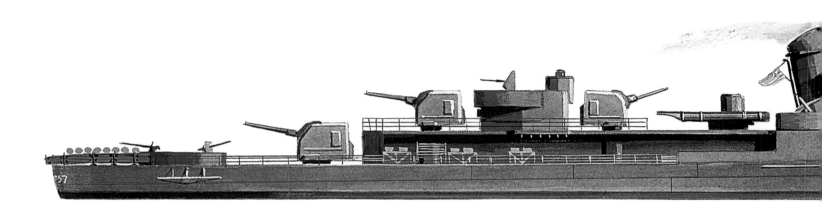

SISTER SHIP: *JOHNSTON*

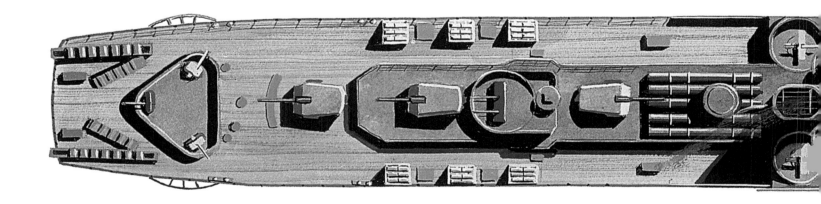

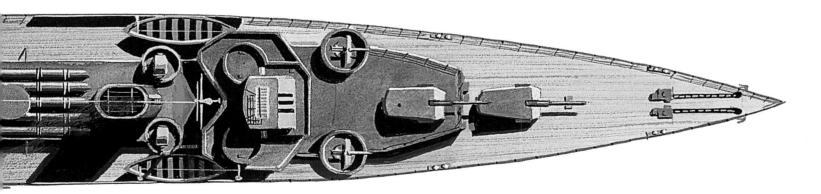

FLETCHER CLASS

The first two of the *Fletcher* class went down the ways in February 1942, and the last four of 175 ships on the same day at Puget Sound Navy Yard. Although the vessels in the *Fletcher* class were generally rushed out to the Pacific on completion, those built on the Atlantic seaboard saw some service in that ocean. The *Fletcher* herself served on convoy-protection duty in the western Atlantic before her deployment to the Pacific in time for the naval actions off Guadalcanal. All the ships of this class were named after U.S. Navy personnel or civilians who had rendered outstanding service.

The Sullivans *served with distinction in World War II, taking part in intense combat, rescuing downed aviators, and earning nine battle stars for service.* The Sullivans *is now a National Historic Landmark.*

Originally laid down as the *Putnam*, in 1943, on 8 February, the destroyer was renamed *The Sullivans* and launched on 4 April by Mrs. Thomas F. Sullivan, mother of the Sullivan boys who died on active service with the U.S. Navy.

The Sullivans deployed to the Pacific in December 1943, and after a period of training she joined Task Group 58.2, where she formed part of the destroyer screen covering aircraft carriers whose air groups were carrying out strikes on targets in the Marshall Islands. Over the next months she operated almost continuously, helping beat off numerous Japanese air attacks on the U.S. task groups and bombarding shore targets.

The Japanese air attacks grew in intensity during the last half of 1944. On the evening of 12 October, 1944, for example, as strike aircraft returned to the carriers after attacks on Formosa and the Ryukyu Islands, radar detected a wave of Japanese aircraft coming down from the north. For the next six hours, approximately 50–60 Japanese aircraft subjected the American task force to continuous air attacks. Nearly 45 minutes after sunset, *The Sullivans* sighted a Mitsubishi G4M Betty coming in low on the starboard side, and opened fire on

it. During the next 15 minutes, the formation to which *The Sullivans* was attached shot down three aircraft; between 1856 and 1954, the destroyer herself engaged five aircraft. The air attacks continued into the small hours of the morning, the American warships making smoke whenever Japanese flare-dropping aircraft appeared. Meanwhile, *The Sullivans* and the other ships in formation executed 38 simultaneous turn movements at speeds between 22 and 25 knots as their guns kept up a steady fire to repel the attackers.

During the remainder of October, *The Sullivans* operated in support of the Allied landings at Leyte, in the Philippines, during which she survived a typhoon that sank several other vessels. In March 1945 she took part in the invasion of Okinawa, beating off numerous kamikaze attacks and participating in the rescue of crews from stricken U.S. ships. She also survived a spell on radar picket duty, a task in which several American destroyers were sunk. Her last combat operation of World War II took place on 14 May, 1945, when she shot down a kamikaze while screening the aircraft carrier *Enterprise*.

REACTIVATED INTO SERVICE
Her tour in the Pacific at an end, *The Sullivans* returned to the USA in July 1945, and after being overhauled she was placed

in the Reserve Fleet in 1946. She was reactivated in 1951, following the outbreak of the Korean War, and sailed to join Task Force 77, operating off the east coast of Korea. In addition to screening the carrier task force, she carried out a number of bombardments against shore targets, mainly targeting railways.

In 1953, *The Sullivans* joined the U.S. Sixth Fleet in the Mediterranean, and supported the landing of U.S. Marines in Lebanon in 1958. In October 1962, after an overhaul in the USA, she was deployed as part of the U.S. naval forces imposing a blockade during the Cuban Missile Crisis.

MEMORIAL SHIP

Following service as a training ship, *The Sullivans* was decommissioned in 1965. She was later donated as a memorial to the Buffalo and Erie County Naval and Military Park in Buffalo, in New York State, where she remains today.

Interior view

The engine room of a destroyer was a hot, sweaty, and cramped place. Reeking of fuel oil and lubricants, it did not offer a pleasant environment to work in.

(1) **Turbines:** The two-shaft General Electric geared turbines of the *Fletcher* class gave the boats a respectable maximum speed of 38 knots.

(2) **Flush-Decked Hull:** One reason the space was so cramped was the flush-decked hull, which added strength but reduced internal hull volume.

(3) **Instruments:** The engine room instrument panel was large and well designed, with the dials well spaced and easy to read.

(4) **Valves:** The valves that needed to be opened to release steam pressure were operated by large control wheels, conveniently positioned.

(5) **Seamen:** The seaman at work in the engine room is being supervised by a senior engineering technician. Both are wearing "khakis," or working dress.

(6) **Pipes:** All piping in the engine room was well insulated and protected against rupture.

TYPE XXI U-BOAT

The Type XXI U-Boat was a milestone in the development of the submarine, and a significant step forwards on the evolutionary road that led to the nuclear-powered vessels of today. In all, 121 units were commissioned, but relatively few became operational.

MACHINERY
The Type XXI class was powered by two-shaft diesel/electric motors. It was the first submarine to be faster underwater than on the surface. It also had creeping electric motors designed for silent running.

HULL
The Type XXI class had a distinctive streamlined double-pressure hull and a low faired-in conning tower.

BATTERY COMPARTMENT
The battery compartment was more sophisticated than found in other classes. It had three 124-cell batteries for 33,900 ampere/hours, which was some three times the capacity of the earlier Type XXI class.

SNORKEL

The Type XXI was fitted with a *schnorkel* (snorkel), a simple pipe with a valve on one end, which extended above sea level while the boat was submerged. The device enabled the U-boat to run on diesel engines even when underwater.

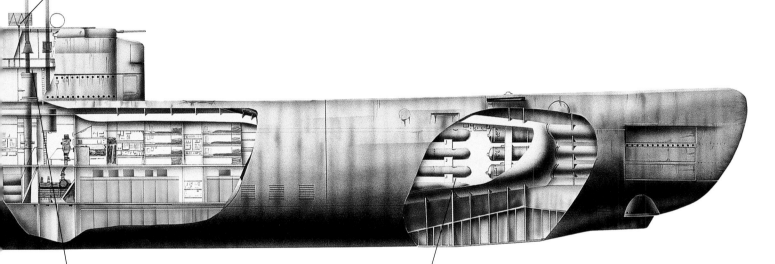

ARMAMENT

Although Type XXI had provision for four 30-mm (1.18-in) guns in twin mountings, four 20-mm (0.79-in) guns were usually carried.

TORPEDOES

The Type XXI class was fitted with six 533-mm (21-in) torpedo tubes, with storage for 23 torpedoes or 14 torpedoes plus 12 mines. The torpedoes were self-loading.

TYPE XXI – SPECIFICATION

Country of origin: Germany
Type: Submarine
In production: 1943–45
Builder: Blohm & Voss, Hamburg; AG Weser, Bremen; F. Schichau, Danzig
Launched: 19 April, 1944
Fate: N/A
Complement: 57

Dimensions:
Displacement: (standard) 1621 tonnes (1787 tons): (full load) 2100 tonnes (2315 tons)
Length: 76.7 m (251 ft 8 in); **Beam:** 8 m (26 ft 3 in); **Draught:** 5.3 m (17 ft 5 in)

Powerplant:
Propulsion: 2 x supercharged 6-cylinder diesel engines delivering 2.9 MW (4000 shp); 2 x double-acting electric motors delivering 3.7 MW (4959 shp); 2 x silent-running electric motors delivering 166 kW (222.5 shp)
Speed (surfaced): 15.9 knots (diesel); 17.9 knots (electric)
Speed (submerged): 17.2 knots (electric); 6.1 knots (silent-running motors)
Range (surfaced): 28,706 km (15,500 nm) at 10 knots
Range (submerged): 630 km (340 nm) at 5 knots

Armament & Armour:
Armament: 4 x 20-mm (0.79-in) cannon; 6 x 533-mm (21-in) torpedo tubes (23 torpedoes)

The ocean-going U-boat proved a fearsome weapon in World War II, and one that came close to bringing Britain to her knees in the bitter conflict known as the Battle of the Atlantic. Had the Type XXIs been available earlier in numbers, they might have massacred the Allied Atlantic convoys.

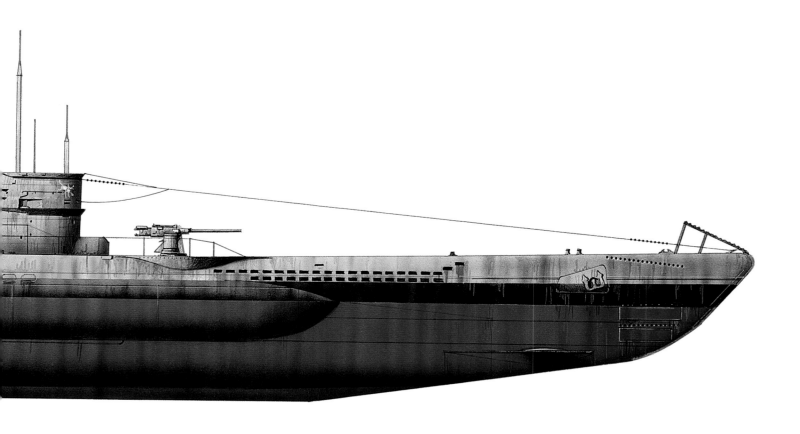

TYPE VII U BOAT: U47

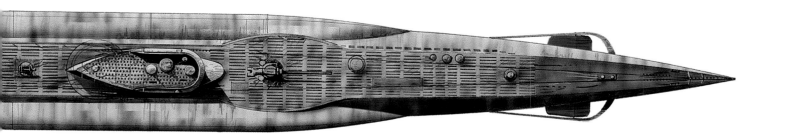

TYPES XXI AND XXIII

In the latter months of the war Germany launched a massive submarine construction programme, the aim of which was to get two types of submarine – the Type XXI and the Type XXIII – into service as quickly as possible. By the end of the war 55 Type XXIs were operational and 57 Type XXIIIs were either at sea, in various stages of construction, or projected. The building programme was severely disrupted by Allied bombing. This was fortunate indeed for the Allies, because both boats were utterly lethal war machines.

With the Battle of the Atlantic being won by the Allies, the requirement for building the Type XXI was so urgent that Germany decided to begin series production before a prototype had even been tested. They also decided to build the boat in sections.

Because no testing had taken place, the first six Type XXIs proved to be unfit for operational service and were relegated to training duties. Three types of shipyard were engaged in the work of construction. The first built the sections of pressure and external hulls and bulkheads, the plating and frames having been received already cut and set to shape by the steelmakers. Some 32 shipyards and structural engineering firms were engaged in this stage, and a massive dispersal programme had to be implemented because of Allied bombing. The sections were then transported to 16 other firms, usually by water, and all the wiring, pipework and main and auxiliary engines were installed. Finally, the sections were welded together in three building yards and the completed vessel was subjected to testing.

Although the first Type XXI U-Boat, *U2501*, was launched in May 1944, she was one of the boats found to be defective and the type did not become operational until

Close-up

The Type XXIs were ocean-going boats capable of fully submerged operations using the *schnorkel* and conventional diesel/electric drive. Their hulls were streamlined.

1. **Design:** Prior to 1943 U-boats were constructed on conventional lines. Some 16 firms were involved, using designs prepared by the German Admiralty.

2. **Prefabrication:** In 1943, a programme of dispersal and prefabrication was set up because of the increase in bombing and to make better use of resources.

3. **Hull:** 32 German shipyards were made responsible for the fabrication of pressure and external hulls, as well as bulkheads.

4. **Transport:** The sections were sent, usually by water, to 16 other firms for installation of all wiring, pipework and engines.

5. **Welding:** The various sections were then welded together by three building yards, which carried out initial trials before handing the U-boats over to the navy.

6. **Hull:** In the Type XXI, surface sea-keeping qualities and gun armament were sacrificed to give a streamlined hull for higher submerged speed.

This photograph shows a Type XXI being launched. The first six Type XXIs were unfit for operational use. Some of the factories producing the plating and frames had worked to excessive tolerances, so the six examples they built were relegated to training duties.

March 1945, with the *U2511*. Although 740 Type XXIs were ordered, only 21 were completed, and of the 55 commissioned, only two made operational sorties. The first operational boat, *U2511*, deployed to the Norwegian port of Bergen and set out on her first and only war patrol early in May. On the 4th, she sighted a British cruiser, but her captain, having been advised that the German surrender was imminent, elected to set up only a dummy attack on the warship, so saving its crew and probably his own.

SUPER-LIGHT BATTERIES

The Type XXI was a double-hulled vessel, with a high submerged speed and the ability to run silently at 3.5 knots thanks to her electric "creeper" motors. The outer hull was constructed of light plating to aid streamlining, while the inner hull was reinforced with 28–37 mm (1.1–1.45 in) of thick carbon steel plating. With her new, super-light batteries, she could maintain a submerged speed of 16 knots for one hour; at four knots, she could remain submerged for three days on a single charge.

The Type XXIs were eagerly seized by the Allies at the end of the war. The *U2518*, surrendered to Britain, went to France in 1947 and was extensively tested as the *Roland Morillot*, forming the basis for the French Navy's *Narval* class of five boats laid down between 1951 and 1956. Their long range enabled them to make a fast transit to France's overseas colonies, followed by a patrol of seven to 14 days. Another boat, the *U2540*, was salvaged and recommissioned by the West German Bundesmarine as the *Wilhelm Bauer*.

ONE TYPE XXI SURVIVING

The Soviet Union's first post-war submarine, the "Whiskey" class, was essentially a modified version of the Type XXI. The Russians went on to mass-produce 236 submarines between 1949 and 1957.

The first Type XXI, *U2501*, spent her operational career on training duties in the Baltic. On 3 May, 1945, she was scuttled by her crew in Hamburg. Only six Type XXIs survived the war intact. One was salvaged and is today preserved as a museum exhibit in Bremerhaven.

Modern Ships 1950–Present

During the early years of the Cold War era it was apparent that the aircraft carrier, like the battleship before it, was becoming increasingly vulnerable to attack from the air and under the sea, and it needed powerful defensive measures to support it.

The Sovremenny *Class destroyers were designed to engage hostile ships by means of missile attack, and to provide warships and transport ships with protection against ship and air attack.*

In the 1950s, the Americans and Russians both began to explore the concept of the nuclear-powered ballistic missile submarine, a vessel capable of remaining submerged for lengthy periods, making use of the polar ice-cap and various oceanic features to remain undetected. Armed with nuclear-tipped rockets, it would be the ultimate deterrent. The world's first nuclear-powered submarine was the American *Nautilus*, launched on 21 January 1954.

FIRST NUCLEAR SUBMARINE

Although the Americans were the first to make the nuclear-powered submarine breakthrough, with an early class of boat based on the prototype *Nautilus*, what the U.S. Navy really wanted was to merge the new technologies of ballistic missiles, smaller thermonuclear weapons, and inertial guidance systems into a single weapon system. They succeeded with the deployment, in 1960, of the first Fleet Ballistic Missile (FBM) submarine, armed with the Polaris A1 missile. The Russians' first nuclear submarine design was the "November" class, which was designed for the anti-ship rather than the anti-submarine role. Armed with nuclear torpedoes, the task of these boats was to attack carrier battle groups. They were very noisy underwater and were prone to reactor leaks, which did not endear them to their crews. They were involved in numerous accidents.

The inability of the USSR to match the United States in terms of sea power was apparent in October 1962, when the Americans imposed a blockade of Cuba following the infiltration of Soviet strategic and tactical missiles, as well as Il-28 jet bombers, into the island. Lacking the means to break the quarantine, and unwilling to risk all-out nuclear war, Premier Khrushchev was compelled to back down and order the removal of the missiles and bombers.

MISSILE-CARRYING WEAPONS

The Cuban Crisis taught the Russians a stern lesson in the importance of sea power, and future Soviet naval policies were amended accordingly.

The USS Nimitz *and her sister ships form the nucleus of a US fleet's Battle Force, the principal task force in the US Navy.* Nimitz *forms part of Carrier Strike Group 11.*

A pattern of bi-annual exercises was established in 1963; in March and April seven surface units plus support vessels exercised near the Lofotens, and in August a similar force conducted exercises in the Iceland-Faeroes Gap. Part of this group circumnavigated the British Isles before returning to the Baltic. Inter-fleet transfers between the Northern, Baltic and Black Sea Fleets continued and intensified. The exercises of 1964 saw the introduction of the latest missile-carrying warships; fleet strengths were increased and the scope and type of exercises between North Cape and the Faeroes Gap revealed more imagination and expertise.

The proliferation of Soviet nuclear attack submarines, and the consequent increased threat to American carrier task groups, led to the development of new escort vessels dedicated to anti-submarine warfare. Foremost among these were frigates, fitted with twin-shaft gas turbine engines with controllable-pitch propellers, giving them the power necessary to pursue high-speed

nuclear-powered submarines. These vessels are at the cutting edge of naval technology, making their design and construction prohibitively costly for smaller navies, which usually prefer to buy them off the shelf from the principal maritime powers.

CRUISE MISSILE SUBMARINE

Development of the Soviet submarine fleet in the 1980s was impressive. In 1985, 10 submarine classes were under construction and two conversion programmes were under way, culminating in the "Oscar"-class cruise missile submarine. The underwater equivalent of a *Kirov* class cruiser, the first "Oscar I" class cruise missile submarine (SSGN) was laid down at Severodvinsk in 1978 and launched in the spring of 1980, starting sea trials later that year. The second was completed in 1982, and a third of the class–which became the first "Oscar II" completed in 1985, followed by a fourth, fifth and sixth at intervals of a year. The primary task of the "Oscar" class was to attack NATO carrier battle groups with a variety of submarine-launched

Tarawa was the first of five ships in a new class of general-purpose amphibious assault ships, and combined in one ship type the functions previously performed by four different types.

The Visby *class was originally designed to be divided into two subcategories where some ships were optimized for surface combat and others for submarine hunting; however, this was changed due to cutbacks.*

cruise missiles. Perhaps the most famous "Oscar II" boat, for tragic reasons, was the *Kursk*, described in this work.

DEFINITE PATTERN

The naval operations that took place in the latter years of the twentieth century, in support of UN-authorised actions in the Balkans, Afghanistan, Iraq and elsewhere, set a definite pattern for those that are likely to occur in the twenty-first. Sea warfare will never be the same again. The titanic mid-ocean battles that were a scenario of the Cold War will never be enacted. Instead, future naval battles will be fought along coastlines against developing countries or regional powers which present a threat to the international community, and for this reason diesel-electric submarines like

the Dutch *Zeeleeuw*, and mine warfare vessels such as the Tripartartite Minehunter, have assumed a new importance.

"The sea is a medium in which military and political power may be projected to critical areas of the world ... an activity associated largely with aircraft carriers and amphibious forces."

Hugh Faringdon, Military Analyst

163

Nautilus (SSN-571) 1954

The world's first nuclear-powered submarine was the American *Nautilus*, launched on 21 January, 1954. Apart from her revolutionary propulsion system, she was designed along conventional lines. She became the first submarine to pass under the Arctic ice cap.

ESCAPE HATCH

The upper and lower hatches, as well as the escape door on one side, permitted several men at a time to make an emergency escape from the ship while submerged. The escape door also served as the torpedo loading hatch.

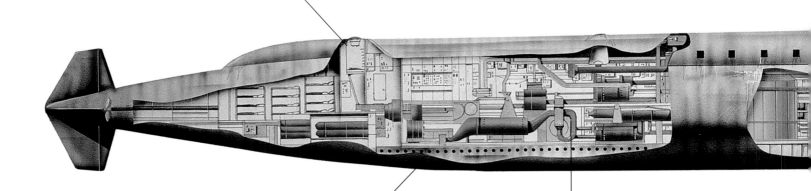

HULL

In order to avoid unnecessary risk, the hull was designed conventionally, with reactor safety being given absolute priority.

MACHINERY

Twin screws driven by steam turbines using superheated steam generated by an S2W nuclear reactor via a heat exchanger.

CONTROL CENTRE

The Central Operating Compartment was the third compartment aft and was also divided into two levels. The Diving Stand, with aircraft-type controls, was located in the forward end of the compartment.

ARMAMENT

Nautilus was fitted with six 533-mm (21-in) bow torpedo tubes. The stowage racks for the torpedoes, known as "skids," were immediately aft of the tubes.

ACCOMMODATION

A partial deck divided the crew accommodation into two sections. The upper room was the officers' quarters, consisting of the wardroom, the pantry, and six staterooms. The crew's living area was below the officers' quarters.

NAUTILUS (SSN-571) – SPECIFICATION

Country of origin: USA
Type: Submarine
Laid down: 14 June, 1952
Builder: General Dynamics
Launched: 21 January, 1954
Commissioned: 30 September, 1954
Decommissioned: 3 March, 1980
Fate: Retained by navy as museum
Complement: 13 officers, 92 crew

Dimensions:
Displacement: (submerged) 3712 tonnes (4092 tons); (surface) 3205 tonnes (3533 tons)

Length: 97.5 m (320 ft)
Beam: 8.5 m (28 ft)
Draught: 7.9 m (26 ft)

Powerplant:
Propulsion: Two-shaft nuclear steam turbines/electric motors producing 10 MW (13,400 hp)
Speed: 23 knots
Range: Unlimited

Armament
Armament: 6 x 533-mm (21-in) torpedo tubes

Early trials with *Nautilus* established new records. This included travelling nearly 2245 km (1213 nm) submerged in 90 hours at 20 knots. At that time, this was the longest period spent underwater by an American submarine, as well as being the fastest speed submerged.

NAUTILUS

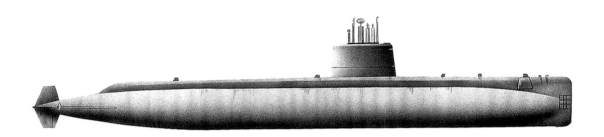

AMERICAN SSBN: *GEORGE WASHINGTON*

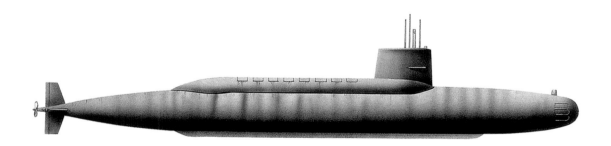

AMERICAN SSN: *SKATE*

AMERICAN SSN: *TRITON*

NAUTILUS AND *SEAWOLF*

There were in fact two prototype nuclear attack submarines. The other vessel, *Seawolf*, was launched in July 1955 and was the last U.S. submarine to feature a traditional conning tower, as distinct from the fin of later nuclear submarines. *Nautilus* was the more successful of the two. *Seawolf* was designed around the S2G nuclear reactor, intended as a backup to the S2W, but it had many operational problems and was replaced by an S2W in 1959. *Nautilus* was decommissioned in 1979 and preserved as a museum exhibit in 1982.

During the period 22 July to 5 August 1958, *Nautilus*, the world's first atomic-powered ship, added to her list of historic achievements by crossing the Arctic Ocean from the Bering Sea to the Greenland Sea, passing submerged beneath the geographic North Pole.

During the late 1940s, the major navies of the world made strenuous efforts, and carried out much experimentation, to find ways of improving the effectiveness of their submarine fleets. The U.S. Navy, however, was already forging ahead with developments that would revolutionize undersea warfare.

Work on a Submarine Thermal Reactor (STR), a nuclear reactor for submarines, began in 1948. It was developed by Westinghouse into the STR Mk 2 (later re-designated S2W) in collaboration with the Argonne National Laboratory, where key parts of the world's first atomic bomb had been established. Development of the associated technology was

Interior view

In operating conditions, a number of limitations in the design and construction of *Nautilus* became apparent, but these failings were put right in subsequent submarines.

(1) **Planesmen:** *Nautilus* had two "planesmen," one operating the bow planes to control the boat's depth when submerged and one to control ascent and descent.

(2) **Seating:** The planesmen and helmsman, who sat between them, had the benefit of comfortable aircraft-type seats.

(3) **Helmsman:** As his name implies, the helmsman steered the boat both on the surface and underwater. To do this, he had to work closely with the planesmen.

(4) **Instruments:** For such a revolutionary craft, these were surprisingly simple, although most instruments, like the compass, had a backup.

(5) **Speed:** Built around a conventional hull form, *Nautilus* was limited to a top speed of about 20 knots.

(6) **Gyrocompass:** Navigation beneath the Arctic ice sheet was difficult. A gyrocompass was installed to aid the boat's passage.

Nautilus *is shown here about to berth in a French port during her Mediterranean deployment. The French yachts in the background are decked with bunting as a sign of welcome.*

the responsibility of a team of scientists and engineers at the Naval Reactors Branch of the Atomic Energy Commission, led by an energetic U.S. Navy officer, Captain Hyman G. Rickover. On 12 December, 1951, when the Department of the Navy was satisfied that the STR was a viable proposition, the U.S. Navy decided to order a hull for the new reactor. The name chosen for the revolutionary new boat was *Nautilus*, which commemorated not only two previous U.S. submarines, but also Robert Fulton's submersible of 1800 and the fictional boat in Jules Verne's book *Twenty Thousand Leagues Under the Sea.*

The keel of the latest *Nautilus* was laid by President Truman at the Electric Boat Division of General Dynamics in Groton, Connecticut, on 14 June, 1952. Work progressed rapidly, the *Nautilus* (SSN-571) being launched on 21 January, 1954, and commissioned eight months later.

From 1955–57, *Nautilus* underwent various trials to investigate the effects of increased submarine speeds and endurance. On 4 February, 1957, she logged her 60,000th nautical mile, matching the endurance of Jules Verne's fictional vessel, and in May she deployed to the Pacific to take part in exercises with the Pacific Fleet. Later in the year

she toured NATO naval bases in the North Atlantic area and participated in NATO exercises, which demonstrated that most of the methods of submarine detection then in use were virtually ineffective against a nuclear-powered vessel.

"*NAUTILUS* NINETY DEGREES NORTH"

In July 1958 she sailed north from Pearl Harbor in the Pacific and passed under the polar ice cap, an achievement marked by the historic signal "*Nautilus* Ninety Degrees North" sent to the U.S. Admiralty by her skipper, Commander William R. Anderson. She carried on from the North Pole and, after 96 hours and 2945 km (1,590 nm) under the ice, surfaced northeast of Greenland, having completed the first successful submerged voyage across the roof of the world.

The journey had not been without its dangers. In the Bering Strait, ice extended as much as 18 m (60 ft) below sea level. During the initial attempt to traverse the Bering Strait, there was insufficient room for the submarine to pass between the ice and the sea bottom. During the second, successful attempt, the submarine passed through a known channel close to Alaska, a route taken in order to avoid detection and the ice.

Long Beach (CGN-9) 1959

The first U.S. surface warship to be powered by nuclear energy, *Long Beach* was originally intended to be no larger than a frigate. However, during the design stage she rapidly reached the dimensions of a heavy cruiser.

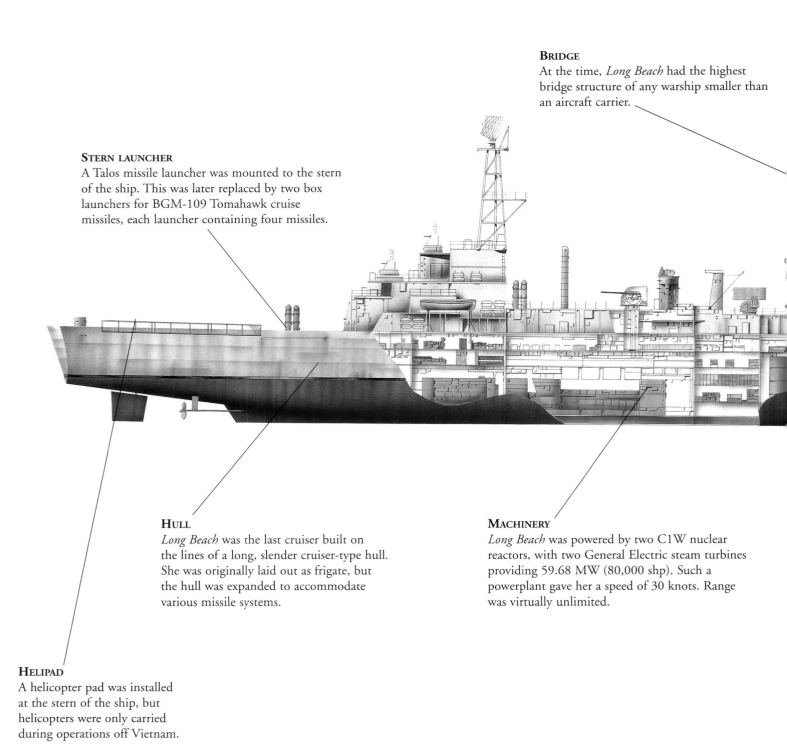

BRIDGE
At the time, *Long Beach* had the highest bridge structure of any warship smaller than an aircraft carrier.

STERN LAUNCHER
A Talos missile launcher was mounted to the stern of the ship. This was later replaced by two box launchers for BGM-109 Tomahawk cruise missiles, each launcher containing four missiles.

HULL
Long Beach was the last cruiser built on the lines of a long, slender cruiser-type hull. She was originally laid out as frigate, but the hull was expanded to accommodate various missile systems.

MACHINERY
Long Beach was powered by two C1W nuclear reactors, with two General Electric steam turbines providing 59.68 MW (80,000 shp). Such a powerplant gave her a speed of 30 knots. Range was virtually unlimited.

HELIPAD
A helicopter pad was installed at the stern of the ship, but helicopters were only carried during operations off Vietnam.

SUPERSTRUCTURE
The high box-like superstructure housed the SCANFAR radar system, comprising the AN/SPS-32 and AN/SPS-33 phased array radars.

FORWARD LAUNCHERS
There were two forward launchers for the Terrier and Talos surface-to-air missiles. These were later replaced by the longer-range Standard missile.

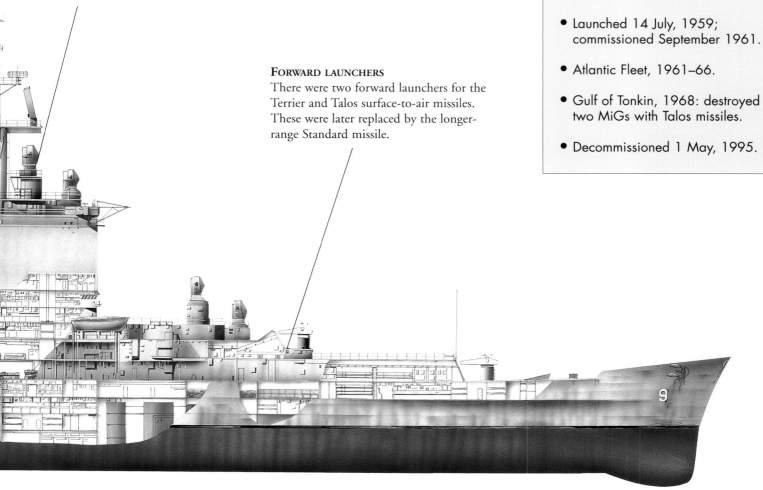

LONG BEACH (CGN-9) – SPECIFICATION

Country of origin: USA
Type: Missile cruiser
Laid down: 2 December, 1957
Builder: Bethlehem Steel Co., Fore River Shipyard, Massachusetts
Launched: 14 July, 1959
Commissioned: 9 September, 1961
Decommissioned: 1 May, 1995
Fate: Struck 1 May, 1995
Complement: 1160 officers and men

Dimensions:
Displacement: (standard) 14,098 tonnes (15,540 tons); (full) 15,898 tonnes (17,525 tons)
Length: 220 m (721 ft 3 in); **Beam:** 21.79 m (71 ft 6 in); **Draught:** 9.32 m (30 ft 7 in)

Powerplant:
Propulsion: 2 C1W nuclear reactors, 2 General Electric turbines producing 59.68 MW (80,000 shp)
Speed: 30 knots
Range: Unlimited

Armament & Armour:
Armament: 2 x 127-mm (5-in) Mk 30 guns; 2 x Mk 10 missile launchers Standard missiles (ER), 2 x Mk 141 Harpoon missile launchers; 1 x Mk 16 ASROC missile launcher; Mk 46 torpedoes from two Mk 32 triple mounts; 2 x 20-mm (0.79-in) Phalanx CIWS; 2 x armoured box launchers for Tomahawk cruise missiles
Armour: N/A
Aircraft: None. Helicopter launch pad

Long Beach was the third ship to be named after the city of Long Beach, California. The first was a converted German cargo ship, seized in 1917, and the second was a patrol frigate, which had served in the U.S. Navy from 1943–45.

AMERICAN GUIDED MISSILE CRUISER: *LEAHY*

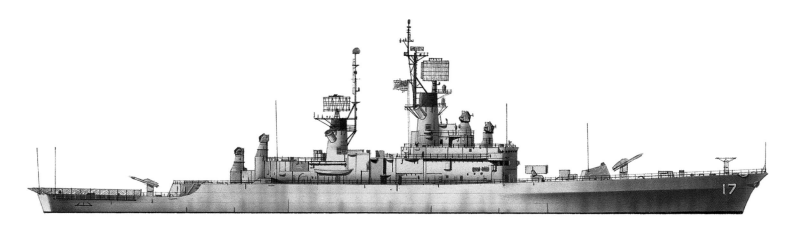

LONG BEACH

In May 1964, *Long Beach* joined the nuclear-powered aircraft carrier *Enterprise* (CVN-65) and the guided missile frigate *Bainbridge* (DLGN-25) to form the all-nuclear-powered Task Force 1, the first such battle force of its kind in the history of naval operations. At the end of July, the three warships began Operation Sea Orbit, a two-month unrefuelled cruise around the world. The task force left Gibraltar on 31 July, sailed down the Atlantic and around Africa, across the Indian and Pacific Oceans and round Cape Horn, completing the 55,793 km (30,216 nm) voyage in 65 days.

AMERICAN GUIDED MISSILE CRUISER: *BELKNAP*

AMERICAN AIR DEFENCE CRUISER: *TICONDEROGA*

Long Beach *(CGN-9) was the first U.S. surface warship powered by nuclear energy. During the Vietnam War in 1967–68 her long-range TALOS SAM systems engaged North Vietnamese MiGs on several occasions.*

***Long Beach* was a one-ship class. The reason for this was that she was an experimental platform for her phased array radar system, a precursor of the AN/SPY-1 system installed in later Aegis guided-missile warships.**

In 1966, *Long Beach* deployed to the Western Pacific for her first tour of duty off Vietnam. She was stationed mainly in the northern part of the Gulf of Tonkin, where the U.S. Navy had created a Positive Identification Radar Advisory Zone (PIRAZ). From this position she maintained constant radar surveillance to ensure that North Vietnamese intruder aircraft did not evade identification by attempting to mingle with returning U.S. strike aircraft. *Long Beach* also provided facilities for an on-board search-and-rescue helicopter. During this initial tour, one of her Air Intercept Controllers (AIC) directed a U.S. Navy F-4 Phantom to shoot down an Antonov An-2 Colt aircraft that was attempting to engage South Vietnamese naval craft.

Long Beach returned to the USA in July 1967 and returned to the Gulf of Tonkin in 1968. During this deployment, her Talos missiles destroyed two North

Vietnamese MiG-17s at a range of 112 km (70 miles). This was the first recorded use, in combat conditions, of naval surface-to-air missiles.

COMPASSIONATE RESCUE DUTIES

After Vietnam, *Long Beach* carried out routine duties in the Western Pacific, and in 1975 she was part of the task force assembled to rescue American seamen captured by the Khmer Rouge when their ship was seized. In 1980, she was involved in the rescue of 114 Vietnamese "boat people," fleeing the Communist regime.

As a result of experiences in the Vietnam War, in 1968, a conventional SPS-12 air search radar was fitted to *Long Beach* in order to supplement her fixed arrays. In 1970, an integral Identification Friend/Foe (IFF) and digital Talos fire-control system were fitted to the ship as well.

By 1979 the Talos system was growing obsolete, so the launchers and radars were removed and two quadruple Harpoon surface-to-surface missile launchers were installed. In the following year the fixed-array radar systems (which had proved less than adequate) were removed and replaced by SPS-48 and SPS-49 radars, the original planar array panels on the superstructure being replaced by armour plate.

In 1981 the Terrier missiles were replaced by Standard SM-2ER SAMs, and two armoured box launchers for Tomahawk cruise missiles were installed in 1986, the Harpoons being repositioned along the superstructure to make room. Kevlar armour and a Tactical Flag Command Centre were also fitted. For additional defence, two Phalanx Close-In Weapon Systems (CIWS) were added.

In 1987, *Long Beach* provided support during Operation Nimble Archer. In this operation American warships attacked Iranian oil platforms that were allegedly being used by Iranian forces as command-and-control posts with radars to track shipping in the area and that had been equipped with communications gear to relay messages between the mainland and Iranian forces operating near the platforms. Then, in 1991, *Long Beach* operated as part of the UN task force during Operation Desert Storm.

AWAITING RECYCLING

Long Beach was deactivated on 1 May, 1995, having seen more than 33 years of operational service. By the year 2010, she was still awaiting recycling at the Puget Sound Naval Shipyard, Bremerton, Washington.

Close-up

Long Beach was propelled by two nuclear reactors – one for each propeller shaft – and was capable of speeds in excess of 30 knots.

(1) **Launcher:** The rear launcher for the Talos was replaced with two Tomahawk cruise missile box launchers. Each launcher held 4 missiles.

(2) **Safety Nets:** These were an essential feature around a helicopter landing pad, as protection against the powerful downwash from the rotor blades.

(3) **Crewman:** A crewman in a distinctive yellow jacket guides the helicopter down to a spot landing.

(4) **Hull:** *Long Beach* was designed as an "all-missile" ship from the very beginning. She was also the last cruiser built on a traditional long, lean cruiser hull.

(5) **Helicopter:** The one seen here is a Kaman SH-2 Sea Sprite, which had both anti-submarine and anti-surface-vessel warfare capabilities.

(6) **Helicopter Scanner:** The SH-2Fs were fitted with a forward-looking infrared scanner under the nose.

Fearless 1963

The *Fearless*-class ships were designed to provide amphibious assault lift capabilities, using an onboard naval assault group/brigade headquarters unit with a fully equipped assault operations room. From such a room, the assault commander could mount and control all the air, sea, and land force assets required for an operation.

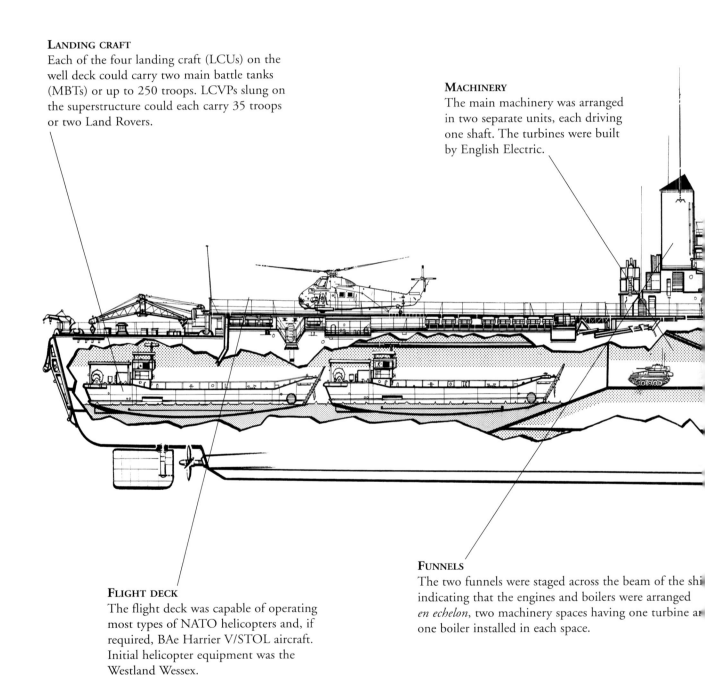

LANDING CRAFT
Each of the four landing craft (LCUs) on the well deck could carry two main battle tanks (MBTs) or up to 250 troops. LCVPs slung on the superstructure could each carry 35 troops or two Land Rovers.

MACHINERY
The main machinery was arranged in two separate units, each driving one shaft. The turbines were built by English Electric.

FLIGHT DECK
The flight deck was capable of operating most types of NATO helicopters and, if required, BAe Harrier V/STOL aircraft. Initial helicopter equipment was the Westland Wessex.

FUNNELS
The two funnels were staged across the beam of the ship, indicating that the engines and boilers were arranged *en echelon*, two machinery spaces having one turbine and one boiler installed in each space.

ELECTRONICS

Fearless and *Intrepid* were fitted with a Type 978 navigation radar, a Type 994 air and surface search radar, and a satellite communication and countermeasures system.

ARMAMENT

Fearless carried an anti-aircraft armament comprising four Short Seacat SAM launchers (there were two on *Intrepid*), and two 40-mm (1.57-in) AA guns. The Seacat was replaced by the Phalanx Close-in Warfare System (CIWS) during the 1991 refit.

FACTS

- Launched 19 December, 1963; commissioned November 1965.

- Royal Navy's first Landing Platform Dock (LPD).

- Last steam-powered ship in Royal Navy service.

- Command ship for anti-terrorist operations in Aden, 1967

- HQ ship for 3 Commando Brigade, Falklands War, 1982.

- Refit 1985–89. Recommissioned 1991.

- Decommissioned 2002. Broken up at Ghent Harbour, Belgium, 2008.

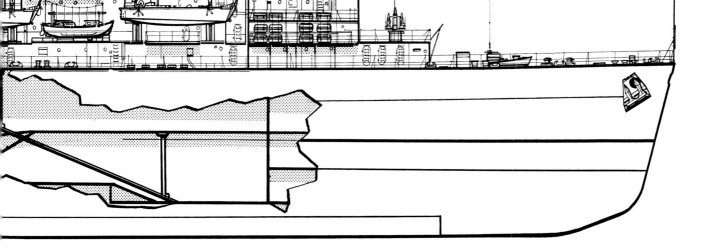

FEARLESS – SPECIFICATION

Country of origin: United Kingdom
Type: Amphibious transport dock
Laid down: 25 July, 1962
Builder: Harland and Wolff, Belfast, Northern Ireland
Launched: 19 December, 1963
Commissioned: 25 November, 1965
Decommissioned: 18 March, 2002
Fate: Scrapped 2008
Complement: 580

Dimensions:
Displacement: (full load) 109,878 tonnes (121,120 tons)
Length: 160 m (520 ft); **Beam:** 24 m (80 ft);

Draught: 6.4 m (21 ft)

Powerplant:
Propulsion: 2 x English Electric dual-shaft geared steam turbines producing 8.2 MW (11,000 shp)
Speed: 21 knots
Range: 9260 km (5000 nm)

Armament & Armour:
Armament: 2 x 20-mm (0.78-in) BMARC GAM BO1 single mounts; 2 x Phalanx CIWS
Armour: N/A
Aircraft: Landing platform for up to five Sea King helicopters

**The 1982 Falklands War proved that the
amphibious task force was still one of the most
effective methods of projecting power over long
distances. In the case of the Falklands, it was the
only means of force projection at Britain's disposal.**

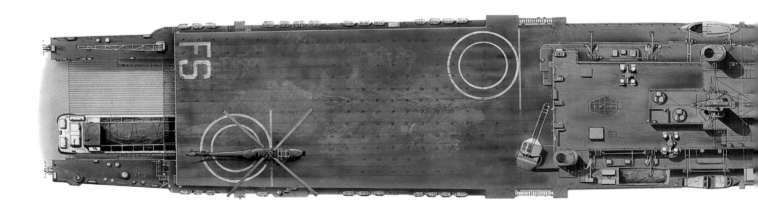

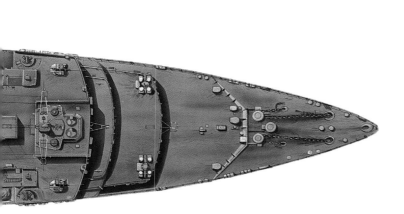

FEARLESS AND *INTREPID*

The assault ships *Fearless* and *Intrepid* formed the core of the Royal Navy's Amphibious Warfare Squadron for nearly three decades. They carried landing craft that could be floated through the open stern by flooding compartments of the ship and lowering her in the water. The ships could deploy tanks, vehicles, and men, and they had seakeeping qualities much superior to those of tank landing ships, together with greater speed and range. They could also serve as command ships at sea for transit operations and as headquarters ships in the assault area.

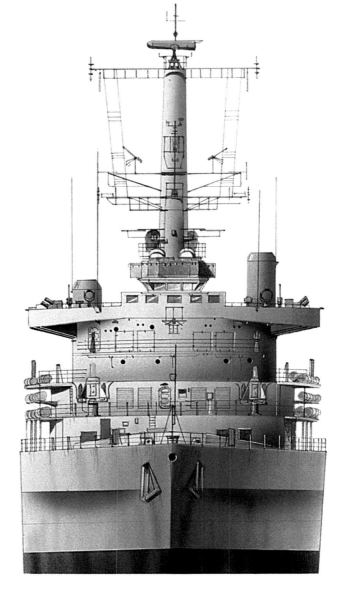

***Fearless* soon demonstrated her value. Not long after she was commissioned, she was deployed in support of anti-insurgent operations in the British Protectorate of Aden, from where Britain was about to withdraw.**

In 1966, during her Middle East deployment, *Fearless* landed elements of the Irish Guards on the beach at Dhofar in support of the Sultan of Oman's forces, which were engaged in quelling dissident factions. Her main task, however, was to act as a command ship and to provide helicopter support for the British forces covering the withdrawal from Aden. Soon after this, in 1968, her name hit the headlines when she served as a floating venue for talks between British Prime Minister Harold Wilson and Rhodesian Prime Minister Ian Smith, whose government had unilaterally declared independence from Britain.

Fearless undertook much service around the world in support of British interests, but in April 1982 she went to war in earnest. On 6 April, she sailed from Portsmouth with

Close-up

Fearless was the first purpose-built landing platform dock (LPD) used by the Royal Navy. She was also the Royal Navy's last steam-powered ship.

(1) **Communications:** *Fearless* was one of the few vessels fitted with modern satellite communications equipment during the Falklands War.

(2) **Armament:** Despite being large and valuable, *Fearless* carried only a light armament. She had four LCM (9) landing craft in davits amidships.

(3) *Fearless* was downgraded in 1981, but was available in emergency. She arose in 1982, when Argentina invaded the Falklands.

(4) **Funnels:** A distinctive recognition feature of *Fearless* was her staggered twin funnel arrangement, the funnel on the port side being set well forwards.

(5) **Anti-aircraft Gun:** For a short time an Argentine anti-aircraft gun was fitted to the flight deck and manned at action stations before being handed on to a logistics ship.

(6) **Landing platform:** *Fearless's* landing platform, here occupied by a Harrier, could take up to five Sea King helicopters.

This bird's-eye view of Fearless *emphasizes the ship's extensive flight deck, and also makes clear the offset arrangement of her funnels, the vessel's major recognition feature.*

elements of 3 Commando Brigade, having been designated Amphibious Headquarters Ship for the Falklands Task Force. After stopping at Ascension Island, where she was joined by her sister ship *Intrepid* (which had the remainder of 3 Commando Brigade embarked) she sailed for the Falklands and made a night approach to San Carlos Water, where she was to disembark her troops. In the early stages of the operation, aircraft of the Argentine Air Force and Navy repeatedly attacked *Fearless* and other ships in the anchorage. *Fearless* escaped with slight damage, a few injuries, and some very near misses, and was credited with a share of four Argentine jets shot down.

Fearless then became headquarters ship for the officer commanding 3 Commando Brigade, General Jeremy Moore, while also supporting elements of the 5th Infantry Brigade and 846 Naval Air Squadron. The force headquarters staff remained embarked throughout the final battle for Port Stanley. At times the ship was host to more than 1500 people and overall the flight deck saw more than 5000 helicopter deck landings, as well as a passing visit from a Sea Harrier.

After the capture of Goose Green, much Argentinean equipment was discovered, put in working order by *Fearless* personnel and, in some cases, put to use. For a short time an Argentine anti-aircraft gun was fitted to the flight deck and manned at action stations before being handed on to a logistics ship that had a greater need for it. Several helicopters were found in working condition and were soon utilized, albeit with a fresh paint scheme. *Fearless* spent the final week of her deployment off Port Stanley, lending support to the reconstruction effort ashore.

ULTIMATELY SCRAP

In 1985 *Fearless* was decommissioned for two years prior to undergoing a two-year refit at Devonport, in Plymouth. Recommissioned in 1991, she subsequently supported the seagoing phase of initial officer training as part of the Dartmouth Training Squadron.

She was decommissioned again in 2002 and awaited disposal in Fareham Creek, Hampshire, alongside *Intrepid*. Efforts to preserve her as a museum ship failed, and she was broken up at Ghent, Belgium, in 2008. *Intrepid* suffered a similar fate, being scrapped at Liverpool.

Resolution 1966

In February 1963 the British government stated its intention to order four or five *Resolution*-class nuclear-powered ballistic missile submarines, armed with the American Polaris SLBM, to take over the British nuclear deterrent role from the RAF in 1968.

ELECTRONICS
The vessel was fitted with one Type 1007 surface-search radar, one Type 2001 bow sonar, one Type 2007 sonar, one Type 2023 retractable towed-array sonar, one Type 2019 intercept sonar, and one ESM suite, as well as extensive communications equipment.

TORPEDO TUBES
Although designed for strategic missile attack, the *Resolution*-class boats were fitted with six 533-mm (21-in) torpedo tubes in the forward part of the hull.

HULL
The hull was assembled on the berth from sections prefabricated in the assembly shop. The fore and aft parts of the ship were built up simultaneously, the prefabricated missile sections, complete with missile tubes, being fitted into the space between.

CREW
Normal crew on *Resolution* was 154. Each Ship Submersible Ballistic Nuclear (SSBN) had two crews, known as "port" and "starboard," alternating on each voyage of approximately three months' duration.

MISSILES

Resolution had launch tubes for each of her 16 Polaris A3 SLBMs. Her Polaris system was updated in 1984 with the Chevaline IFE (Improved Front End). This included two new warheads and re-entry bodies, as well as super-hardened penetration aids to resist anti-ballistic missile (ABM) attack, replacing the original three ET.317 warheads.

MACHINERY

Resolution's powerplant was a pressurized water-cooled reactor powering two steam turbines driving a single shaft, giving the boat a speed of at least 25 knots underwater.

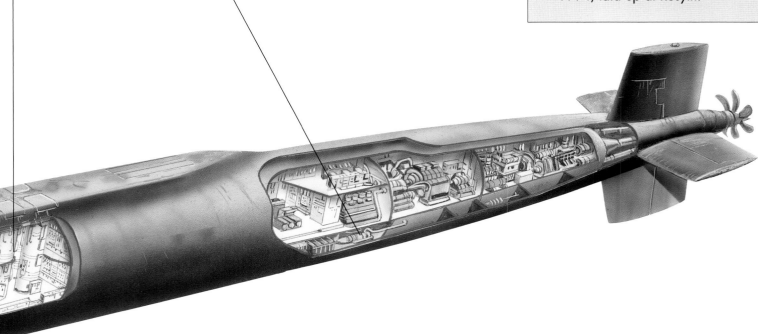

FACTS

- Launched 15 September, 1966; commissioned 2 October, 1967.

- First live firing of Polaris missile, 15 February, 1968.

- First operational patrol, 15 June, 1968.

- Carried out 69 operational patrols, including one of 108 days (in 1991).

- Decommissioned 22 October, 1994; laid up at Rosyth.

RESOLUTION – SPECIFICATION

Country of origin: United Kingdom
Type: Submarine
Laid down: 26 February, 1964
Builder: Vickers Shipbuilding Ltd, Barrow-in-Furness, England
Launched: 15 September, 1966
Commissioned: 2 October, 1967
Decommissioned: 22 October, 1994
Fate: Laid up at Rosyth Dockyard, Scotland
Complement: 143

Dimensions:
Displacement: (surfaced) 6804 tonnes (7500 tons); (submerged) 7620 tonnes (8400 tons)
Length: 130 m (425 ft); **Beam:** 10 m (33 ft); **Draught:** 9.17 m (30 ft 1 in)

Powerplant:
Propulsion: 1 x Vickers/Rolls-Royce PWR.1 pressurized-water nuclear reactor, 2 steam turbines
Speed: (surface) 20 knots; (submerged) 25 knots
Range: Unlimited

Armament:
Armament: 16 x Polaris A3TK IRBMs; 6 x 533-mm (21-in) torpedo tubes

Resolution was the first of four similar vessels in her class. The second, *Repulse*, followed in September 1968, with *Renown* and *Revenge* following in November 1968 and December 1969 respectively.

U.S. SSBN: *LAFAYETTE*

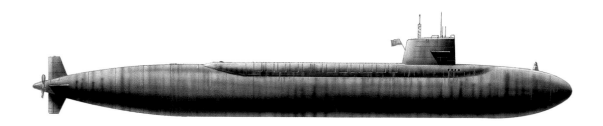

BRITISH SSN: *VALIANT*

BRITISH SSBN: *"R" CLASS*

BRITISH SSN: *DREADNOUGHT*

POLARIS MISSILES

The project to develop the Polaris SLBM began in the mid-1950s and, at the time, was considered extremely ambitious. The weapon became operational in 1960, the original missile being the Polaris A-1 with a single 0.5mT warhead. In 1962 the A-2 missile was introduced, with more powerful rocket motors and better in-flight control; the A-3 appeared in 1974, with more powerful fuel, better guidance, and multiple warheads. *Resolution*'s Polaris system originally had three ET.17 warheads mounted on each missile, but this was updated in 1984 with the Chevaline IFE (Improved Front End) system. This included new warhead re-entry bodies, with penetration aids super-hardened to resist ABM attack.

A Royal Navy Sea King helicopter winches up a crewman from the deck of Resolution. *Exchanges of personnel, and sometimes the evacuation of sick personnel, by helicopter were not uncommon.*

The design, construction, and deployment of the *Resolution* class was claimed to have been the only British defence procurement programme to have been completed under budget.

Resolution (S22) was the first of a class of four ballistic missile submarines built for the Royal Navy. She was based on the U.S. Navy's *Lafayette* class. These submarines allowed the Royal Navy to assume a Quick Reaction Alert (QRA) posture, taking over responsibility for Great Britain's strategic nuclear deterrent from the RAF's Blue Steel-armed Vulcan and Victor V-Bomber force, as agreed at the 1962 Nassau Conference. The four submarines (a fifth was cancelled) used U.S. Polaris missiles, missile tubes, and fire control systems plus British engines and other equipment.

Resolution's keel was laid down at the Vickers yard, Barrow-in-Furness, on 26 February, 1964. Colossal planning and design effort went into the Polaris submarine programme, which involved half a million man-hours of planning. More than 10,000 carefully detailed drawings were prepared, all of which had to be translated into the physical business of construction. Additionally, a full-scale wooden "mock-up" was built. Not only did this allow the exact positioning of any piece of equipment to be planned and the routes for cables, pipes, and trunking to be decided upon, but it enabled crew to undergo training and become familiar with their new boat before they even set foot on her.

PROGRAMME POLITICALLY CURTAILED

The British Polaris boats lacked the fin-mounted diving planes of the original *Lafayette*s, and instead borrowed certain features from the British *Valiant* class of nuclear attack submarines. To guarantee that one submarine would always remain on patrol, the Royal Navy planned to build a fifth submarine. However, it was cancelled by the incoming Labour government in 1964 as an economic measure and to placate those calling for nuclear disarmament. Officially, there was never a gap in submarine QRA patrols. Unofficially, it is believed that the RAF's Vulcans took back the strategic deterrent commitment on at least one occasion in the late 1960s.

Launched in September 1966, *Resolution* was completed in October 1967, and went on her first patrol in 1968 as planned after completing live firing trials with Polaris off of Florida. To improve the ability of the Polaris missile to penetrate the USSR's increasingly sophisticated anti-ballistic missile (ABM) defences, Britain embarked on an expensive and ambitious upgrade programme code-named Chevaline, adding decoys to the Polaris warhead.

As with U.S. and French SSBNs, two crews (port and starboard) were used to make the best use of time spent at sea, each patrol lasting around three months. When based ashore, the crews took leave and did refresher training with the 10th Submarine Squadron, based at Faslane on the River Clyde, Scotland. A considerable spell of leave was necessary after a seagoing tour, because three months underwater could produce physical symptoms. For example, it took a crew member some time before his eyes again adjusted to long-distance viewing after the submarine's confined spaces.

New Trident-armed *Vanguard*s replaced the *Resolution*-class submarines starting in 1995. *Revenge* was withdrawn in 1992, and *Resolution* followed in 1994. The remaining two submarines in the class were withdrawn during 1995–96.

Interior view

The four *Resolution* class SSBNs (Ship Submersible Ballistic Nuclear) served the Royal Navy well, but after 20 years in service suffered problems with their reactors.

(1) **Confined Space:** Crew members spend months underwater in a confined space, and find that it takes days for their eyes to adjust to long distance again.

(2) **Bombers:** In the Royal Navy, ballistic missile submarines are referred to as "bombers."

(3) Modern ballistic missile submarines are usually designed to launch their weapons at keel depth, typically less than 50 m (164 ft).

(4) **Features:** The *Resolution* class incorporated several enviable features, such as a machinery loading hatch, automated hovering system, and welded hull valves.

(5) **Construction:** The construction was unusual in that the bow and stern were constructed separately before being assembled together.

(6) **Design:** This was a modification of the *Valiant*-class fleet submarine, but extended to incorporate the missile compartment between the fin and the nuclear reactor.

Sturgeon 1966

Until the introduction of the *Los Angeles* class, the *Sturgeon* class was the backbone of the U.S. Navy's attack submarine fleet, dedicated to seeking out and destroying enemy submarines.

MACHINERY
Sturgeon was fitted with a Westinghouse S5W pressurized-water reactor powering two steam turbines driving one shaft, giving a speed of 18 knots on the surface and 26 knots underwater.

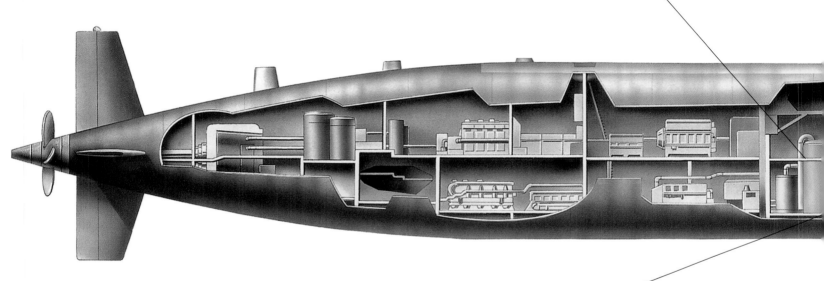

COMPARTMENTS
Some of the *Sturgeon*-class boats were modified with compartments for Special Forces troops and their associated equipment.

ELECTRONICS

The original electronics fit comprised one BPS-15 surface-search radar, a BQQ-5 sonar suite (later including towed array), a Mk 117 torpedo fire control system, a satellite communications system, and an underwater telephone.

CONTROL CENTRE

The control centre of an attack submarine includes a Target Motion Attack (TMA) system, which allows the submarine to track targets using only passive sonar bearings.

ARMAMENT

Sturgeon's original armament of 533-mm (21-in) torpedoes was upgraded to include Sub-Harpoon and Tomahawk submarine-launched ballistic missiles.

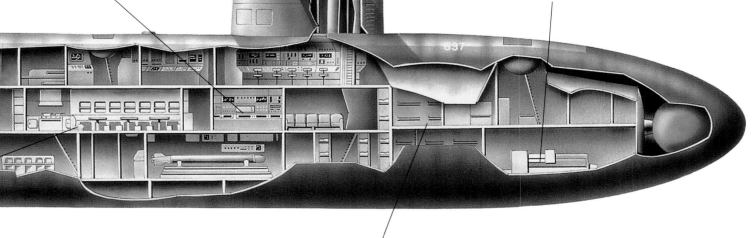

TORPEDO ROOM

Data on each torpedo tube is displayed on a control panel in the control centre and relayed to the submarine's combat system.

STURGEON (SSN-637) – SPECIFICATION

Country of origin: USA
Type: Attack submarine
Laid down: 10 August, 1963
Builder: General Dynamics Electric Boat, Connecticut, USA
Launched: 26 February, 1966
Commissioned: 3 March, 1967
Decommissioned: 1 August, 1994
Fate: Scrapped
Complement: 14 officers, 95 men

Dimensions:

Displacement: (light) 3638 tonnes (4010 tons); (full) 3909 tonnes (4309 tons)

Length: 89 m (292 ft): **Beam:** 9.7 m (32 ft); **Draught:** 8.8 m (29 ft)

Powerplant:
Propulsion: S3G Core 3 reactor with a S5W steam plant producing 11.2 MW (15,000 shp)
Speed: 26 knots
Range: Unlimited

Armament & Armour:
Armament: 4 x 533-mm (21-in) torpedo tubes

Apart from its high-tech sensory systems, the main
advantage of the hunter-killer submarine is that it
can remain submerged on patrol for virtually
unlimited periods. Its diving depth can match, and
often exceed, that of a ballistic missile submarine.

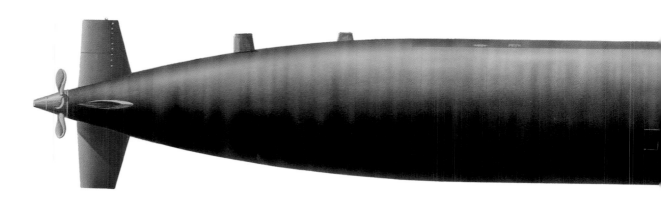

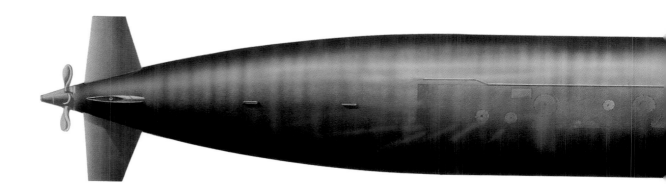

HUNTER-KILLER SUBMARINES

The USA and USSR both began developing hunter-killer submarines in the late 1940s, but their development paths diverged over the years. The Americans concentrated on boats armed with weapons launched by torpedo tubes, these craft being designated SSNs, whereas the Russians developed submarines capable of launching both torpedoes and anti-ship missiles. Such submarines carry the designation SSGN.

SSNs hunt their quarry by listening with sensitive sonar devices mounted on the hull. The most advanced of these sensors use lightweight plastic sheets fastened to the hull. These generate electric impulses in response to minute acoustic pressure waves, and process the resulting signals using a computer.

Modern SSNs are designed to be very quiet. When cruising on patrol at low speed, a nuclear submarine may radiate only 0.01 watt of acoustic power, less than the noise of a car passing along a motorway.

The U.S. Navy's first SSN was the *Skipjack* class. These were built in the late 1950s and remained the U.S. Navy's fastest submarine for 30 years. The first American SSN with advanced sonar equipment and deep-diving capability was the *Thresher* class, which could dive to a maximum depth of 600 m (1970 ft). These boats were later renamed the *Permit* class after the prototype, *Thresher*, was lost with all 129 crew during its diving trials off the New England coast in April 1963.

SUBROC MISSILES

The *Permit* class of submarine introduced the SUBROC anti-submarine missile, which was a nuclear depth charge propelled by a solid-fuel rocket motor. SUBROC followed a short underwater course after launch from a submarine's

Interior view

The control centre of a nuclear attack submarine is a busy place, and many people are crammed into a small space, so teamwork must be of the highest order.

(1) **Drills:** To keep the skills of the crew honed and their minds sharp, daily drills simulate responses to various threats and combat situations.

(2) **Navigation:** The navigation and plotting areas are at the rear of the compartment.

(3) **Consoles:** All consoles providing information on the control of the boat are compact, concisely laid out, and simple to interpret.

(4) **Periscope:** In the middle of the control room is a raised platform with the periscopes mounted in it.

(5) **OOD:** The forwards part of the control room is the watch station for the officer of the deck (OOD).

(6) **On Standby:** Helmsman and planesmen stand by to control the submerged boat. Diving is a carefully controlled and balanced procedure.

A sister boat to Sturgeon *was* Queenfish *(SSN-651), seen here travelling at speed on the surface. In 1970,* Queenfish *undertook the assignment of mapping the ocean floor under the Arctic ice cap.*

torpedo tube, before transferring to an air trajectory for the major portion of its journey to the target. At a pre-determined point, the depth charge separated from the rocket booster and followed a ballistic trajectory to enter the water close to the target, after which it sank to a pre-determined depth and detonated. SUBROC reached a maximum speed of Mach 1.5 and had a maximum range of 55 km (30 miles). Its five-kT W55 fission warhead had a lethal range of 5–8 km (3–5 miles) from the detonation point. *Sturgeon* and other later American SSNs carried SUBROC. A longer-range weapon, known as Sea Lance, was intended to replace it in 1990, but this was cancelled. Then, in 1989, SUBROC was withdrawn.

INTELLIGENCE GATHERING

Sturgeon was an enlarged and improved version of the *Thresher/Permit* design with additional "stealth" features and electronic systems. The *Sturgeon*-class SSNs were the largest class of nuclear-powered submarines until the advent of the *Los Angeles* class, and were frequently used in intelligence gathering, which involved carrying special equipment and National Security Agency personnel. In 1982, *Cavalla* was

converted at Pearl Harbor to undertake a secondary amphibious assault role by carrying a swimmer delivery vehicle (SDV). *Archerfish*, *Silversides*, *Tunny*, and *L. Mendel Rivers* were similarly equipped, while *William H. Bates*, *Hawkbill*, *Pintado*, *Richard B. Russell*, and others were modified to carry the Navy's Deep Submergence and Rescue Vehicles (DSRV).

Sturgeon began her operational patrols in 1968, her main task being interspersed with exercises and equipment evaluation. During one series of exercises, she played a key part in the evaluation of new equipment mounted in the U.S. Navy's maritime patrol aircraft. Her longest deployment took place in 1974, when she was detached to the U.S. Sixth Fleet in the Mediterranean for a six-month period.

Sturgeon was decommissioned and stricken from the Naval Register in August 1994. She subsequently entered the Nuclear Powered Ship and Submarine Recycling facility at Bremerton, Washington, where work on dismantling her began. By 11 December, 1995, all but one fragment of her ceased to exist.

In September 1995 her sail was transferred with due ceremony to the Undersea Museum in Keyport, Washington, where it was erected in the museum carpark.

Sjöormen 1967

Nuclear-powered submarines are expensive, and diesel/electric boats like the Royal Swedish Navy's *Sjöormen* class provided a cost-effective solution to the problem of maintaining an undersea presence in territorial waters.

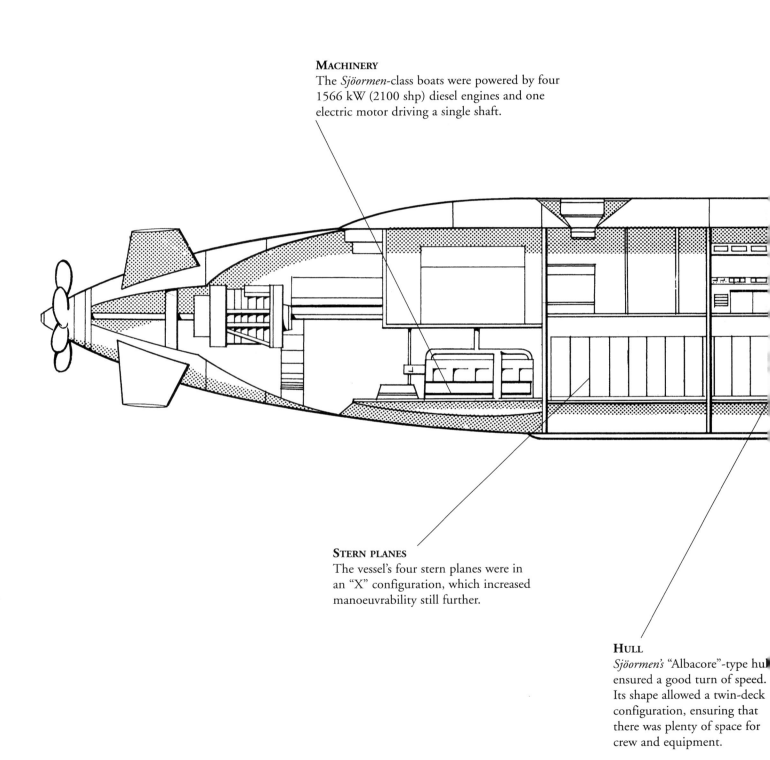

MACHINERY
The *Sjöormen*-class boats were powered by four 1566 kW (2100 shp) diesel engines and one electric motor driving a single shaft.

STERN PLANES
The vessel's four stern planes were in an "X" configuration, which increased manoeuvrability still further.

HULL
Sjöormen's "Albacore"-type hull ensured a good turn of speed. Its shape allowed a twin-deck configuration, ensuring that there was plenty of space for crew and equipment.

HYDROPLANES

The hydroplanes were mounted on the sail, which greatly increased the boat's underwater manoeuvrability. In the Baltic, manoeuvrability was of greater importance than diving depth.

ARMAMENT

The basic armament load was eight 533-mm (21-in) Type 61 anti-ship wire-guided torpedoes or 16 influence ground mines, plus four Type 42 wire-guided anti-submarine torpedoes.

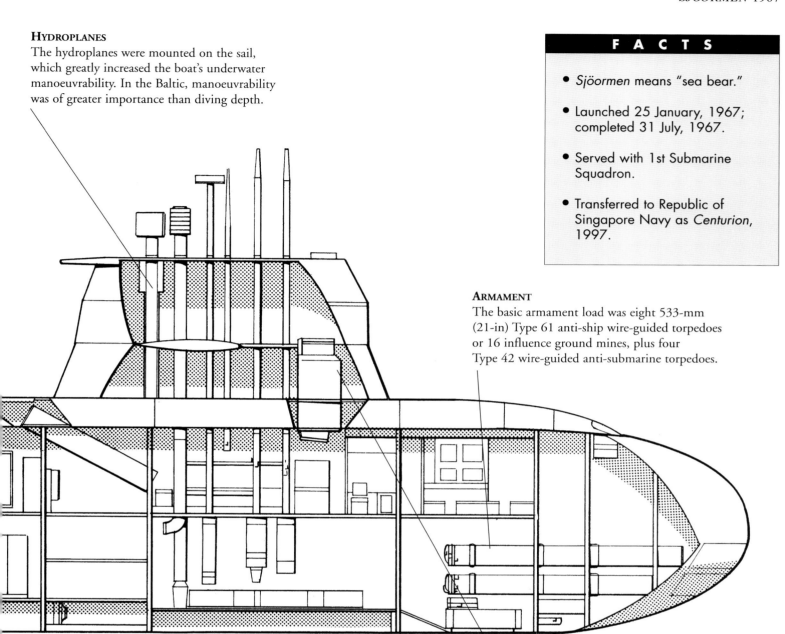

ELECTRONICS

Electronics on the vessel included one Terma surface search radar, one low-frequency sonar, and one IBS-A17 torpedo fire control/action information system.

SJÖORMEN – SPECIFICATION

Country of origin: Sweden
Type: Submarine
Laid down: 1966
Builder: Kockums, Malmö
Launched: 25 January, 1967
Commissioned: 31 July, 1968
Decommissioned: 1997
Fate: Sold to Singapore in 1997
Complement: 25 officers and enlisted crew

Dimensions:
Displacement: (surfaced) 1130 tonnes (1246 tons); (submerged) 1210 tonnes (1191 tons)

Length: 50.5 m (165 ft 8 in)
Beam: 6.1 m (20 ft)
Draught: 5.8 m (19 ft 9 in)

Powerplant:
Propulsion: 2 x Hedemora Diesel generators delivering 1566 kW (2100 shp), single shaft, electric motor
Speed: 20 knots (dived)
Range: N/A

Armament:
Armament: 4 x 533-mm (21-in) torpedo tubes; 2 x 400-mm (15.8-in) torpedo tubes for 10 and 4 torpedoes respectively

Sjöormen was developed as a counter to
Soviet diesel-electric vessels, such as the
"Foxtrot" class, seen here, which operated
extensively in the Baltic.

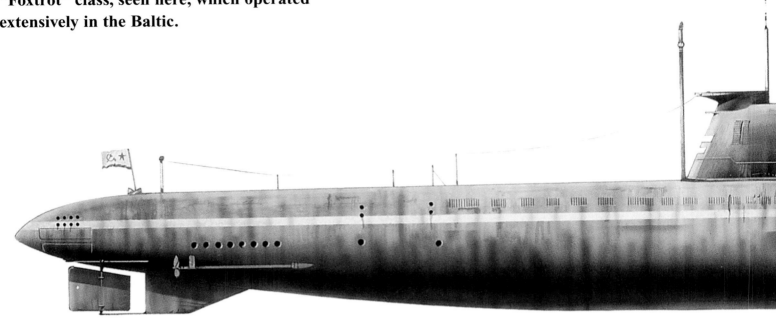

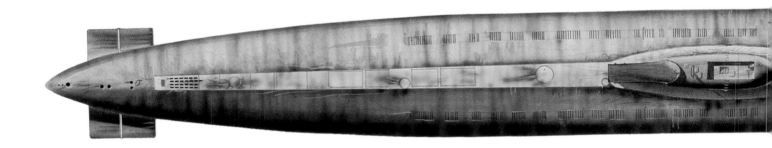

ALBACORE-TYPE HULL

Sjöormen's Albacore-type hull, so called because it was first used in the design of the American submarine *Albacore*, is shaped like a teardrop. The emphasis of such a design is on hydrodynamic flow, and the benefits include increased speed and a smaller acoustic signature, which makes the submarine more difficult to detect. The foreplanes are located so as not to interfere with the sonar. There are several design variations. American designers moved the foreplanes to the sail, where they could be tilted upwards to aid in piercing thin ice. The British often located the foreplanes forwards, at the level of the deck, and designed them to fold upwards so as to not foul harbour structures.

RIVAL: "FOXTROT"

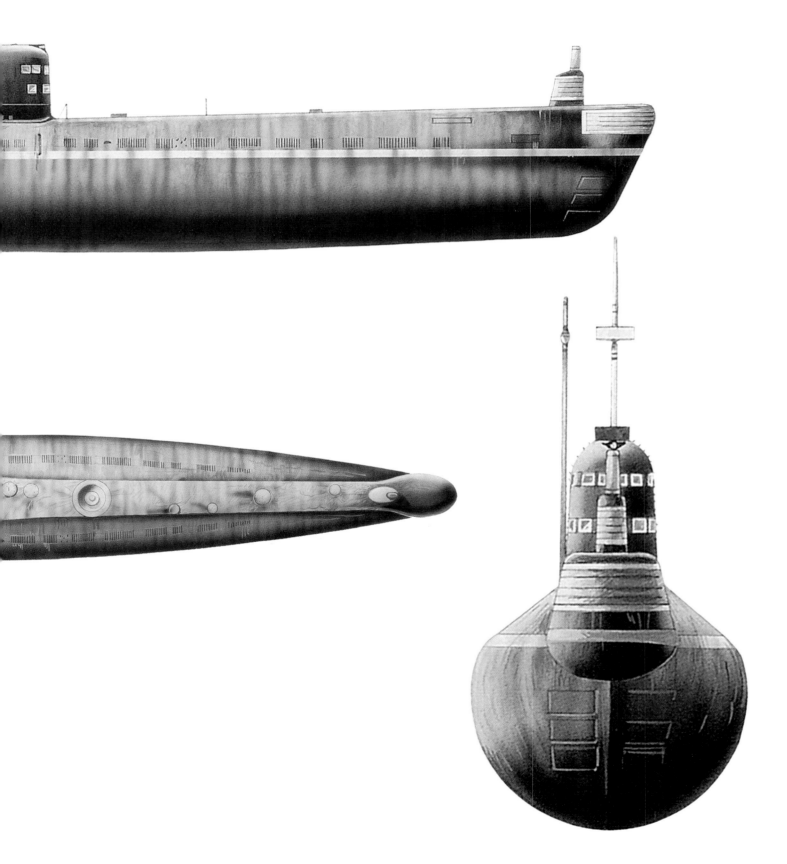

The key to the success of the Sjöormen-*class vessels was their manoeuvrability, which made them ideal for operations in confined waters. This factor in particular made them attractive to the navy of the Republic of Singapore.*

All five boats of the *Sjöormen* class were built within a year at the Kockums and Karlskrona yards. The names of the other four were *Sjölejonet* (sea lion), *Sjöhunden* (sea dog), *Sjöhästen* (sea horse), and *Sjöbjörnen* (sea bee).

The five boats of the *Sjöormen* class were the first modern type of submarines to enter service with the Royal Swedish Navy. They were optimized for service in the relatively confined waters of the Baltic Sea, which are notoriously difficult to navigate. The average width of the Baltic is only about 200 km (125 miles) and the average depth between 100–200 m (330–650 ft). Although the Baltic is practically tideless, strong north-easterly winds can whip up choppy seas, and these can create hazardous navigating conditions for small craft. Worryingly too, the Swedish and Finnish coasts are heavily indented, with a liberal scattering of rocky islands, while the eastern and southern shores are characterized by dunes, sandspits, lagoons, and estuaries.

The *Sjöormen*-class vessels were designed in the early 1960s and construction was equally divided between Kocklums of Malmö (the designer) and Karlskrona Varvet.

With an Albacore-type hull for speed and a twin-deck arrangement, the excellent manoeuvrability of the boats greatly enhanced the Royal Swedish Navy's ASW operations in the area. The control surface and hydroplane arrangements were such that, together with the hull design, they enabled the submarine to make the best use of its manoeuvrability throughout the full underwater speed range, although they were most effective at the lower end. For example, a 360-degree turn could be achieved in five minutes within a 230-m (755-ft) diameter circle at a speed of 7 knots underwater. Increasing the speed to 15 knots meant that the same turn would take only two and a half minutes. As a result, this class could easily out-turn most of the Warsaw Pact ASW escorts encountered in the Baltic, as well as most of their NATO counterparts.

INTELLIGENCE GATHERING

All five boats were upgraded in 1984–85 with new Ericsson IBS-A17 combat date/fire control systems. In the 1990s they were progressively replaced by the new A19 class, which incorporated a fully integrated combat system, more extensive sensors, and even quieter machinery to permit their use on offensive hunter-killer ASW patrols.

In 1995, personnel of the Republic of Singapore Navy arrived in Sweden to undergo an intensive submariners' training course on four boats of the *Sjöormen* class, which had now been retired from service with the Swedish navy. This course would eventually qualify them to form the crews of Singapore's first-ever submarines.

RELAUNCHED FOR TROPICAL CONDITIONS

The first to be transferred was *Sjöbjörnen*, which was modified and upgraded for tropical conditions in 1996–97 and relaunched as *Challenger* on 26 September, 1997. The other vessels in the *Challenger* class are *Centurion* (formerly *Sjöormen*), *Conqueror* (formerly *Sjölejonet*) and *Chieftain* (formerly *Sjöhunden*), which together form 171 Submarine Squadron. The weapons options for the reconditioned boats include a combination of FFV Type 613 anti-ship torpedoes (10 carried) and four FFV Type 431 ASW torpedoes.

Close-up

A comprehensive tropicalization programme, involving a number of modifications, was carried out to make the vessels suitable for service with the navy of the Republic of Singapore.

① **New Systems:** Refurbishing four of the *Sjöormen* boats obtained by Singapore was a major exercise, involving the fitting of new systems.

② **Engine:** The twin-engine *Sjöormen* runs on diesel-electric power and has the capability of navigating underwater at a speed of up to 16 knots.

③ **Hull:** *Sjöormen*'s distinctive double-deck hull is clearly visible in this photograph.

④ **Modernization:** This involved installing air conditioning, marine growth protection systems and corrosion-resistant piping.

⑤ **Armament:** The weapons for the boats comprised a combination of FFV Type 613 anti-ship torpedoes and FFV Type 431 ASW torpedoes.

⑥ **Hydroplane:** The control surface and hydroplane arrangements were the same as those fitted to the later Swedish submarine classes.

California 1971

Originally intended to have been a class comprised of five nuclear-powered guided missile frigates, the *California* class was cut back to only two vessels. These were commissioned as frigates and were then later redesignated as cruisers.

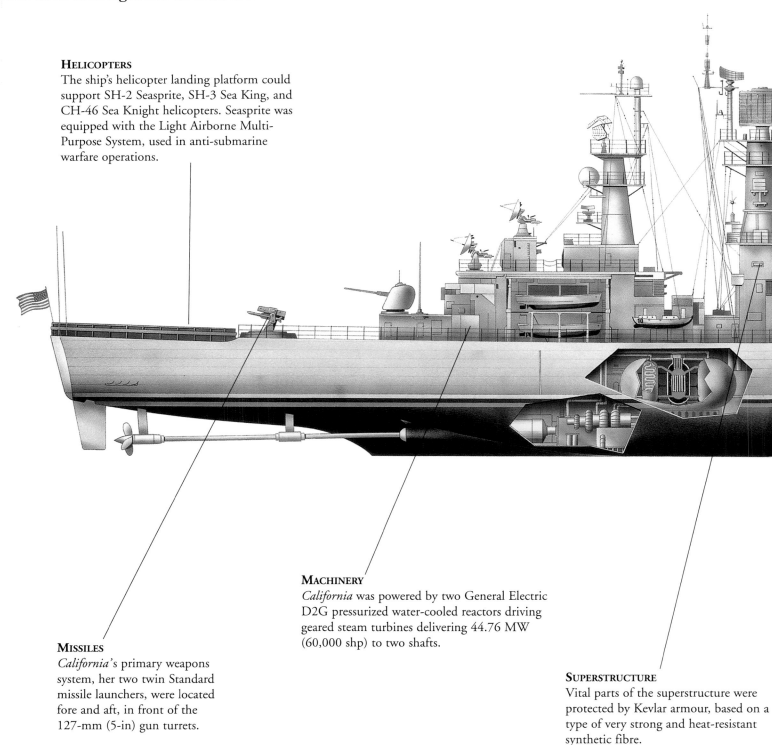

HELICOPTERS
The ship's helicopter landing platform could support SH-2 Seasprite, SH-3 Sea King, and CH-46 Sea Knight helicopters. Seasprite was equipped with the Light Airborne Multi-Purpose System, used in anti-submarine warfare operations.

MISSILES
California's primary weapons system, her two twin Standard missile launchers, were located fore and aft, in front of the 127-mm (5-in) gun turrets.

MACHINERY
California was powered by two General Electric D2G pressurized water-cooled reactors driving geared steam turbines delivering 44.76 MW (60,000 shp) to two shafts.

SUPERSTRUCTURE
Vital parts of the superstructure were protected by Kevlar armour, based on a type of very strong and heat-resistant synthetic fibre.

SENSORS

Sensors included an SPS-48A 3D air search radar, 2D air search radar, and an array of surface search radars and fire control radar systems. These enabled the vessel to engage targets up to 130 km (70 nm) distant.

F A C T S

- Launched 22 September, 1971; completed 16 February, 1974.

- Sixth ship to bear the name of the state of California.

- Nicknamed "The Golden Grizzly."

- Circumnavigated the globe in 1980.

- Decommissioned 1999, scrapped 2000.

GUN ARMAMENT

California's main gun armament comprised two 127-mm (5-in) Mk 45 guns. The gun mount featured an automatic loader with a capacity of 20 rounds.

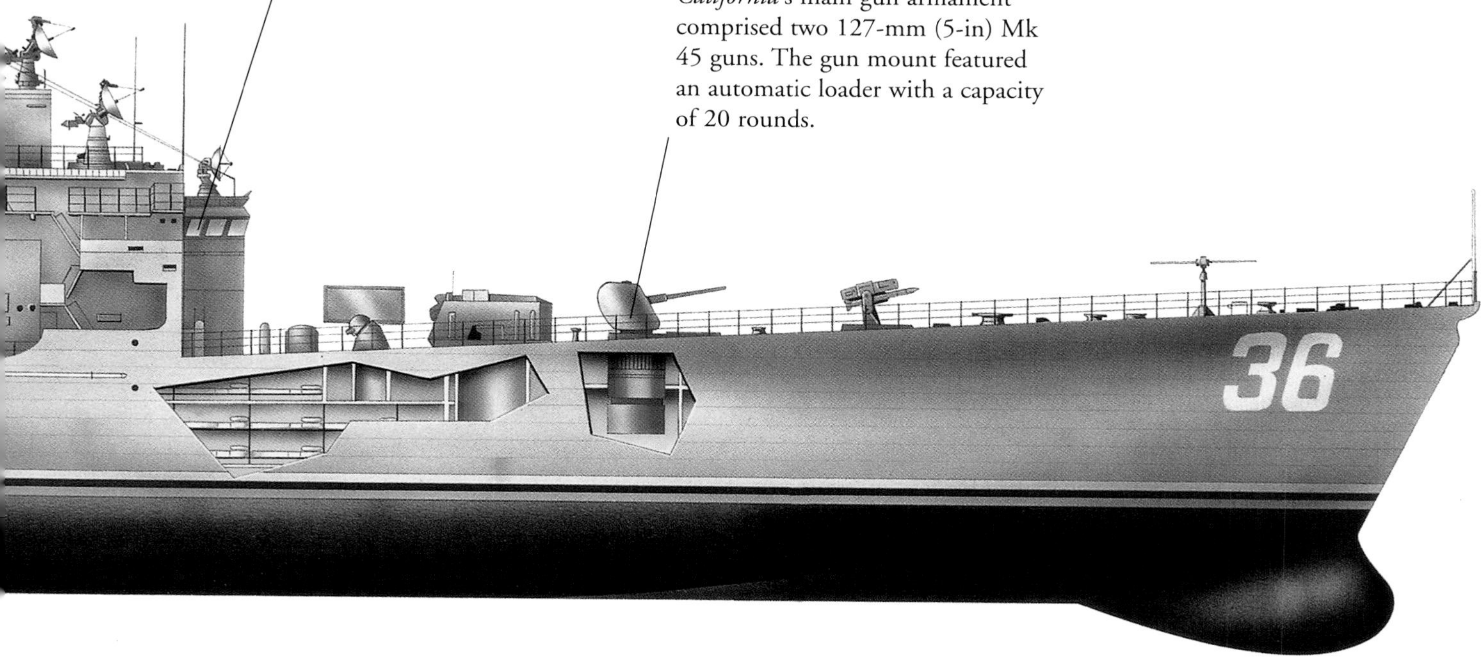

CALIFORNIA – SPECIFICATION

Country of origin: USA
Type: Cruiser
Laid down: 23 January, 1970
Builder: Newport News Shipbuilding, Virginia
Launched: 22 September, 1971
Commissioned: 16 February, 1974
Decommissioned: 9 July, 1999
Fate: Nuclear ship recycling
Complement: 40 officers and 544 enlisted crew

Dimensions:
Displacement: 10,814 tonnes (11,920 tons)
Length: 181.6 m (596 ft);

Beam: 18.5 m (61 ft); **Draught:** 10 m (33 ft)

Powerplant:
Propulsion: 2 x General Electric nuclear reactors
Speed: 32 knots
Range: Nuclear

Armament & Armour:
Armament: 2 x Mk 141 Harpoon missile launchers; 2 x 127-mm (5-in) Mk 45 guns; 2 x 20-mm (0.79-in) Phalanx CIWS; 1 x ASROC missile launcher; 2 x Mk 13 missile launchers; Mark 46 torpedoes for anti-submarine use
Aircraft: Helicopter deck

California's principal task was to act in the "goalkeeper" role as escort to an aircraft carrier, her missiles eliminating any air threats that leaked through the carrier task group's outer defence zone.

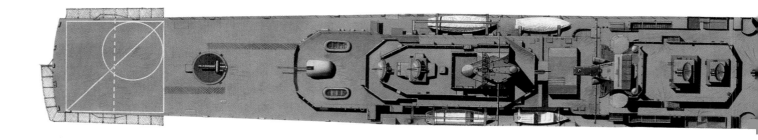

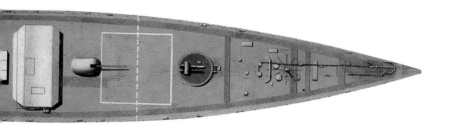

SAM

California's main weapon, the semi-active radar homing Standard SAM, began development in the early 1960s as a replacement for the Tartar and Terrier systems, two models with different ranges and altitude limits, being designed to replace the earlier weapons. After entering service beginning in 1968 on warships undergoing refits or on newly built vessels, both models underwent several subsequent upgrades to improve their reliability. These improvements considerably enhanced the Standard SAM's capabilities against high-performance aircraft and missiles. The SM-2 version of the missile, which is at the heart of the Aegis missile defence system, has almost double the range of the first model.

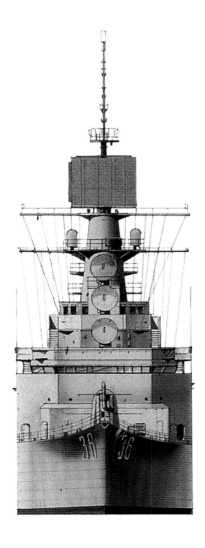

California's sister ship, *South Carolina*, had an even more active life than the class leader. Among other assignments, she supported NATO operations off the coast of the former republics of Yugoslavia. She, too, was scrapped in 2000.

Two nuclear-powered *California*-class cruisers were built for the U.S. Navy after plans for a pair of guided missile destroyers fell through. They proved to be very different from their cancelled predecessors, because they incorporated a host of new systems, the most important of which were their nuclear powerplants. As a consequence, their research and development escalated sharply and funding was only released by the Pentagon after Congress intervened to rewrite the budget, as often happens in the U.S. procurement system, and in 1975 the *California*s were redesignated as nuclear-powered cruisers (CGNs).

UPDATED ARMAMENT

The original design had specified heavyweight 127-mm (5-in) main guns and tubes for Mk 48 torpedoes, but the

Close-up

California and her sister ship, *South Carolina*, were designed to counter every conceivable threat, in the air, on the surface or underwater.

(1) **Flight Deck:** *California*'s extensive flight deck near the stern was designed to accommodate Seasprite, Sea King, or Sea Knight helicopters.

(2) **Launchers:** *California* was equipped with launchers, fore and aft, for the Standard surface-to-air missile.

(3) **Main Gun:** The main gun armament was a lightweight Mk 45 127-mm (5-in) gun, two of which were fitted.

(4) **Vital Areas:** Extensive measures were taken to make the vital areas, such as the bridge, resistant to missile impact and heat.

(5) **Sensor:** Sensors were designed to detect any threat long before it could penetrate the carrier task group's outer defence zone.

(6) **Speed:** With both nuclear reactors running, *California* could reach a speed of 32 knots.

California *is pictured here turning at speed. After a long and distinguished career, she was deactivated on 28 August, 1998, at the Puget Sound Naval Shipyard in Bremerton, Washington.*

guns were replaced with lighter weapons of the same calibre and the torpedo tubes were deleted. Standard surface-to-air missiles replaced the earlier Tartars and *California* was fitted with a greatly improved reactor design, with three times the reactor fuel life of the nuclear powerplants installed on earlier nuclear-powered cruisers. A helicopter deck was also fitted, but there was no hangar.

California was launched in September 1971 (as DLGN 36) and completed in February 1974. An anti-submarine rocket (ASROC) system was installed under the bridge behind the forward gun, and remained there until 1993. *California* underwent several upgrades over the years. Kevlar armour protection was installed over vital areas of the superstructure and her original SPS-40 radar was replaced by an improved SPS-49.

For a decade after her commissioning, *California* operated successively in the Atlantic and Indian oceans as well as the Mediterranean, serving three times with the Sixth Fleet and twice with the Seventh Fleet. Her first Mediterranean cruise was from July 1976 to February 1977. In the summer of 1977, she represented the United States surface fleet at the Silver Jubilee Review in Portsmouth, England, where more than 150 warships from

18 nations had assembled to celebrate the twenty-fifth anniversary of Queen Elizabeth's coronation.

ON STANDBY IN A CRISIS
Two years later, during the crisis that developed following the seizure of the U.S. Embassy in Iran, she deployed from Livorno, Italy, to the North Arabian Sea as part of an all-nuclear task group and remained on station in the Indian Ocean for the next five months, returning to the U.S. in May 1980 after a nine-month overseas deployment.

In April 1990, *California* entered the Puget Sound Naval Shipyard in Bremerton, Washington, for a three-year refuelling procedure and overhaul that included the installation of two new D2G high-endurance reactor cores in her engineering plant with adequate fuel capacity to power the ship for more than 20 years of normal operations. After the overhaul, in January 1993, *California* began a series of exercises and evaluations in preparation for deployment. This took place in June 1994, when she joined the *Kitty Hawk* and her battle group in the Western Pacific. In January 1998, *California* deployed to the Eastern Pacific and the Caribbean Sea in support of a counter-drug task force. She was decommissioned in August 1998 and scrapped in 2000.

Nimitz (CVN-68) 1972

The *Nimitz*-class nuclear-powered supercarriers, in service with the U.S. Navy, are the largest capital ships in the world. The ship was named for Fleet Admiral Chester W. Nimitz, who commanded the U.S. Pacific Fleet in World War II.

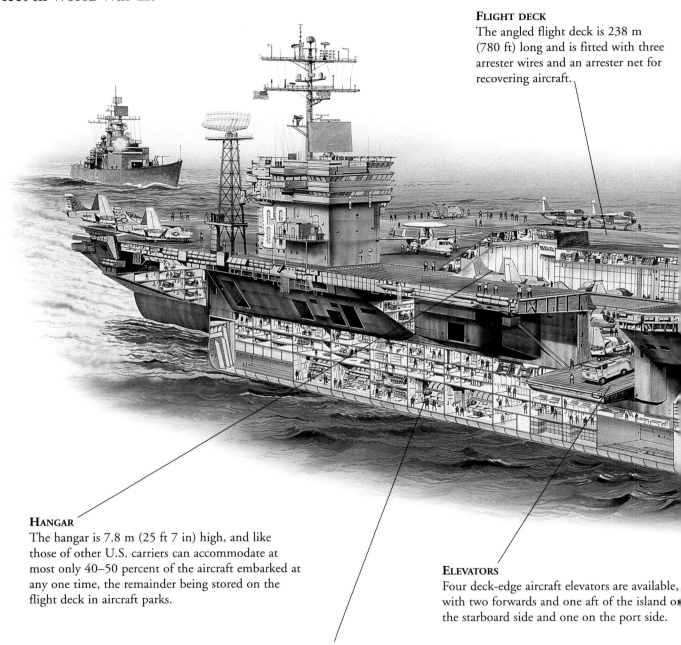

FLIGHT DECK
The angled flight deck is 238 m (780 ft) long and is fitted with three arrester wires and an arrester net for recovering aircraft.

HANGAR
The hangar is 7.8 m (25 ft 7 in) high, and like those of other U.S. carriers can accommodate at most only 40–50 percent of the aircraft embarked at any one time, the remainder being stored on the flight deck in aircraft parks.

ELEVATORS
Four deck-edge aircraft elevators are available, with two forwards and one aft of the island on the starboard side and one on the port side.

MACHINERY
Nimitz is powered by two Westinghouse A4W nuclear reactors and four steam turbines, generating 194 MW (260,000 shp).

FACTS

- Launched 13 May, 1972; commissioned May 1975.
- The *Nimitz* reaches more than 23 storeys high from the keel to the top of the mast.
- First deployment to the Mediterranean, July 1976, with Carrier Air Wing 8 embarked.
- Built to have an active service life of at least 50 years.
- There are 10 *Nimitz*-class carriers, the last of which (CVN-77 *George H.W. Bush*) was commissioned in 2009.

Complement
Nimitz has a complement of 3200, plus a further 2480 manning the air group. The *Nimitz* can stock at least 70 days' supply of refrigerated and dry storage goods. The Food Services Department can provide 18,000–20,000 meals a day.

Aircraft
Nimitz's Carrier Air Wing includes four squadrons of F/A-18 Hornets/Super Hornets, an electronic attack squadron with EA-8B Prowlers, an early warning squadron with E-2C Hawkeyes, and an ASW squadron with SH-60 helicopters.

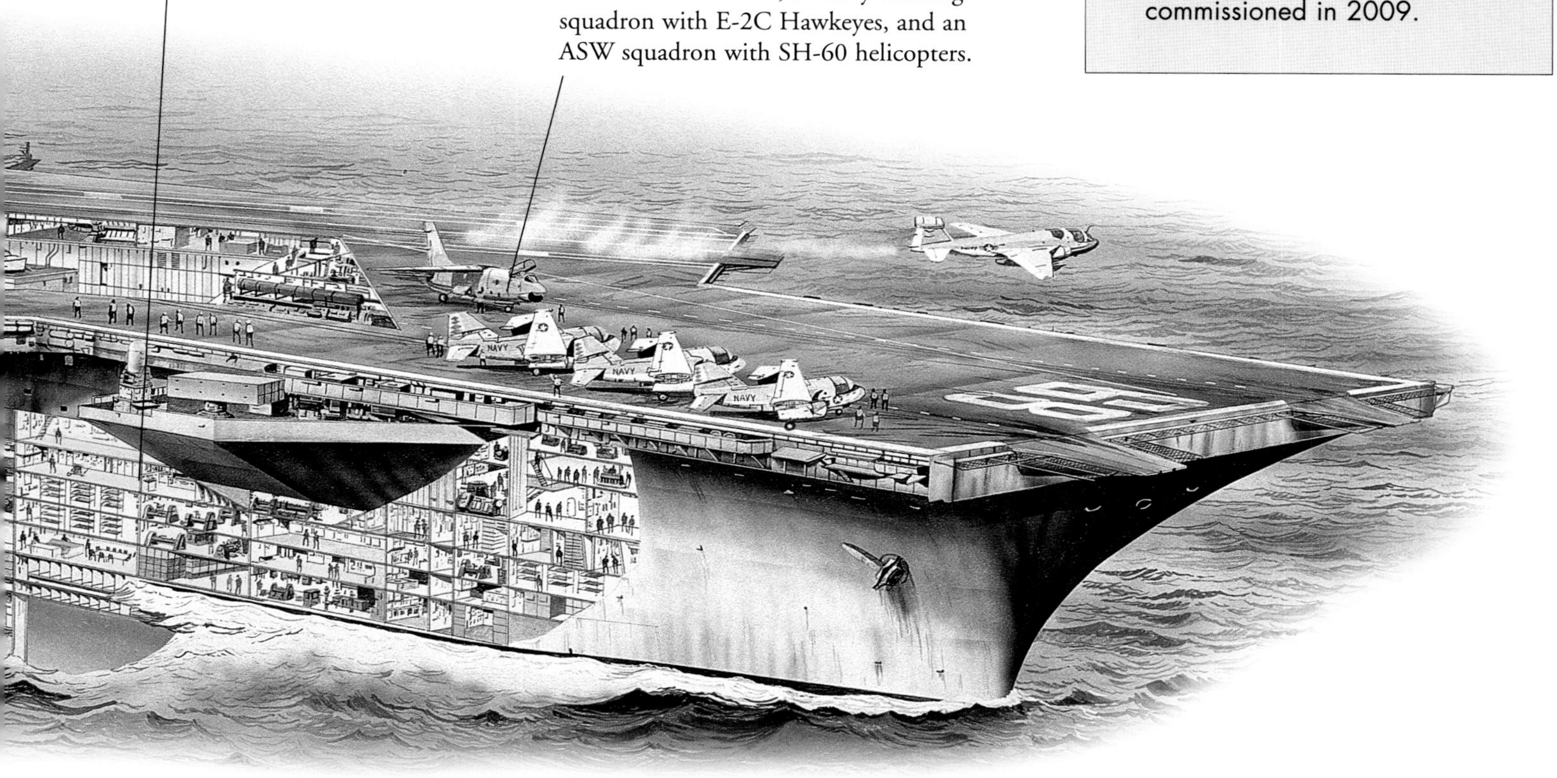

NIMITZ (CVN-68) – SPECIFICATION

Country of origin: USA
Type: Supercarrier
Laid down: 22 July, 1968
Builder: Newports News Shipbuilding
Launched: 13 May, 1972
Commissioned: 3 May, 1975 (still in service)
Complement: Ship's company: 3200; Air wing: 2480

Dimensions:
Displacement: 102,621 tonnes (113,120 tons)
Length: 332.8 m (1092 ft)
Beam: 76.8 m (252 ft)
Draught: 11.3 m (37 ft)

Powerplant:
Propulsion: 2 x Westinghouse A4W nuclear reactors, quadruple shafts producing 194 MW (260,000 shp)
Speed: 31.5 knots
Range: Unlimited

Armament & Armour:
Armament: 2 x 21-cell Sea RAM; 2 x MK29 Sea Sparrow
Armour: Classified
Aircraft: 90 fixed-wing and helicopters

Nimitz-class carriers have a formidable nuclear-strike capability. Their magazines are capable of accommodating more than 100 nuclear weapons for tasks ranging from anti-submarine warfare to area attacks on cities.

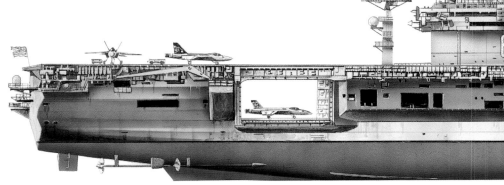

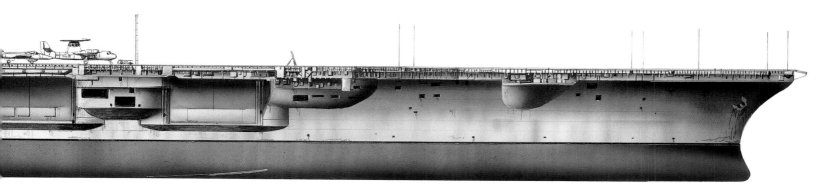

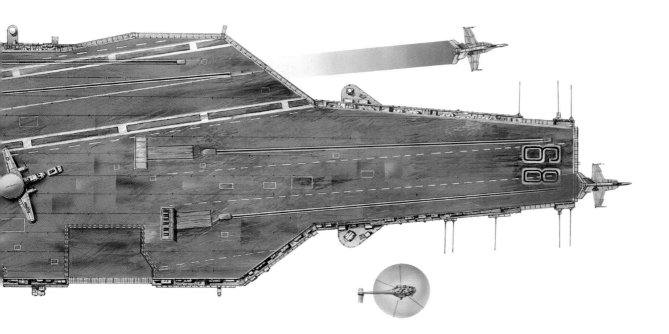

NIMITZ

In time of war, the Mediterranean-based U.S. Sixth Fleet would make an important, and probably decisive, contribution to the security of NATO's southern flank. The fleet has eight task forces, covering the whole spectrum of warfare from air strike through amphibious assault to submarine attack. At the heart of the whole organization is the Battle Force. In the case of the Sixth Fleet this is Task Force 60, which comprises two carriers – a nuclear-powered attack carrier, usually a vessel of the *Nimitz* class, and a smaller attack carrier. The larger attack carriers have an air group of 90–95 aircraft, the smaller vessels about 75 aircraft.

An aircraft carrier like Nimitz *is at the core of an extremely powerful battle group, comprising almost every type of warship, including nuclear attack submarines, which protect its flanks.*

The aircraft carrier is a powerful element of U.S. foreign policy. Former president Bill Clinton once said that the first thing any president asked when being told of a new crisis anywhere in the world was, "Where are the nearest carriers?"

The first three *Nimitz*-class carriers were originally designed as replacements for the elderly *Midway* class. They differed from the earlier *Enterprise* in having a new two-reactor powerplant design in two separate compartments, with the ordnance magazines between and forward of them. This increased the internal space available to allow the carrier to accommodate some 2331 tonnes (2570 tons) of aviation weapons and 10.6 million litres (2.8 million gallons) of aircraft fuel, enough for 16 days of continuous flight operations before the stocks need to be replenished.

WORLDWIDE DUTIES

Commissioned in May 1975, *Nimitz* deployed to the Mediterranean in July 1976, with Carrier Air Wing 8

embarked. It was to be the first of several deployments to the Mediterranean and the Middle East. On her third deployment, in 1979–80, she moved to the Indian Ocean and conducted Operation Evening Light, in which her helicopters made an abortive attempt to rescue 52 American hostages held in the U.S. Embassy at Tehran, Iran.

Her sixth and final deployment to the Mediterranean took place in 1986, after which she proceeded to a new station in the Western Pacific. In 1988 she returned to the Middle East and operated in the North Arabian Sea on tanker protection duty, and in February 1991 she deployed to the Persian Gulf, where she relieved *Ranger* in the aftermath of Operation Desert Storm.

In 1996 she returned to the Pacific, patrolling the waters around Taiwan in a show of strength as the Chinese People's Republic conducted missile tests in the area. In the following year she made a round-the-world cruise that ended at Newport News, Virginia, in March 1998. She remained there for the next three years, undergoing an extensive overhaul.

The next decade was a busy one for *Nimitz*. In March 2003 she sailed on her eleventh operational deployment, during which her air group supported operations in Iraq and Afghanistan. On 24 January, 2008, *Nimitz* deployed to the Western Pacific, and on 9 February two Russian Tu-142 aircraft overflew the carrier while she was on station. Four F/A-18s were launched when the Russian aircraft were 800 km (500 miles) away from the U.S. ships, and intercepted them 80 km (50 miles) south of *Nimitz*. Two F/A-18s trailed one of the aircraft, which buzzed the deck of the carrier twice, while the other two F/A-18s trailed another Tu-142 circling about 50 miles (80 km) away from the carrier. Reportedly, there was no radio communication between the U.S. and Russian aircraft. According to the U.S. Department of Defense, one of the two aircraft was said to have flown above *Nimitz* at an altitude of 610 m (2,000 ft). On the same day, Russian aircraft entered Japanese airspace, causing the Japanese to protest to Russia's ambassador in Tokyo. Again, on 5 March, 2008, a Russian maritime surveillance Tu-142 came within 3–5 nm and flew 610 m (2000 ft) above *Nimitz* and her battle group. Two F/A-18 fighters intercepted the Russian aircraft and escorted it out of the area.

In 2009, the *Nimitz* was once again operating in support of Enduring Freedom, the NATO operation in Afghanistan.

Interior view

An aircraft carrier flight deck is one of the most exhilarating and dangerous work environments in the world. Its smooth operations depends on tight and meticulous control.

1. **Directing Flight:** In the Primary Flight Control (Pri-Fly), the air officer (left) and air officer assistant (right) direct all aircraft on the flight deck and within an 8-km (5-mile) radius.

2. **Equipment:** The air officer and air officer assistant have an array of computers and communications equipment.

3. **View:** The excellent view along the whole of the flight deck, facilitated by extensive windows, aids in directing aircraft activity.

4. **Landing Signals Officer:** When an approaching aircraft comes within 1.2 km (0.75 miles), the landing signals officers take over control to direct the landing.

5. **Vulture's Row:** At the same level as the Pri-Fly, crew visitors can walk out onto "vulture's row," a balcony platform with a view of the flight deck.

6. At the next level down from Pri-Fly, the captain directs the ship from the bridge.

Tarawa (LHA-1) 1973

The primary mission of the LHA-1 *Tarawa* class is to land and sustain U.S. Marines on any shore during combat operations. The ships provide the nucleus of a multi-ship Amphibious Readiness Group (ARG).

FLIGHT DECK
The flight deck has nine landings spots. The carrier-type island is to starboard, with the helicopter elevators to port. The flight deck can handle 10 helicopters simultaneously.

AIRCRAFT
The *Tarawa*-class vessels can support 35 aircraft, including AV-8B Harrier IIs, helicopter gunships, and heavy lift and assault helicopters.

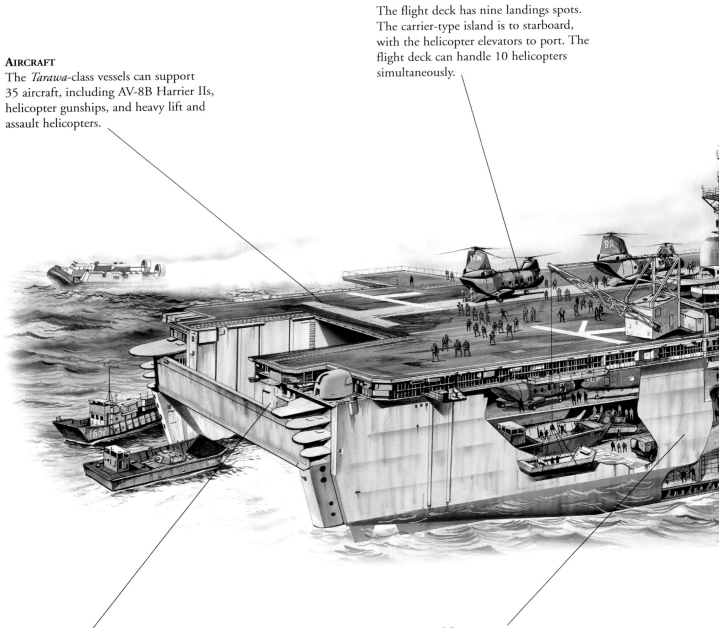

WELL DECK
There is a large well deck in the stern of the ship for a number of amphibious assault craft, including air cushion vehicles. The well deck accommodates up to four LCU 1610 or one LCAC or seven LCM(8) or 17 LCM(6) landing craft.

MACHINERY
The *Tarawa* class is powered by two steam turbines delivering a total of 52.2 MW (70,000 shp) and giving a range of 18,520 km (10,000 miles) at 20 knots. The propulsion system is highly automated.

ACCOMMODATION

The ships can accommodate an average of 960 officers and men and more than 2000 marines. All troops have bunks, and the ships are air-conditioned throughout.

COMMUNICATIONS

Communications systems include SRR-1, WSC-3 UHF, WSC-6 SHF, and USC-38 SHF SATCOM receivers, and an SMQ-11 weather satellite receiver.

F A C T S

- Named after Tarawa Atoll in the Pacific, captured by U.S. Marines after bitter fighting in 1943.

- Launched 1 December, 1973; commissioned May 1976.

- First deployment 1979, with AV-8 Harrier V/STOL aircraft embarked.

- Flagship of amphibious task force in Operation Desert Storm, 1991.

- Deployed in support of Operation Iraqi Freedom, 2005–06.

- Decommissioned 31 March, 2009.

TARAWA (LHA-1) – SPECIFICATION

Country of origin: USA
Type: Amphibious assault ship
Laid down: 15 November, 1971
Builder: Ingalls Shipbuilding
Launched: 1 December, 1973
Commissioned: 29 May, 1976
Decommissioned: 31 March, 2009
Fate: Awaiting disposal
Complement: Over 960 crew and over 2000 marines

Dimensions:
Displacement: 35,289 tonnes (38,900 tons)
Length: 250 m (820 ft); **Beam:** 32 m (106 ft);
    Draught: 7.9 m (26 ft)

Powerplant:
Propulsion: Two shaft, two geared steam turbines, 52.2 MW (70,000 shp)
Speed: 24 knots
Range: 18,520 km (10,000 nm) at 20 knots

Armour & Armament:
Armament: 4 x Mk 38 Mod 1 25-mm (0.98-in) Bushmaster cannons, 5 x 20.7-mm (0.5in) M2HB Browning MGs, 2 x 20-mm (0.98-in) x Mk 15 Phalanx (CIWS), 2 x Mk 49 RAM launchers
Aircraft: Up to 35 helicopters, 8 AV-8B Harrier II VSTOL aircraft

Tarawa **was the first of five ships in a new class of**
general-purpose amphibious assault ships, and
combined the functions previously performed by
four different types: the Amphibious Assault Ship
(LPH); the Amphibious Transport Dock (LPD); the
Amphibious Cargo Ship (LKA); and the Dock
Landing Ship (LSD).

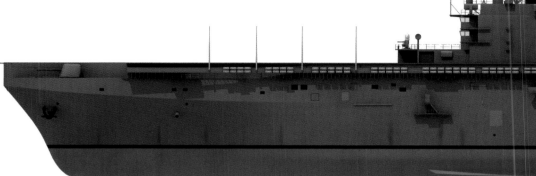

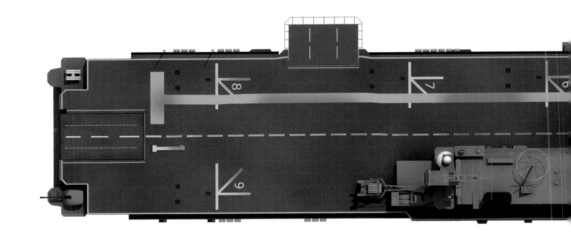

TARAWA'S COMPUTER

The nerve centre of the *Tarawa* class is a tactical amphibious warfare computer, which keeps track of the landing force's positions after leaving the ship, and also tracks enemy targets ashore. The tactical data system can also direct the targeting of the guns and missiles from the ship as well as the support ships. The system maintains air and surface traffic control during the landing phase for the ship's own helicopters, and also provides direction for the task force's supporting ships and assault craft, and for combat air patrols.

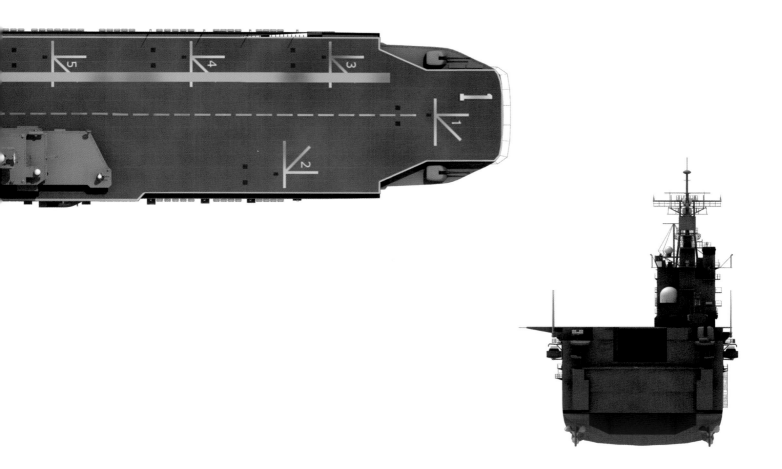

The other ships in the *Tarawa* class were *Saipan*, *Belleau Wood*, *Nassau*, and *Peleliu*. All but the last two ships have been decommissioned.

Tarawa's first deployment took place in 1978, when she spent a period working with her AV-8 Harriers. During this time, she rescued 400 Vietnamese refugees from the South China Sea. Her operations took her worldwide, and 1983 found her in the Mediterranean, where she supported UN peacekeepers in Beirut, Lebanon.

In December 1990, *Tarawa* acted as the flagship of an amphibious assault force consisting of 13 vessels placed off of Iraqi-occupied Kuwait. In January and February of 1991 she took part in a successful deception exercise when her marines landed in Saudi Arabia just outside the border of Kuwait to divert attention from the real Coalition attack, which was to be an armoured thrust through the desert. Her contribution to Operation Desert Storm was quickly followed by a humanitarian mission to cyclone-torn Bangladesh in May 1991, when she supplied rice and equipment for purifying water to the local people.

Interior view

***Tarawa* is equipped with a 300-bed hospital, four medical operating rooms, and three dental operating rooms.**

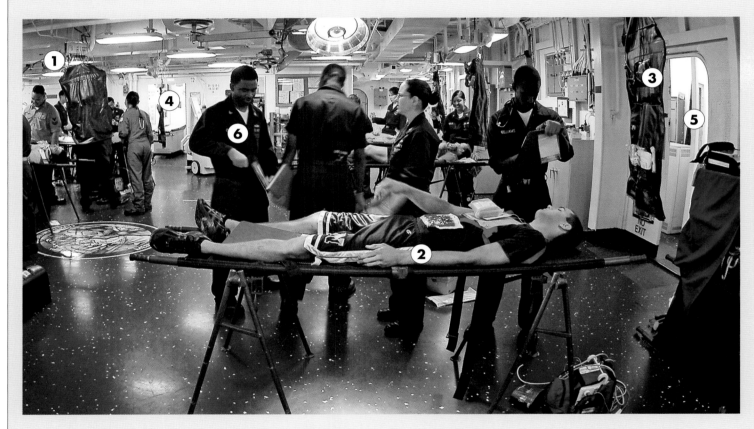

(1) **Medical Facilities: The hospital was fitted out to the same standard as the finest local hospitals in the U.S.**

(2) **Exercises: Emergency exercises are carried out frequently in the hospital to maintain a state of readiness.**

(3) **Dental Care: The mission of the Dental Department was to provide care for active duty Navy and Marine Corps personnel to prevent or remedy diseases.**

(4) **Laboratory: This was equipped with a chemistry analyzer, coulter counter, automated blood gas analyzer, and microbiology capability.**

(5) **Freezer: *Tarawa*'s freezers could store 1000 units of frozen blood and could process six units every 30 minutes for emergency use.**

(6) **The medical staff consists of one general medical officer (department head), one medical administrative officer (division officer), and sixteen other technicians.**

Following four and a half months of providing the setting for intensive individual ship and amphibious refresher training for embarked marines, Tarawa *ended 1978 in her home port of San Diego, California, on Christmas stand-down.*

In May 1992, *Tarawa* deployed for the eighth time to the Western Pacific, and entered the Indian Ocean to participate in a joint U.S./Kuwaiti exercise. The ship also supported the insertion of Pakistani troops into Somalia in support of UN humanitarian relief, and returned to San Diego in November 1992. Her 1992 deployment included visits to Hong Kong, Singapore, the Persian Gulf, Somalia, and Australia.

In April 1996, following an extensive overhaul at Long Beach, California, *Tarawa* set out on her ninth Western Pacific and Indian Ocean deployment, in the course of which she carried out amphibious training exercises with the navies of Thailand, Saudi Arabia, and Jordan. She also helped enforce the "no-fly" zone over southern Iraq, and participated in Operation Desert Strike, a U.S. response to an Iraqi offensive in Kurdistan in 1996.

SUPPORT IN TIMES OF CRISIS

Tarawa was passing through the Strait of Hormuz in the middle of October 2000 on her way into the Persian Gulf when the *Arleigh Burke*-class destroyer *Cole* was attacked by suicide bombers using an inflatable craft.

Upon being notified of the attack, *Tarawa* came about and steamed full ahead to the Port of Aden in Yemen where she joined *Donald Cook*, *Hawes*, and the Royal Navy frigate *Marlborough*, already providing logistical support and harbour security, as the command ship in charge of force protection. *Tarawa* remained with *Cole* until she was secure aboard the Norwegian heavy-lift semi-submersible salvage ship *Blue Marlin* for passage to the U.S. *Tarawa* then returned to duty in the Persian Gulf.

A further deployment in 2005 again took *Tarawa* by way of the Pacific to the Persian Gulf, where she delivered the 13th Marine Expeditionary Unit to Iraq in support of Operation Iraqi Freedom.

Tarawa was decommissioned at San Diego Naval Base, California, on 31 March, 2009. She was the second ship to bear the name. The original *Tarawa* was commissioned in December 1945, too late to serve in World War II. In the early 1950s, she was redesignated an attack carrier (CVA) and then an antisubmarine warfare carrier (CVS). Except for one tour in the Far East, she spent her entire second career operating in the Atlantic and Caribbean.

LOS ANGELES (SSN 688) 1974

The *Los Angeles* class is the mainstay of the U.S. Navy's attack submarine fleet. The vessels in this class are very large, weighing in at about 1800 tonnes (2000 tons) more than their predecessors, the *Sturgeon* class.

COMPARTMENTS
There are two watertight compartments in the *Los Angeles* class. The forward compartment contains spaces for the crew to live, for weapons handling, and control spaces. The aft compartment contains the bulk of the ship's engineering systems.

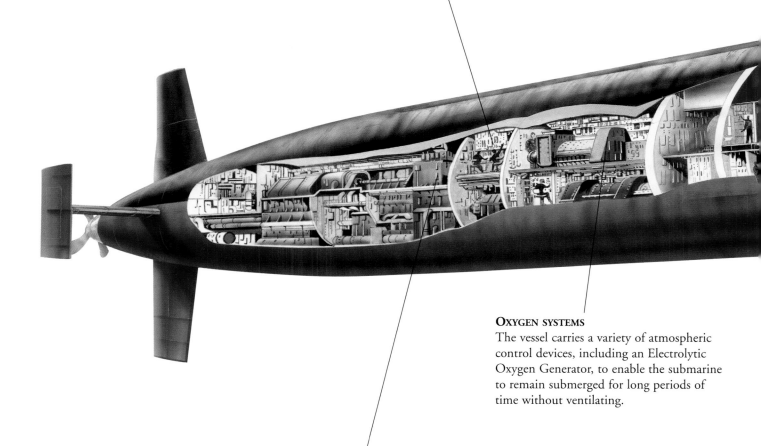

OXYGEN SYSTEMS
The vessel carries a variety of atmospheric control devices, including an Electrolytic Oxygen Generator, to enable the submarine to remain submerged for long periods of time without ventilating.

MACHINERY
Los Angeles is powered by a General Electric S6G nuclear reactor, which delivers pressurized hot water to the steam generator. This in turn drives the steam turbines.

SONAR

Sensors on the *Los Angeles* vessels include a BQR-15 passive-towed sonar array, stowed in a channel on the starboard side of the casing and streamed through a tube on the starboard diving plane.

ARMAMENT

Los Angeles-class submarines carry about 25 weapons launched by torpedo tubes, and all boats of the class are capable of launching Tomahawk cruise missiles in this way. The last 31 boats of this class also have 12 dedicated vertical launch (VLS) tubes for launching Tomahawks.

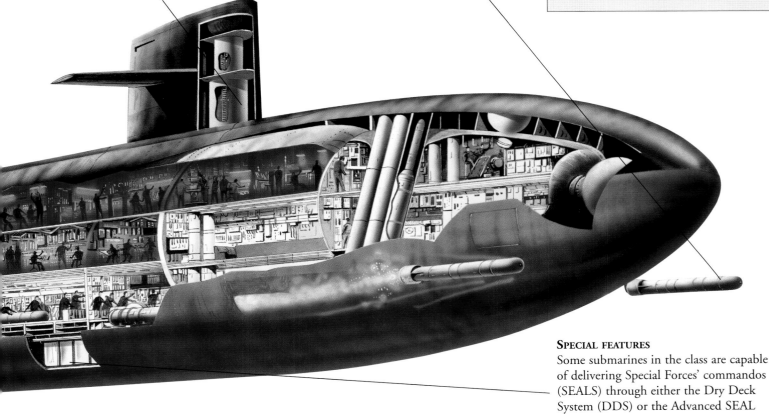

F A C T S
• Launched 6 April, 1974; commissioned 13 November, 1976.
• First operational deployment to the Mediterranean, 1977.
• Transferred to Pacific Fleet, 1978. Assigned to Submarine Squadron 7 and based at Pearl Harbor.
• Deactivated November 2009.

SPECIAL FEATURES

Some submarines in the class are capable of delivering Special Forces' commandos (SEALS) through either the Dry Deck System (DDS) or the Advanced SEAL Delivery System (ASDS).

LOS ANGELES (SSN 688) – SPECIFICATION

Country of origin: USA
Type: Submarine
Laid down: 8 January, 1972
Builder: Newport News Shipbuilding
Launched: 6 April, 1974
Commissioned: 13 November, 1976
Decommissioned: 23 January, 2010
Fate: Not available
Complement: 13 officers, 131 enlisted

Dimensions:
Displacement: 5508 tonnes (6072 tons)
Length: 110.3 m (361 ft 10 in);

Beam: 10 m (32 ft 10 in); **Draught:** 9.4 m (30 ft 10 in)

Powerplant:
Propulsion: S6G nuclear reactor, 2 turbines, 1 shaft producing 26 MW (35,000 shp), 1 auxiliary motor producing 242 kW (325 shp)
Speed: (surfaced) 25 knots; (submerged) 30 knots
Range: Unlimited

Armament & Armour:
Armament: 4 x 533-mm (21-in) bow tubes, Mark 48 torpedo, Harpoon missile, Tomahawk cruise missile

The *Los Angeles*-class submarines were
intended mainly to escort carrier task groups.
For this reason, they were designed to be
capable of making high speeds underwater
in order to keep up with surface forces.

LOS ANGELES

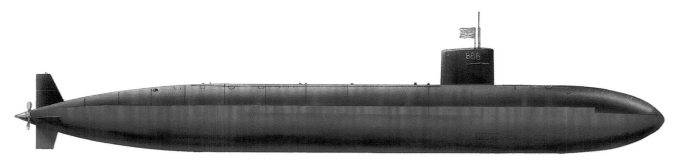

AMERICAN SSN: *SKIPJACK*

AMERICAN SSN: *PERMIT*

AMERICAN SSN: *STURGEON*

LOS ANGELES-CLASS TORPEDOES

The original primary weapon of the *Los Angeles*-class submarines was the 533-mm (21-in) heavyweight torpedo. A long-range, variable-speed, wire-guided dual-role weapon, it was developed beginning in 1957, when feasibility studies were initiated to meet an operational requirement that was eventually issued in 1960. The weapon was intended as both a surface- and submarine-launched torpedo, but the former requirement was dropped when surface-launched torpedoes were supplanted by anti-ship missiles. The latest variant is the Mk 48 MkMod 5, which has a higher-powered sonar to improve target acquisition and to reduce the effect of decoys and anechoic coatings.

This dramatic and atmospheric photograph shows a Los Angeles-*class submarine travelling at speed on the surface, looking more like a colossal marine creature than a machine of war. In* Los Angeles, *the U.S. Navy acquired some of the fastest and quietest submarines ever built.*

The *Los Angeles* (SSN 688) was the lead ship in her class. She was launched in April 1974 and completed in November 1976. Total production was 62 units, making this class by far the most important in the U.S. submarine fleet.

Many important changes have been made to the "688s," as the class is commonly known, in the course of their operational life. Starting in 1984 onwards, beginning with the launch of the *Providence* (SSN 619), all the *Los Angeles*-class vessels have been fitted with vertical launch tubes for the Tomahawk land-attack cruise missile, 20 of which can be carried. Earlier vessels can launch Tomahawks from their torpedo tubes, but can only carry eight missiles.

STANDOFF LAND ATTACK

The launch of the *San Juan* (SSN 751) in 1986 marked the appearance of the "Improved 688" class, because it was fitted with the new BSY-1 submarine combat system. A more

obvious change was the replacement of the sail-mounted diving planes with bow planes, permitting better manoeuvrability when the boat was cruising under the ice.

Though they were designed as classic hunter-killer submarines, the role of the *Los Angeles* class has been greatly expanded in the modern U.S. Navy by virtue of a standoff land attack capability. In fact, the fleet of *Los Angeles* SSNs provides the U.S. with a second-tier attack force, quite distinct from the fleet ballistic missile submarines. U.S. Navy attack submarines have been capable of launching nuclear weapons, when the Regulus cruise missile was introduced on a limited scale. However, matching the *Los Angeles* class with the Tomahawk cruise missile has produced a truly deadly combination.

A VERSATILE ASSET

During the latter years of the Cold War, the *Los Angeles*-class SSNs would have gone to sea with some of their BGM-109 Tomahawk missiles armed with 200kT thermonuclear warheads. The nuclear-tipped version of the Tomahawk is no longer deployed, and missiles now carry 450 kg (1000 lb) of high explosive. This switch to the conventional land attack role has made her class a far more useful and versatile asset.

INVISIBLE PRESENCE

Submarines have a covert striking power and can be deployed to a crisis or potential trouble spot without ever betraying their presence. Nine of the class were involved in the Gulf War of 1991, two firing Tomahawk missiles at targets in Iraq from stations in the eastern Mediterranean,

and the *Los Angeles* boats have since supported NATO operations in the Balkans and Afghanistan.

Nineteen years after *Los Angeles* joined the fleet, the commissioning of *Cheyenne* (SSN-773) brought to a close the biggest group of SSNs ever built to a single design. The long production run was due to uncertainty about successors, and by the mid-1990s the design was starting to look dated.

Ten years later, *Los Angeles* was the oldest submarine still on active service with the U.S. Navy. She was inactivated on 2 November, 2009, to await decommissioning and disposal at a later date.

Interior view

The sonar room on *Los Angeles* is where all the information from the boat's sensors is collated and interpreted. In effect, it is the eyes and ears of the submerged submarine.

(1) **Officer of the Deck:** Supervised by the officer of the deck, each console is manned by a senior technician.

(2) **Consoles:** The sonar room is dominated by its consoles, each performing a specific function.

(3) **Lighting:** The colour of the lighting can be altered to suit particular conditions; blue background lighting is often used.

(4) **Modes:** Two modes of sonar observation are used. In the "active" mode, the echoes of sound waves sent out from the sub are timed and analyzed by the operator.

(5) **Towed Sonar:** This is the passive "thin line" array, designed to detect very low-frequency noise at very long ranges.

(6) **Intercept Receiver:** An acoustic intercept receiver alerts the crew that an active sonar is being used.

Ivan Rogov 1976

The appearance of the *Ivan Rogov*-class dock-landing ships in the late 1970s seemed a clear indication that the Soviet Union was intent on projecting its military power worldwide.

MISSILES

An air defence missile system (NATO code-name Gecko) provided defence against anti-ship missiles, aircraft, and surface targets. The system uses semi-active radar homing. The ship was also equipped with two close-range, portable, Strela-3M (Grail) air defence missile systems, each system having a quadruple launcher.

GUNS

The ship had a 75-mm (3-in) multipurpose twin gun, with 1000 rounds of ammunition, and four 30-mm (1.18-in) air defence guns. The latter could be used for engaging airborne threats, small sea targets, floating mines, and light armoured coastal targets.

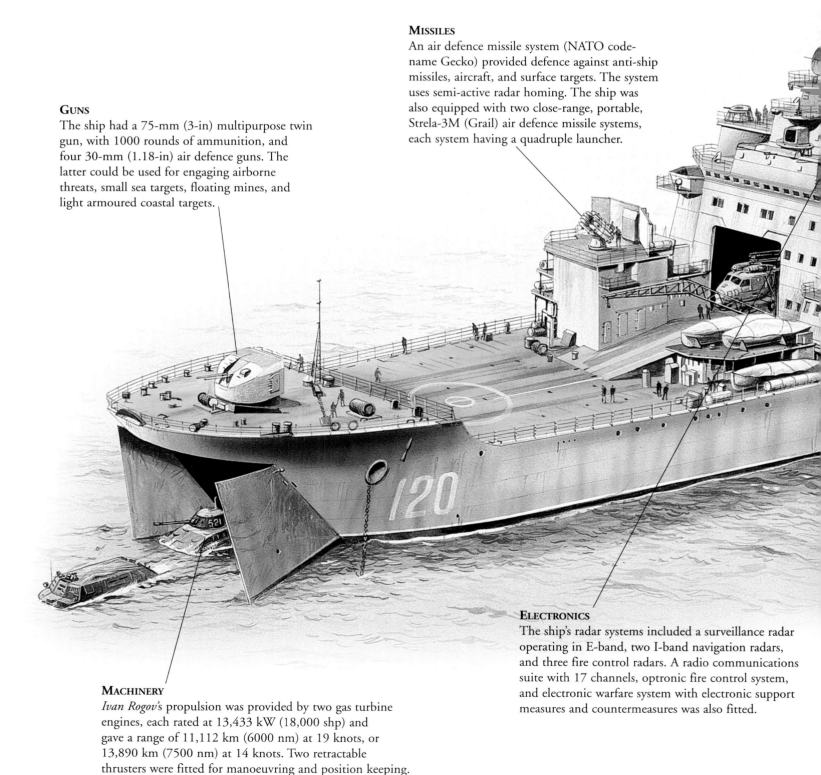

ELECTRONICS

The ship's radar systems included a surveillance radar operating in E-band, two I-band navigation radars, and three fire control radars. A radio communications suite with 17 channels, optronic fire control system, and electronic warfare system with electronic support measures and countermeasures was also fitted.

MACHINERY

Ivan Rogov's propulsion was provided by two gas turbine engines, each rated at 13,433 kW (18,000 shp) and gave a range of 11,112 km (6000 nm) at 19 knots, or 13,890 km (7500 nm) at 14 knots. Two retractable thrusters were fitted for manoeuvring and position keeping.

AIRCRAFT
Ivan Rogov-class ships could carry four Kamov
Ka-27 or Ka-29 helicopters. One landing pad was
located forward of the superstructure and one aft.

F A C T S

- Launched 1976; commissioned 1978.

- Designed with bow ramp for beach landings.

- Served as both LPD and LST.

- Could carry 2270 tonnes (2500 tons) of cargo.

- Capable of carrying 53 tanks or 80 APCs instead of landing craft in docking bay.

- Stricken 1996.

TRANSPORT DECKS
The extensive tank deck was accessed via
the bow ramp. The docking bay, with
doors at the stern of the ship, could be
flooded for amphibious operations using
small landing craft.

IVAN ROGOV – SPECIFICATION

Country of origin: Soviet Union
Type: Large landing ship
Laid down: N/A
Builder: Yantar Baltic Shipbuilding plant, Kaliningrad
Launched: 1976
Commissioned: 1978
Decommissioned: 1996
Fate: Stricken 1996
Complement: 239

Dimensions:
Displacement: (full load) 12,755 tonnes (14,060 tons)
Length: 157 m (515 ft); **Beam:** 23.8 m (78 ft);

Draught: 6.7 m (22 ft)

Powerplant:
Propulsion: 2 shafts, 2 gas turbines, 2 x 13,433 kW
(18,000 shp)
Speed: 19 knots
Range: 13,890 km (7500 nm) at 14 knots

Armament:
Armament: 1 x 2 Osa-M surface-to-air missile launcher; 1 x 2
76-mm (3-in) AK-726 gun; 4 x 6 30-mm (1.18-in) AK-630 air
defence gun; 1 x Grad-m 122-mm (4.8-in) rocket launcher
Aircraft: 4 x Ka-27 "Helix" or Ka-29 helicopters

Some of *Ivan Rogov*'s assault craft were air cushion vehicles. These were ideal for getting troops ashore as quickly as possible, the type of assault the Soviet navy specialized in.

IVAN ROGOV

SUPPORT CRAFT: *LEBED* **CLASS**

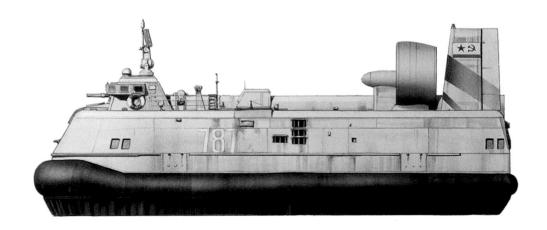

RIVAL BRITISH ASSAULT SHIP: *INTREPID*

SUPPORT CRAFT: *GUS* CLASS

IVAN ROGOV VESSELS

The *Ivan Rogov* vessels were designed with a bow ramp for beach landings, and a flooded well deck to launch amphibious transports or assault boats. This meant they could serve either as Tank Landing Ships (LSTs) or as Dock Landing Ships (LPDs). The ships could carry 2270 tonnes (2500 tons) of cargo, and the typical load would consist of one battalion of 520 marines and 25 tanks. If no landing craft were carried, then the extra space in the docking bay allowed for the transport of 53 tanks or 80 armoured personnel carriers.

Close-up

Ivan Rogov had both a well deck and a helicopter flight deck and hangar, which made it unique in Soviet amphibious ship design.

(1) **Turret:** A twin 76-mm (3-in) dual-purpose gun turret was mounted on the forecastle to engage both land targets and aircraft.

(2) **Vehicle Deck:** The bow doors and internal ramp position provided access to a vehicle parking deck located in the lower forwards part of the ship.

(3) **Accommodation:** Living space for the embarked naval infantry units was located within the superstructure block.

(4) **Radar:** *Ivan Rogov* had two "Don Kay" helicopter control and navigation radars, one "Head Net C" air-search radar and an "Owl Screech" gun control radar.

(5) **Guns:** Four 30-mm (1.18-in) Gatling-type guns were mounted on top of the main superstructure block for close-in air defence.

(6) **Rocket Launcher System:** This was mounted on top of the tall deck house to provide saturation shore bombardment in support of the assault force.

This photograph gives a good view of Ivan Rogov's *massive stern doors, leading to the floodable well deck. This could accommodate up to three pre-loaded* Lebed-*class air cushion vehicles or up to six 145-ton landing craft.*

Only one of the three *Ivan Rogov* vessels, the *Mitrofan Moskalenko*, remained in service in 2009, the *Aleksandr Nikolayev* having been stricken in 1997, a year after *Ivan Rogov* herself.

The lead ship of the *Ivan Rogov* class, designated Project 1174 *Bolshoy Desantnyy Korabl* (Large Landing Ship) was completed at the Kalinin yard in 1978. It was the largest amphibious warfare ship yet built for the Soviet navy. A second unit, the *Aleksandr Nikolayev*, was commissioned in 1982, and the third unit, the *Mitrofan Moskalenko*, in 1990.

Three times as large as the earlier "Alligator"-class amphibious warfare ships, *Ivan Rogov* had both a well deck and a helicopter flight deck and hangar. This allowed the ship to perform not only the traditional role of over-the-beach assault by use of bow doors and ramp, but also the standoff assault role using a mixture of helicopters, landing craft, air cushion vehicles, and amphibious vehicles.

The bow doors and internal ramp position provided access to a vehicle parking deck located in the lower forwards part of the ship. More vehicles could be accommodated in the midships area of the upper deck, access to this being by way of hydraulically operated ramps leading from the bow doors to the docking well. The vehicle deck itself led directly into the floodable well. Living quarters for the embarked Naval Infantry units were located within the superstructure block itself, together with the vehicle and helicopter workshops.

HELICOPTER CAPACITY

The ship had helicopter landing spots, each with its own flight control station, one forward, and one aft located above the well deck. Both spots had access to the massive block superstructure, the forwards pad by a ramp leading up to the hangar and the aft by a set of hangar doors. The helicopters could be brought out of the hangar through two exit doors, one leading to the helicopter landing pad forwards of the superstructure and the other to the landing pad behind it. Both pads had refuelling and replenishment stations. Four helicopters could be carried: two Kamov Ka-27 ("Helix") and two Ka-29 ("Helix-B"). The Ka-27 ("Helix") is a naval anti-submarine helicopter, and the Ka-29 is the combat transport version, with the capacity to ferry 16 fully equipped and armed troops. For cargo carrying, the helicopter can carry two tons in the cabin plus four tons on a sling. In the medical evacuation role the helicopter can lift four stretcher patients and seven seated patients, together with one medical officer.

As well as air defence missiles, *Ivan Rogov*-class ships carried an extensive gun armament, the main weapon being a 76-mm (3-in) AK-726 multipurpose twin gun, with 1000 rounds of ammunition. Its maximum range is almost 16 km (10 miles) and the gun is capable of firing up to 100 rounds per minute. The gun mount can be laid and the fire control carried out in automatic mode using the fire control radar system, and in semi-automatic mode using the Prizma optical sighting device mounted on the turret or in manual mode using the gunner's sights.

Kortenaer 1976

During the Cold War, some European nations, notably the Netherlands and the Federal Republic of Germany, cooperated in frigate design and production. The two countries manufactured vessels like the *Kortenaer* to satisfy a common requirement.

GUN ARMAMENT
Kortenaer was originally fitted with two 76-mm (3-in) guns, but the one mounted on top of the helicopter hangar towards the stern of the ship was replaced by a Goalkeeper CIWS system.

AIRCRAFT
As designed, the *Kortenaer*-class ships had the facility to carry two Westland Sea Lynx anti-submarine helicopters, but as of 1986 the landing pad was replaced by a Standard SAM missile launcher.

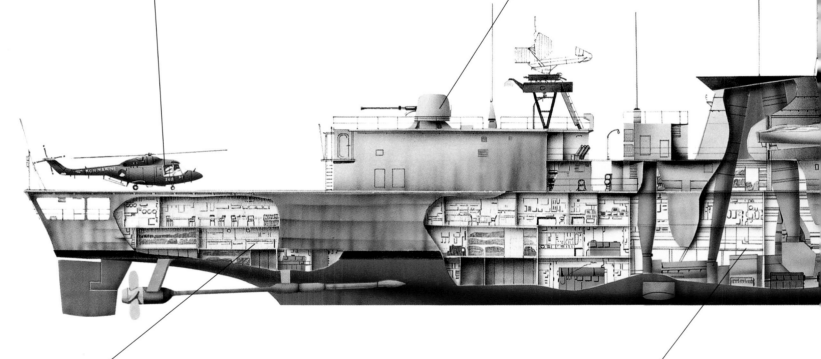

HULL
The hull followed the lines of contemporary French designs, with a continuous upper and main deck, a single rudder of the semi-balanced type, and a clipper bow with negative sheer.

MACHINERY
The *Kortenaer*-class ships use Combined Gas or Gas (COGOG), a propulsion system for ships using gas turbine engines. A high-efficiency, low-output turbine is used for cruising speeds with a high-output turbine being used for high-speed operations.

MISSILE ARMAMENT

The *Kortenaer* class originally carried two quadruple GMLS Mk 141 Harpoon surface-to-surface missile launchers with eight missiles, and one octuple launcher for the GMLS Mk 29 Sea Sparrow surface-to-air missile. The later *Kortenaer*s were fitted with the Standard SAM system.

ELECTRONICS

The electronics fit included an LW-08 air search radar, a WM-25 fire direction radar, a ZW-06 navigation radar, and an AN/SQS-509 hull-mounted sonar.

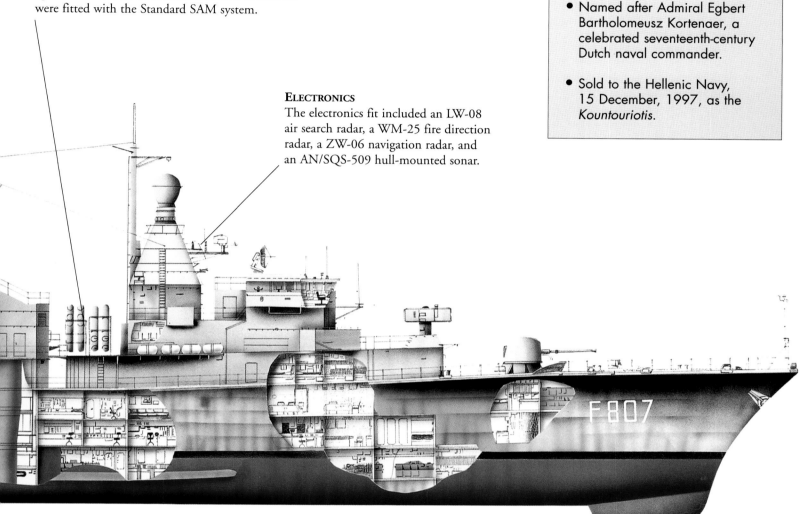

F A C T S
• Launched 18 December, 1976; commissioned 26 October, 1978.
• Named after Admiral Egbert Bartholomeusz Kortenaer, a celebrated seventeenth-century Dutch naval commander.
• Sold to the Hellenic Navy, 15 December, 1997, as the *Kountouriotis*.

KORTENAER – SPECIFICATION

Country of origin: The Netherlands
Type: Frigate
Laid down: 8 April, 1975
Builder: Royal Schelde
Launched: 18 December, 1976
Commissioned: 26 October, 1978
Decommissioned: 1987
Fate: Sold to the Hellenic Navy as *Kountouriotis*
Complement: 176–196

Dimensions:
Displacement: 3538 tonnes (3900 tons)
Length: 130 m (426 ft 6 in); **Beam:** 14.4 m (47 ft 3 in);
  Draught: 4.4 m (14 ft 5 in)

Powerplant:
Propulsion: 2 x Rolls-Royce Tyne RM1C gas turbines, 3700 kW (4900 shp) each or 2 x Rolls-Royce Olympus TM3B gas turbines, 19,200 kW (25,700 shp) each (boost), 2 shafts
Speed: 30 knots
Range: 8704 km (4700 nm) at 16 knots

Armament & Armour:
Armament: 1 x Goalkeeper CIWS; 1 x 76-mm (3-in) gun; 2 x twin Mk46 torpedo tubes; 2 x RGM-84 Harpoon anti-ship missile launchers; 1 x 8-cell Sea Sparrow anti-aircraft missile launchers
Armour: N/A
Aircraft: 2 x Sea Lynx helicopters

Frigates must be at the cutting edge of
naval technology in order to achieve their
primary ASW role, so the cost of building
them can be prohibitive for smaller
navies. Developing the *Kortenaer* class
was a bold step for the Dutch navy.

ITALIAN FRIGATE: *LUPO*

DUTCH FRIGATE: *JACOB VAN HEEMSKERK*

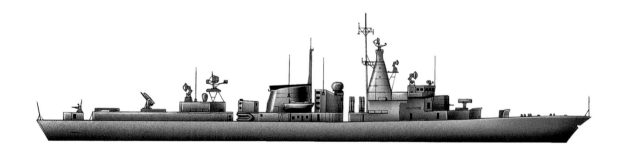

REPLACEMENT: *BREMEN*

KORTENAER-CLASS VESSELS

Ten of the *Kortenaer*-class vessels were built by de Schelde in Flushing and two by Wilten-Fijenoord in Schiedam. Of the 12, 10 served with the Royal Netherlands Navy. Two were sold to Greece while still under construction and replaced by two *Jacob van Heemskerck*-class frigates, which are basically an anti-aircraft variant of the *Kortenaer* class. In Greek service, the frigates were renamed the *Elli* class. Eight similar ships were built by Germany during the same period as the *Bremen* class. By 2003 all ships had been transferred to the navies of Greece and the United Arab Emirates.

This Kortenaer-*class frigate is the* Abraham Crijnssen, *named after a seventeenth-century admiral. The original ship of that name became famous for her escape from Surabaya in World War II disguised as a tropical island.*

The *Kortenaer*-class frigates were very successful vessels, and a powerful asset in NATO's anti-submarine warfare arsenal. Their turbines gave them the level of manoeuvrability and acceleration that are vital when hunting fast nuclear-powered submarines.

Authorized in the late 1960s, the *Kortenaer*-class frigates were intended to replace 12 older anti-submarine warships of the *Holland* and *Friesland* classes, which were then in service with the Royal Netherlands Navy.

A modified version of the *Van Speijk*-class frigate (essentially a British *Leander*-class with Dutch radar) was originally proposed, but was rejected because of its limited cruising range and because the basic design did not allow for upgrading in mid-life. Discussions with the Royal Navy with a view to sharing the hull of a new design with the projected British Type 22 *Broadsword*-class frigate also came to nothing, as did investigations into the possibility of using American and French designs. As a result the Dutch were forced to proceed independently in developing their own "Standard" design, so called as it was planned to build

ASW and AAW versions on a standard, common hull, and because it conformed to NATO requirements for ocean escorts.

Two of the *Kortenaer*-class frigates were built for the Hellenic Navy in 1981, named *Elli* and *Limnos*. Eight more ex-Dutch vessels (*Bankert, Callenburg, van Kinsbergen, Kortenae, Jan van Brakel, Pieter Florisz, Philips van Almonde,* and *Bloys van Treslong*) were transferred in the late 1990s and early 2000s. Six of the eight frigates underwent a mid-life modernization programme, which was completed in 2009.

FROM WARSHIP TO LUXURY YACHT

The two remaining *Kortenaer*-class frigates, *Piet Hein* and *Abraham Crijnssen*, were sold to the United Arab Emirates as the *Al Emirat* and *Abu Dhabi*, and were subsequently converted into luxury super-yachts. An Iranian order for eight *Kortenaer*-class vessels was cancelled following the Iranian revolution of 1979.

Bremen was a "Germanized" modification of the *Kortenaer*, which was an eight-ship class of Type 122 frigates that replaced the German navy's elderly *Fletcher*-class destroyers and *Köln*-class frigates. The first order was placed in 1977, and the first ship was commissioned in

1982. The frigates were primarily intended to be deployed for service in the Baltic, but some were deployed further afield in later years in support of NATO operations.

HELICOPTER CAPACITY

The anti-aircraft variant of the *Kortenaer* class was the *Jacob van Heemskerck* class. It consisted of two units, the other being *Witte de With*. Commissioned in 1986, the intention was to alternate the vessels as the flagship of the Royal Netherlands Navy's 3rd ASW hunter-killer group, assigned to NATO's Channel Command in wartime. The two vessels were to replace the two *Kortenaer*-class frigates that had been sold to Greece. In addition to the Goalkeeper CIWS, they were armed with the Standard and Sea Sparrow SAM systems, and were capable of providing effective area defence of a task group out to a range of 46 km (25 nm) using the D Standard SM-1MR SAM, the Raytheon Sea Sparrow providing medium range backup to 14 km (7.8 nm). The Standard missile replaced the Tartar in NATO service. Both ships were later sold to Chile, with *Jacob van Heemskerck* being renamed *Almirante Blanco Encalada* while *Witte de With* became *Capitan Prat*.

Close-up

The vessel pictured here is the *Kortenaer*-class frigate *Banckert*. It was named after the seventeenth-century Dutch admiral Adriaen van Banckert.

1. **Replacements:** The *Kortenaer* frigates were designed as replacements for the anti-submarine destroyers of the *Holland* and *Friesland* classes.

2. **Layout:** The propulsion plant and machinery layout was taken from the *Tromp* class frigates.

3. **Fin Stabilizers:** A single pair of fin stabilizers was fitted, and as far as possible systems were automated to reduce crew numbers.

4. **Role:** The vessels were built to be a general-purpose frigate able to combat all surface, submarine, and aircraft targets.

5. **CIWS:** In Dutch service the frigates were armed with a Goalkeeper Close-In Warfare System (CIWS), positioned on top of the helicopter hangar.

6. **Escort:** During the Cold War, the *Kortenaers* escorted convoys bringing supplies and reinforcements to allied forces in Europe.

Invincible 1977

In the late 1960s, the British Royal Navy was forced to reappraise its maritime air task following the cancellation of a projected new aircraft carrier, CVA-01. What was needed was a new type of combat aircraft, and a new class of "cut-price" carrier to deploy it effectively. The result was the *Invincible* class, and the remarkable Sea Harrier.

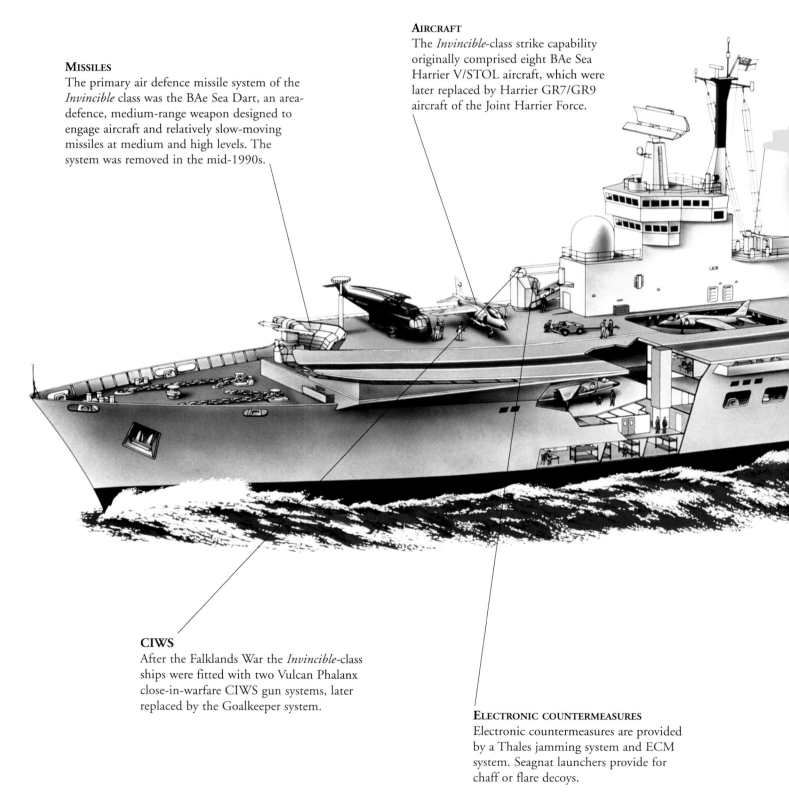

AIRCRAFT
The *Invincible*-class strike capability originally comprised eight BAe Sea Harrier V/STOL aircraft, which were later replaced by Harrier GR7/GR9 aircraft of the Joint Harrier Force.

MISSILES
The primary air defence missile system of the *Invincible* class was the BAe Sea Dart, an area-defence, medium-range weapon designed to engage aircraft and relatively slow-moving missiles at medium and high levels. The system was removed in the mid-1990s.

CIWS
After the Falklands War the *Invincible*-class ships were fitted with two Vulcan Phalanx close-in-warfare CIWS gun systems, later replaced by the Goalkeeper system.

ELECTRONIC COUNTERMEASURES
Electronic countermeasures are provided by a Thales jamming system and ECM system. Seagnat launchers provide for chaff or flare decoys.

HELICOPTERS
Invincible's ASW helicopters were Westland Sea Kings. Operations in the South Atlantic revealed a dire need for airborne early warning, and some Sea Kings were reconfigured for this task.

MACHINERY
The *Invincible*-class ships are powered by four Rolls-Royce Olympus TM3B gas turbine engines, providing 75 MW (97,000 shp) on two shafts.

INVINCIBLE – SPECIFICATION

Country of origin: United Kingdom
Type: Aircraft carrier
Laid down: July 1973
Builder: Vickers Shipbuilding Limited, Barrow-in-Furness, England
Launched: 3 May, 1977
Commissioned: 11 July, 1980
Decommissioned: 3 August, 2005
Fate: In reserve
Complement: 726 ship's company; 384 Air Group personnel

Dimensions:
Displacement: (full load) 18,788 tonnes (20,710 tons)
Length: 210 m (689 ft); **Beam:** 36 m (118.1 ft);

Draught: 8.8 m (28.9 ft)

Powerplant:
Propulsion: 4 x Rolls-Royce Olympus TM3B gas turbines providing 75 MW (97,000 shp), 8 diesel generators
Speed: 28 knots
Range: 12,964 (7000 nm) at 18 knots

Armament & Armour:
Armament: 3 x Goalkeeper CIWS; 2 x 20-mm (0.79-in) guns
Armour: N/A
Aircraft: Sea Harrier "jump jets"; Sea King, Merlin, and Lynx helicopters

Although more flexible in operations than fixed-wing carriers, *Invincible*-class ships suffered from an inadequate complement of fighter/strike aircraft and the absence of fixed-wing early warning aircraft.

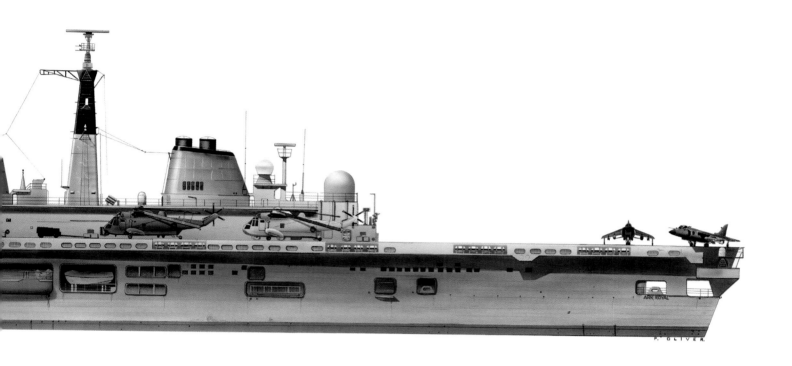

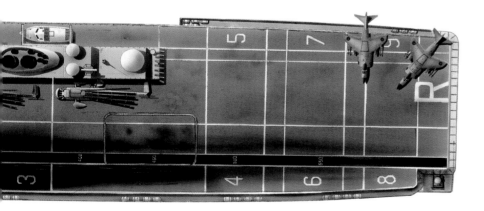

LAUNCHING THE SEA HARRIER

The normal air group deployed aboard *Invincible* and her sister carriers comprised eight British Aerospace Sea Harrier V/STOL strike fighters and 11 Westland Sea King ASW helicopters. In the course of their construction, *Invincible* and *Illustrious* were fitted with a "ski jump" at the foredeck. Inclined at an angle of seven degrees, it enabled a Sea Harrier to launch at a much lower speed than was needed in a flat-deck takeoff at the same gross weight, with a substantial fuel saving. *Ark Royal* was fitted with a 12-degree jump.

"Why not V/STOL planes operating from platforms on ships, without catapult or arrester gear? The argument is unchanged and largely immutable.... The question is, will the cost-effectiveness of a ship-plus-V/STOL aircraft system be worthwhile?"

When those words were written in 1966 by Commander J.W. Powell, DSC, RN (Ret), a former Assistant Director of Naval Warfare, a Defence White Paper had just been published, outlining a policy that envisaged that tactical air power at sea would be provided by land-based aircraft of the Royal Air Force after the Royal Navy's existing aircraft carriers had been retired. Similar ideas had proved to be completely unworkable in the past, for example, in the Far East at the end of 1941. However, the thinking here was that Royal Navy surface forces in their NATO role could rely, in theory, on an air "umbrella" provided from NATO air bases ashore. There was, of course, no inkling that the Royal Navy would one day have to fight a war some 12,800 km (8000 miles) from the nearest RAF land base.

Close-up

The *Invincible*-class carriers were designed specifically to operate short/vertical takeoff aircraft like the British Aerospace Sea Harrier, seen here taking off from the carrier's "ski jump."

(1) **Sea Harrier:** The Sea Harrier FRS.2 was an upgrade of the original FRS.1, with improved radar.

(2) **Ski Jump:** *Invincible* and her sister ship *Illustrious* were both fitted with a "ski jump" inclined at seven degrees.

(3) **Missile System:** *Invincible* was initially armed with the Sea Dart surface-to-air missile system, but this was later removed to provide more deck space.

(4) **Countermeasures:** These were provided by a Thales jamming system and ECM system, together with chaff and decoy launchers.

(5) **CIW:** *Invincible* had a close-in warfare (CIW) anti-aircraft and anti-missile gun system, and also two 20-mm (0.79-in) cannon.

(6) **Control Centre:** The command and control centre enabled *Invincible* to exercise control over a naval task group and to direct anti-submarine warfare operations.

Invincible is seen here with her complement of Sea King anti-submarine warfare helicopters on the flight deck, their rotor blades folded. The carrier's air group comprised eight Harriers and 12 Sea Kings.

AN AIRCRAFT CARRIER BY ANY OTHER NAME

The kind of vessel advocated by Commander Powell came to fruition, albeit in a rather roundabout fashion. In the late 1960s, the Naval Staff began studies of a new class of ship, much smaller than the cancelled CVA-01, and without catapults or wires, which was intended for operations with a rotary-wing anti-submarine warfare (ASW) group in NATO waters. The proposed vessel had a through deck and so was therefore theoretically capable of operating V/STOL aircraft. However, this fact was played down. The design was committed to manufacture in 1972 as *Invincible*, the first of three new ASW carriers.

During the design period and while she was being built, at a time when the term "aircraft carrier" had been politically discredited in the UK, *Invincible* was variously described as a "through deck cruiser," "command cruiser," and "anti-submarine cruiser." Nevertheless, she was an aircraft carrier, regardless of her other roles, and the more imaginative titles were gradually dropped with the growing realization, stemming from major exercises, that naval forces could not be satisfactorily protected solely by shore-based air power, not even in NATO waters.

Invincible's sister ships, *Illustrious* and *Ark Royal*, were laid down in 1976 and 1978 respectively.

On 2 April, 1982, an Argentine amphibious group invaded the Falkland Islands. Britain's response was to assemble a task force to recapture them, with the carriers *Hermes* and *Invincible* at its core. Both sailed from Plymouth on 5 April. Without the two supporting aircraft carriers and their Sea Harriers, together with RAF Harrier ground attack aircraft brought in as reinforcements, a British victory in the Falklands would have been impossible. Aircraft from *Hermes* and *Invincible* accounted for 33 of the enemy, in the air and on the ground.

SUPPORTING NATO OPERATIONS

Returning from the South Atlantic, *Invincible* resumed duties in northern waters. During the next 20 years she served in support of NATO operations in the Balkans and Iraq. In 1999, her Harriers were involved in air strikes on targets in the former Yugoslavia, while her Sea Kings aided refugees.

In June 2005 the UK Ministry of Defence decided that *Invincible* was to be deactivated until 2010, but would still remain available for reactivation at 18 months' notice.

Kirov/Admiral Ushakov 1977

When the Soviet Union launched the missile cruiser *Kirov* in December 1977, she was the largest warship – apart from aircraft carriers – built by any nation since World War II. She was reminiscent of the battlecruisers of bygone years.

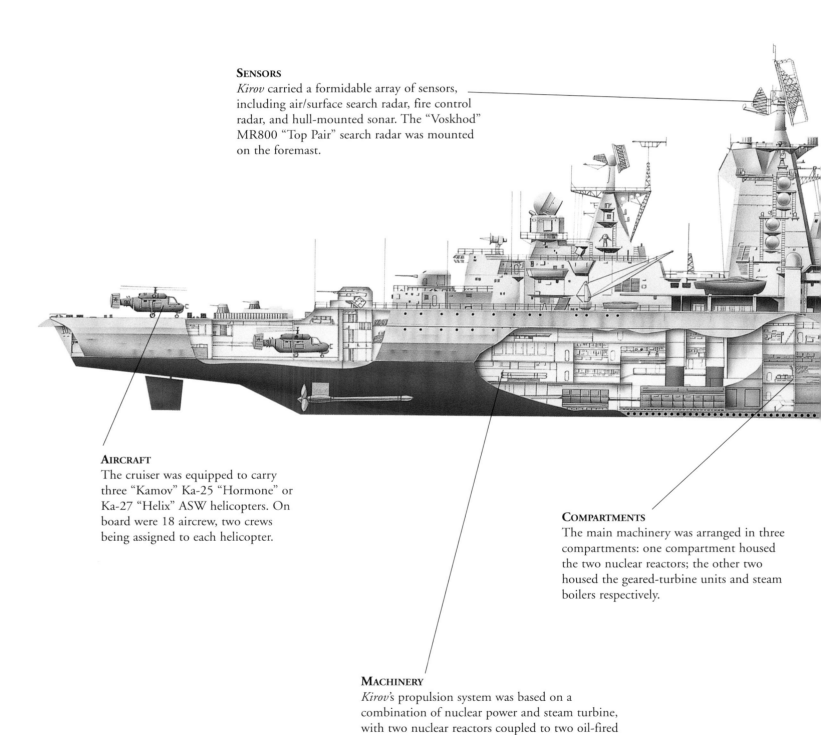

SENSORS
Kirov carried a formidable array of sensors, including air/surface search radar, fire control radar, and hull-mounted sonar. The "Voskhod" MR800 "Top Pair" search radar was mounted on the foremast.

AIRCRAFT
The cruiser was equipped to carry three "Kamov" Ka-25 "Hormone" or Ka-27 "Helix" ASW helicopters. On board were 18 aircrew, two crews being assigned to each helicopter.

COMPARTMENTS
The main machinery was arranged in three compartments: one compartment housed the two nuclear reactors; the other two housed the geared-turbine units and steam boilers respectively.

MACHINERY
Kirov's propulsion system was based on a combination of nuclear power and steam turbine, with two nuclear reactors coupled to two oil-fired boilers, which superheated the steam produced in the reactor plant to increase the power output available during high-speed running.

ARMAMENT

Primary armament of the *Kirov* was the "Granit" (SS-N-19 "Shipwreck") long-range anti-ship missile. Twenty missiles were installed under the upper deck, mounted at an angle of 60 degrees.

BOW

One of the prominent features of the *Kirov*-class warships was the sharply raked bow, a feature of all Soviet warships designed in the latter years of the Cold War.

F A C T S

- Launched 26 December, 1977; commissioned 30 December, 1980.

- First Soviet nuclear-powered surface warship.

- Assigned to the Soviet Northern Fleet.

- Reactor accident while on deployment to the Mediterranean, 1990.

- Placed in reserve and renamed *Admiral Ushakov*, 1992.

- Name *Admiral Ushakov* assigned to a destroyer, 2004.

- Awaiting dismantling in 2010.

KIROV/ADMIRAL USHAKOV – SPECIFICATION

Country of origin: Soviet Union
Type: Missile cruiser
Laid down: 27 March, 1974
Builder: Baltiysky Naval Shipyard, Leningrad
Launched: 26 December, 1977
Commissioned: 30 December, 1980
Decommissioned: 1990
Fate: Awaiting dismantling
Complement: 727, aircrew 18, flagstaff 15

Dimensions:
Displacement: (full load) 25,401 tonnes (28,000 tons)
Length: 252 m (827 ft); **Beam:** 28.5 m (94 ft); **Draught:** 9.1 m (30 ft)

Powerplant:
Propulsion: 2-shaft CONAS, nuclear-powered with steam turbine boost producing 104.4 MW (140,000 shp)
Speed: 32 knots
Range: 1852 km (1000 nm) at 30 knots; essentially unlimited with nuclear power at 20 knots

Armour & Armament:
Armament: 10 x 533-mm (21-in) torpedo tubes; 20 x SS-N-19 "Shipwreck" cruise missiles; 14 x SS-N-14 cruise missiles; rocket launchers, and guns
Armour: 76-mm (3-in) plating around reactor compartment
Aircraft: 3 x Kamov Ka-27 "Helix" or Ka-25 "Hormone" helicopters

Kirov was originally designed as a large anti-submarine warship to search for and engage enemy ballistic missile submarines. After the introduction of the Granit anti-ship missile system, its role was then expanded to engage large surface targets and to provide air and anti-submarine protection to naval forces.

KIROV

SOVIET CRUISER: *MOSKVA*

SOVIET CRUISER: "KARA"

SOVIET CRUISER: *KRASINA*

SOVIET SURPRISES

In the last three decades of the Cold War, Soviet naval architects produced many surprises. In December 1977, the Soviet navy – which by then had expanded its operations worldwide to become a true blue-water fleet – launched the nuclear-powered *Kirov*, the largest warship built by any nation since World War II apart from aircraft carriers. Designated *Raketnyy Kreyser*, the 24,385-tonne (24,000-ton) vessel was more akin, in terms of appearance and firepower, to the obsolete battlecruiser category. Three more vessels of the *Kirov* class were completed: the *Frunze*, *Kalinin*, and *Yuri Andropov*.

The Kirov *was one of the most handsome warships produced by Russian shipyards and was certainly one of the most effective. She has been photographed here at Severomorsk, the primary base of the Northern Fleet.*

In 1984, the Soviet Northern Fleet conducted a large-scale deployment to the Norwegian Sea. It was the largest exercise of its type yet seen. At its heart was the new nuclear-powered cruiser, *Kirov*.

The ability of the Russians to deploy so many warships and supporting units at one time – and with speed – alarmed NATO planners. If the Soviet navy could achieve similar surprise at the outset of a real conflict, it could secure the northern part of the Norwegian Sea and prevent deployment of NATO reinforcements to northern Norway in the event of a Soviet offensive. A further factor that alarmed the Supreme Allied Commander Atlantic (SACLANT) was not so much the current Soviet naval force levels, but the realization that the NATO nations were no longer numerically equal to their potential enemy in shipbuilding terms.

Another even more disquieting trend was the closing of the quality gap that SACLANT had once enjoyed over the Warsaw Pact. This was due partly to the assimilation of huge amounts of published Western military technology that was freely available to the Warsaw Pact, but also to the enormous resources the Soviet Union had devoted to improving the capability of its naval forces. Each successive naval platform had far greater capability in terms of improved weapons and electronics, and an increased durability for sustained operations. By the mid-1980s, almost every unit in the Soviet maritime inventory was armed with a missile of some sort, including very effective sea-skimming anti-ship weapons.

THE "SHIPWRECK" MISSILE

In the case of *Kirov*, there was the Granit long-range anti-ship missile system, known in the West as the "Shipwreck" missile. Twenty Granit antiship missiles were installed under the upper deck, mounted at a 60-degree angle. The long-range missiles could not be controlled once launched, but they had what was known as a multivariant target engagement programme. When ripple-fired, the missiles shared information while in flight. The lead missile assumed a high-level flight trajectory, enabling it to increase its target acquisition capability, while the other missiles followed at a lower level. If the lead missile was destroyed, one of the other missiles automatically assumed the lead role.

In 1990, the mighty *Kirov* suffered a reactor accident while deployed in the Mediterranean. Repairs were never carried out, partly because of a lack of funds and partly because of the rapidly changing political situation. As a result, in 1992, the warship was placed in reserve, laid up at Severomorsk and renamed *Admiral Ushakov* after an

eighteenth-century Russian naval officer. In 1999 Russia's lower parliament, the Duma, authorized repair work to be carried out on the warship, but it never happened. Instead, she was cannibalized for spare parts in order to keep her sister ships in commission.

Of the latter, *Frunze* was renamed *Admiral Lazarev* and by 2009 was awaiting deployment to the Pacific. *Kalinin* was mothballed in 1999 but was reactivated as *Admiral Nakhimov* in 2005, while *Yuri Andropov*, which was not commissioned until 1998, was renamed *Pyotr Velikiy* (Peter the Great) and by 2009 was serving as flagship of the Russian Northern Fleet.

Close-up

Kirov/Admiral Ushakov was fitted with state-of-the-art control and communications systems. Their sophistication came as something of a shock to Western naval analysts.

(1) Gunnery System: The main components of the gunnery system are a computer-based control system with a multi-band radar, television, and optical target sighting.

(2) Gun: The gun can be operated under fully automatic remote control interfaced to the radar control system.

(3) Modules: Two command modules and six combat modules are installed on the ship. The command module provides autonomous operation by detecting any threats.

(4) Target Tracking: The combat module tracks the target with radar and television.

(5) Radar Arrays: The main radar arrays are the Voskhod MR-800 (top pair) 3D search radar on the foremast, the Fregat MR-710 (top steer) 3D search radar on the main mast, and the "Palm Frond" navigation radar, on the foremast.

(6) Sonar: The cruiser is fitted with the "Horse Jaw" LF hull sonar and "Horse Tail" VDS (Variable Depth Sonar).

Sovremennyy 1977

The name *Sovremennyy* translates from the Russian as "modern." The designation was ideally suited to this formidable class of warship, its weapon system upgraded to counter the American *Spruance*-class multi-role destroyers.

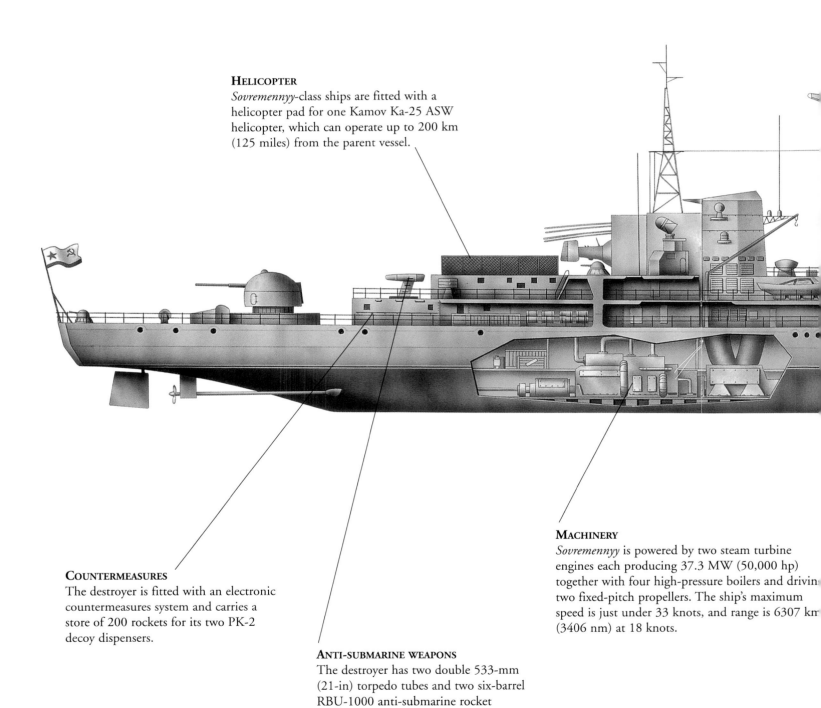

HELICOPTER
Sovremennyy-class ships are fitted with a helicopter pad for one Kamov Ka-25 ASW helicopter, which can operate up to 200 km (125 miles) from the parent vessel.

COUNTERMEASURES
The destroyer is fitted with an electronic countermeasures system and carries a store of 200 rockets for its two PK-2 decoy dispensers.

ANTI-SUBMARINE WEAPONS
The destroyer has two double 533-mm (21-in) torpedo tubes and two six-barrel RBU-1000 anti-submarine rocket launchers, with 48 rockets. The rocket is armed with a 55-kg (122-lb) warhead and has a range of 1000 m (3280 ft).

MACHINERY
Sovremennyy is powered by two steam turbine engines each producing 37.3 MW (50,000 hp) together with four high-pressure boilers and drivin two fixed-pitch propellers. The ship's maximum speed is just under 33 knots, and range is 6307 km (3406 nm) at 18 knots.

FACTS

- Laid down under the designation Project 956 *Sarych* (Buzzard).

- Primary role is to attack enemy warships while providing sea and air defence for warships and transports under escort.

- Launched November 1977; completed 25 December, 1980.

- Decommissioned 1998; scrapped 2003.

COMBAT SYSTEMS

The ship's combat systems can use target-designation data from the ship's active and passive sensors, from other ships in the fleet, from surveillance aircraft, or via a communications link from the ship's helicopter.

ARMAMENT

The *Sovremennyy* class is armed with 44 air-defence missiles, eight anti-ship missiles, torpedoes, mines, long-range guns and a sophisticated electronic warfare system.

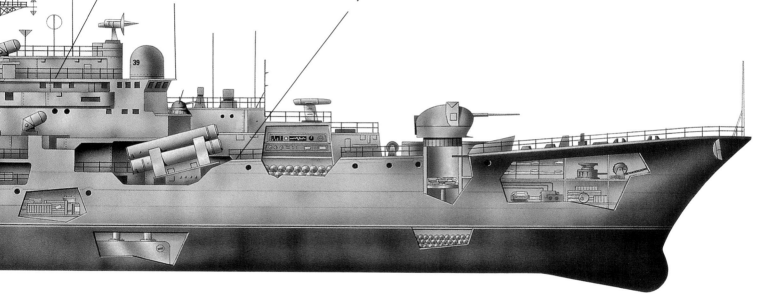

SOVREMENNYY – SPECIFICATION

Country of origin: Soviet Union
Type: Destroyer
Laid down: 1976
Builder: Severnaya Verf (Zhdanov Shipyard), Leningrad (St Petersburg)
Launched: 1977
Commissioned: 1980
Decommissioned: 1998
Fate: Scrapped 2003
Complement: 350

Dimensions:
Displacement: 7203 tonnes (7940 tons)
Length: 156 m (512 ft); **Beam:** 17.3 m (56.8 ft);
  Draught: 6.5 m (21.3 ft)

Powerplant:
Propulsion: 2 shaft steam turbines, 74.6 MW (100,000 hp)
Speed: 32 knots
Range: 6307 km (3406 nm) at 18 knots

Armament & Armour:
Armament: 2 x 4 SS-N-22 "Sunburn" Moskit SSM; 2 x 1 SA-N-7 "Gadfly" SAM; 4 x 130-mm (5.1-in) guns; 4 x 30-mm (1.18-in) AK-630 Gatling guns; 4x 553-mm (21-in) torpedo tubes; 2 x RBU-1000 ASW rockets
Armour: N/A
Aircraft: 1 x Ka-25 "Helix" helicopter

Sovremennyy-class destroyers were part of a
determined drive by the Soviet navy to deploy a
true blue-water fleet capable of sustaining
combat operations anywhere in the world with
powerful Surface Action Groups.

SOVREMENNYY-CLASS DESTROYERS

The *Sovremennyy*-class destroyers made their first appearance in strength in March 1984, during a large-scale exercise in
the north Norwegian Sea, with about half the Soviet Northern Fleet's major surface combatants and a high proportion of
the submarine order of battle participating. Two aggressor groups, simulating NATO forces, carried out an incursion into
northern waters, one group deploying from the Northern Fleet and one from the Baltic. Defending forces included a large
task force consisting of the new 22,680-tonne (25,000-ton) cruiser *Kirov*, medium anti-surface-vessel destroyers of the
Sovremennyy class, anti-submarine destroyers of the *Udaloy* class, and other older classes of warship.

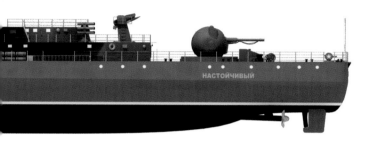

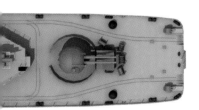

The Sovremennyy-*class destroyer* Bezuderzhnyy *(Impetuous) gets under way in the Baltic. This vessel was commissioned in 1991 and was inactive by 2010, although her exact status was unclear.*

In 2009 only five of the *Sovremennyy*-class destroyers remained active. One was operating with the Pacific Fleet, and two each with the Northern and Baltic Fleets. Five more were laid up, and the rest had been scrapped.

The *Sovremennyy* was the first of a class of 20 missile cruisers (actually designated as destroyers in the Russian navy) which replaced the "Kresta" class in production at Zhdanov. The project was initiated in late 1960s, when it was becoming apparent in the Soviet navy that, while naval guns (as distinct from missiles) still had an important function, especially in support of amphibious landings, existing gun cruisers and destroyers badly needed replacing. The new vessels used basically the same hull and the same pressure-fired steam plants, and had broadly similar armament as the "Kresta," albeit with the addition of fore and aft turrets housing twin 130-mm (5.1-in) guns. These new weapons were liquid-cooled and were capable of firing 32-kg (70.5-lb) shells over a range of just under 30 km (16 nm) at a rate of 40 rounds per minute per barrel.

The system included a computer control system with electronic and television sighting. The guns can be operated in fully automatic mode from the radar control system, under autonomous control using the turret-mounted Kondensor optical sighting system, and can also be laid manually.

Sovremennyy is also armed with four six-barrelled AK-630 gun systems with a rate of fire of 5000 rounds per minute. These can engage low-flying aircraft or surface-skimming missiles at a range of up to 4000 m (4376 yards) and light surface targets at up to 5000 m (5470 yards).

As an alternative, the *Sovremennyy* class can be fitted with the CADS-N-1 Kashtan CIWS.

SURFACE-TO-AIR SYSTEM
The primary surface-to-air missile used by the ship is the Shtil (SA-N-7, NATO reporting name "Gadfly"), with six guidance channels available for the two 24-round launchers. The system uses the ship's three-dimensional circular scan radar for target tracking. Up to three missiles can be aimed at once. The range is up to 25 km (13.5 miles).

The primary offensive weapon is the 3M80E Moskit, a

deadly anti-ship missile system with two four-cell launchers installed port and starboard of the forwards island and set at an angle of about 15 degrees. The ship carries a total of eight Moskit 3M80E missiles (the NATO designation for which is SS-N-22 "Sunburn"). The missile is a sea-skimming weapon with velocity of Mach 2.5, and is armed with a 300-kg (661-lb) high-explosive or a 200kT nuclear warhead. It has a range of up to 120 km (65 nm).

Sovremennyy-class ships were originally conceived as amphibious assault support ships, but they were revised to have a more general multipurpose role, operating alongside the heavy *Slava*-class cruisers and *Udaloy*-class destroyers. *Sovremennyy* was laid down in March 1976, launched in November 1977, and completed on 25 December, 1980. The Zhdanov shipyard went on to complete a further 19 vessels. Two of these were sold to China before completion, and two more vessels, incorporating various upgrades, were built specifically for China in 2005–06.

Close-up

The primary role of the *Sovremennyy* destroyers is to attack enemy warships while also providing sea and air defence for warships and transports under escort.

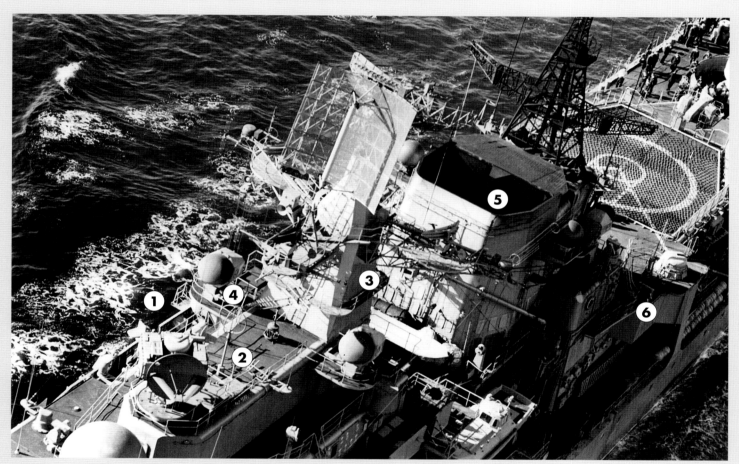

(1) **Turbines:** Although the Soviet navy had moved to gas turbine propulsion, steam turbines were selected for *Sovremennyy*, which was designated Project 956 *Sarych* (Buzzard).

(2) **Rockets:** *Sovremennyy* carried a store of 200 rockets for the two decoy dispensers, model PK-2.

(3) **Sensors:** The sensor suite included the "Top Steer" 3D surveillance radar and "Band Stand" for SS-N 22 missile guidance.

(4) **Data:** The ships are equipped with a secure datalink system, which is their primary means of exchanging data such as radar tracking information beyond line of sight.

(5) **Funnel:** *Sovremennyy* has a large, square funnel positioned immediately behind the very large "Top Dome" radar array.

(6) **Sonar:** The *Sovremennyy* class is fitted with the MGK-355 Medium and High Frequency (M/HF) Platina integrated sonar system.

Ohio (SSBN/SSGN-726) 1979

When she was commissioned in 1981, the nuclear ballistic missile submarine *Ohio* provided the U.S. Navy with a virtually undetectable undersea launch platform. Until the deployment of the Soviet Union's mighty "Typhoon"-class boats, the *Ohio* was the largest submarine in the world.

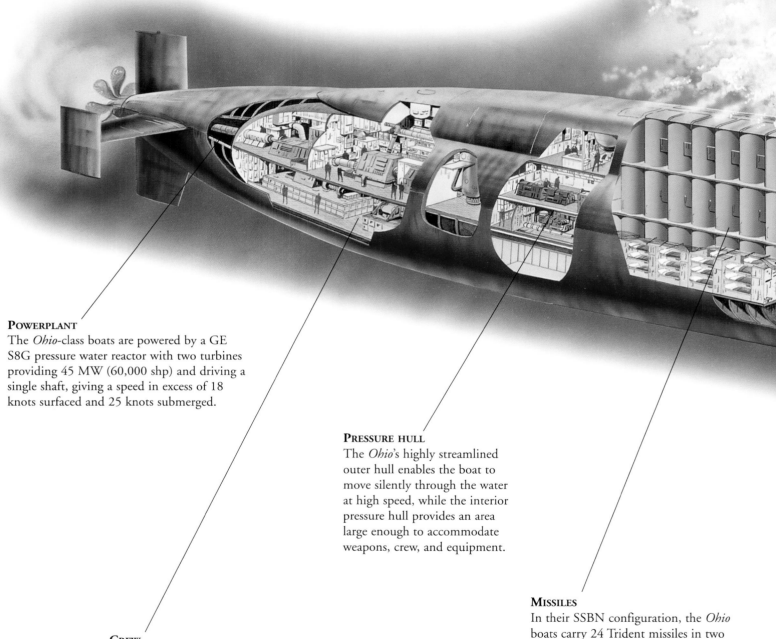

POWERPLANT
The *Ohio*-class boats are powered by a GE S8G pressure water reactor with two turbines providing 45 MW (60,000 shp) and driving a single shaft, giving a speed in excess of 18 knots surfaced and 25 knots submerged.

PRESSURE HULL
The *Ohio*'s highly streamlined outer hull enables the boat to move silently through the water at high speed, while the interior pressure hull provides an area large enough to accommodate weapons, crew, and equipment.

CREW
When on Strategic Deterrent Patrol the *Ohio* boats carry a crew of around 170, spending 70 days at sea. Two crews are assigned to each SSBN, these being designated "Blue" and "Gold" crews. Each crew has its own captain.

MISSILES
In their SSBN configuration, the *Ohio* boats carry 24 Trident missiles in two rows of 12. Each Trident is capable of carrying up to 12 MIRVs (Multiple Independent Re-entry Vehicles) each with a yield of 100kT, although the Strategic Arms Limitation Treaty (SALT) limited this to eight per missile.

TORPEDOES

The *Ohio*-class boats were fitted with four 533-mm (21-in) torpedo tubes with a Mk 118 digital torpedo fire control system. The torpedoes were Gould Mk 48s, a heavyweight weapon with a 290-kg (640-lb) warhead.

F A C T S

- Launched on 7 April, 1979, by Annie Glenn, wife of former astronaut and senator John H. Glenn.

- First Trident Submarine Strategic Deterrent Patrol, October 1982.

- *Ohio* and three sister boats converted as conventional cruise missile submarines and re-deployed as SSGNs, 2006.

SONAR

Ohio's sonar suite includes IBM BQQ 6 passive search sonar, Raytheon BQS 13, BQS 15 active and passive high-frequency sonar, and an active Raytheon BQR 19 navigation sonar.

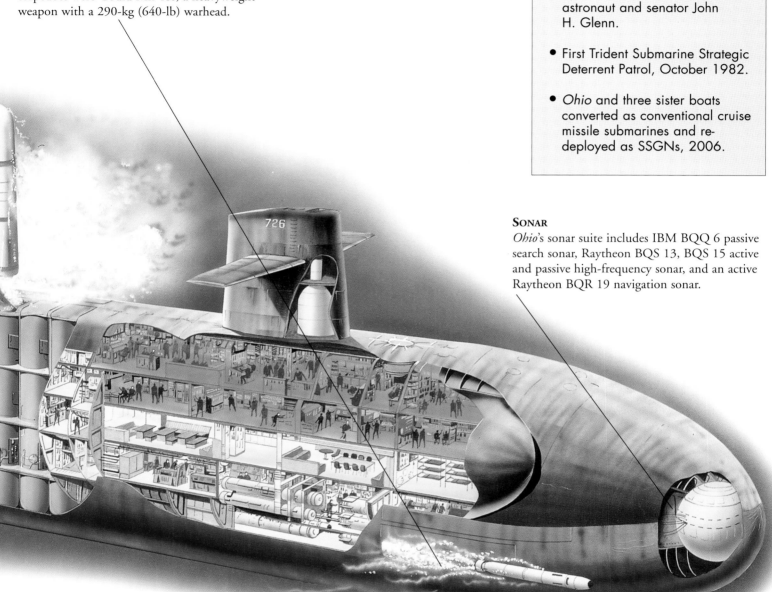

OHIO (SSBN/SSGN-726) – SPECIFICATION

Country of origin: USA
Type: Ballistic missile submarine
Laid down: 10 April, 1976
Builder: General Dynamics Electric Boat
Launched: 7 April, 1979
Commissioned: 11 November, 1981. Still in active service.
Complement: 15 officers, 140 enlisted crew

Dimensions:
Displacement: (surfaced) 15,208 tonnes (16,764 tons); (submerged) 16,969 tonnes (18,750 tons)
Length: 170 m (560 ft); **Beam:** 13 m (42 ft); **Draught:** N/A

Powerplant:
Propulsion: 1 S8G PWR nuclear reactor, 2 geared turbines, 1 x 242 kW (325 hp) auxiliary motor, 1 shaft @ 45 MW (60,000 shp)
Speed: (surfaced) 18 knots; (submerged) 25 knots
Range: Unlimited

Armament:
Armament: 4 x 533-mm (21-in) bow torpedo tubes; 24 x Trident missiles

Ohio **is the lead ship of a large class of nuclear missile submarines (SSBN), originally intended to form the third arm of the United States' nuclear triad. Boats of the class can remain submerged for up to 70 days. Eighteen *Ohio*-class boats were in commission in the 1980s.**

PREDECESSOR: *BENJAMIN FRANKLIN*

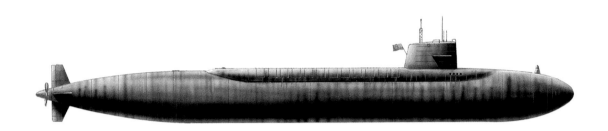

SOVIET SSN: "SIERRA"

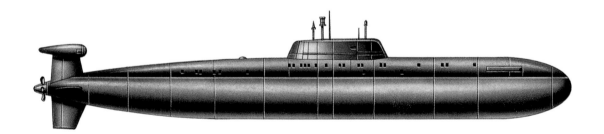

OHIO

SOVIET SSGN: "OSCAR"

DETERRENT-ROLE *OHIO* CLASS

The 18 boats of the *Ohio* class originally deployed in the strategic deterrent role were the *Ohio* (SSBN 726), *Michigan* (SSBN 727), *Florida* (SSBN 728), *Georgia* (SSBN 729), *Henry M. Jackson* (SSBN 730), *Alabama* (SSBN 731), *Alaska* (SSBN 732), *Nevada* (SSBN 733), *Tennessee* (SSBN 734), *Pennsylvania* (SSBN 735), *West Virginia* (SSBN 736), *Kentucky* (SSBN 737), *Maryland* (SSBN 738), *Nebraska* (SSBN 739), *Rhode Island* (SSBN 740), *Maine* (SSBN 741), *Wyoming* (SSBN 742), and *Louisiana* (SSBN 743). Of these, four were reconfigured as cruise missile launchers.

***Ohio* was commissioned on 11 November, 1981. At the ceremony, the principal speaker, George H.W. Bush, then vice president of the United States, remarked to the 8000 assembled guests that the boat introduced "a new dimension in our nation's strategic deterrence."**

Ohio (SSBN 726) was the first in a class of 18 nuclear-powered SSBNs built for the U.S. Navy. The first eight boats in the class were delivered with Trident C4 missiles, with 14 further vessels armed with the longer-range Trident D5. Trident is as accurate as ground-based ICBMs, with the same response time and greater destructive effect. The *Ohio*-class programme was subject to considerable delays, so that *Ohio*, scheduled for delivery in 1977, was not launched until April 1979, and did not complete her trials until 1981.

Interior view

The complex, yet compact, ship control area on *Ohio* is the nerve centre of the boat, and is manned by specialist crew members who "fly" the vessel underwater.

(1) Diving Officer: From behind the control area the diving officer issues instructions to the helmsman and planesman in front of him.

(2) Equipment: This is where the multitude of valves, tanks and other equipment needed to dive and surface the boat are located.

(3) Manual Valves: Situated on top of the ballast control panel, the manual valves are used to blow the tanks in an emergency and permit a rapid ascent to the surface.

(4) Controls: Each control area specialist is responsible for either the rudder and bow planes, or the horizontal stabilizer.

(5) Periscope: A submarine is at its most vulnerable while surfacing, as it generates a lot of noise. It first rises to periscope depth so a sweep for surface vessels can be made.

(6) Seat Belts: The seats on the control area are fitted with seat belts, because underwater manoeuvres can sometimes be violent.

After a thorough overhaul, Ohio *resumed strategic deterrent patrols in January 1995 as part of Submarine Squadron 17, Submarine Group Nine, Pacific Submarine Force.*

Ohio was commissioned on 11 November, 1981, and immediately sailed on a shakedown cruise. On 13 March, 1982, the submarine launched its first Trident I training missile. The following August the vessel was loaded with operational missiles for the first time and on 1 October, *Ohio* sailed on her first deterrent patrol.

SILENT RUNNERS

The *Ohio* class was a major improvement over the previous *Lafayette*-class SSBNs, being faster, quieter, easier to maintain, and having far superior crew facilities, including two onboard libraries. Because each *Ohio* carried 24 Trident missiles, compared to the 16 carried by a *Lafayette*, the U.S. Navy replaced all of its 31 *Lafayette*-class boats with the 18 *Ohio*s, which still provided a far superior striking force.

Ohio boats are among the quietest nuclear-powered submarines in service anywhere because they have been fitted with an advanced turbo-electric drive for silent running. Despite their sophistication, *Ohio*s are robust, and have a remarkably high serviceability record. This means they are capable of averaging 66 percent of their time at sea, usually following 70 days at sea with a 25-day schedule of maintenance.

In June 1993 *Ohio* went into Puget Sound Naval Dockyard in Seattle, for an overhaul, receiving extensive upgrades to her sonar, fire control and navigation systems.

Ohio resumed strategic deterrent patrols in January 1995 as part of Submarine Squadron 17 in the Pacific Submarine Force. In 2002 *Ohio* was due to be retired, but the U.S. Navy decided to modify her and three sister vessels as conventional missile submarines (SSGNs). Modification involved converting 22 of the boats' 24 missile launch tubes to accommodate the Tomahawk TLAM (land attack) or Tactical Tomahawk cruise missiles. Each submarine was to be armed with up to 154 missiles. The launch tubes were adapted by Northrop Grumman Electronic Systems, which had developed a multiple all-up round canister that gives storage and launch of up to seven Tomahawks from each tube.

DELIVERING SEALS

The modified submarines are equipped with the Raytheon AN-BYG-1 combat data system. They are also capable of conducting special operations missions, with accommodation for Northrop Grumman advanced SEAL delivery systems and 102 special operations troops.

Ohio began conversion in November 2002 and rejoined the fleet in January 2006, following sea trials. The other converted *Ohio*-class boats were *Florida*, *Michigan*, and *Georgia*. In November 2007, *Ohio* carried out final trials off Hawaii before beginning her first deployment as an SSGN in the Western Pacific.

"Tripartite" Minehunter 198

The "Tripartite" minehunters were an unusual exercise in collaboration. Belgium provided most of the electronics, France the minehunting equipment, and the Netherlands the propulsion systems.

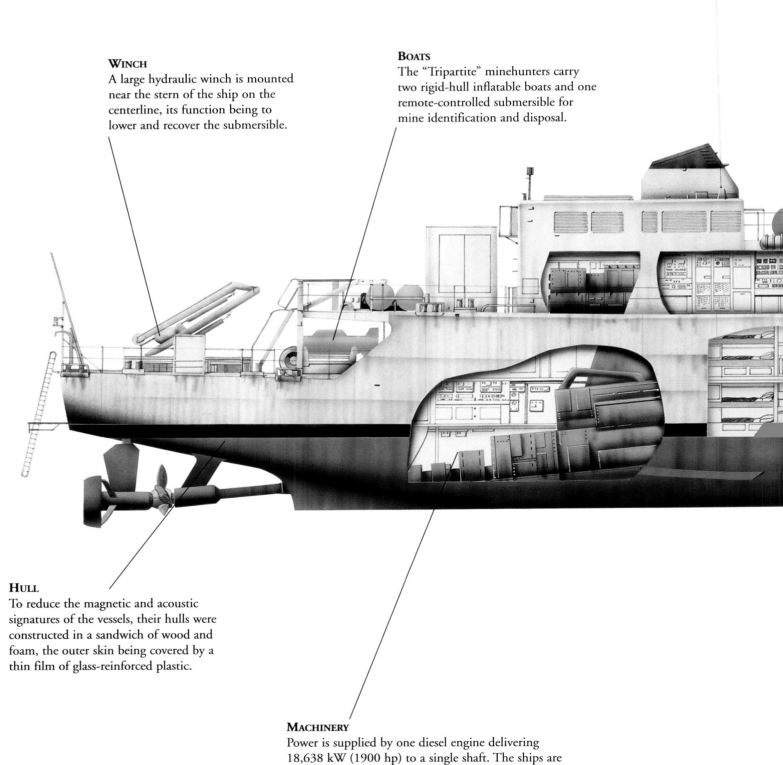

WINCH
A large hydraulic winch is mounted near the stern of the ship on the centerline, its function being to lower and recover the submersible.

BOATS
The "Tripartite" minehunters carry two rigid-hull inflatable boats and one remote-controlled submersible for mine identification and disposal.

HULL
To reduce the magnetic and acoustic signatures of the vessels, their hulls were constructed in a sandwich of wood and foam, the outer skin being covered by a thin film of glass-reinforced plastic.

MACHINERY
Power is supplied by one diesel engine delivering 18,638 kW (1900 hp) to a single shaft. The ships are fitted with an "active rudder" system for minehunting.

SUPERSTRUCTURE
The superstructure and deckhead are a composite of wood and fibreglass resin. All the propulsion systems can be operated from the bridge.

BOW PROPELLER
The "Tripartite" vessels are fitted with a bow propeller to enhance their manoeuvrability when operating in confined areas, such as harbours and estuaries.

"TRIPARTITE" MINEHUNTER – SPECIFICATION

Countries of origin: Belgium, France, the Netherlands
Type: Minehunter
Laid down: 1981
Builders: N/A
Launched: 1981
Commissioned: 1981. Still in service.
Complement: 4 officers, 15 non-commissioned officers, 17 sailors

Dimensions:
Displacement: (full) 605 tonnes (667 tons)
Length: 51.5 m (169 ft); **Beam:** 8.96 m (29.4 ft);
   Draught: 3.6 m (12 ft)

Powerplant:
Propulsion: 1 x 18,638 kW (1900 shp) Werkspoor RUB 215 V12 diesel
Speed: 15 knots
Range: 5556 km (3000 nm) at 12 knots

Armament & Armour:
Armament: (French navy) 1 x 20-mm (0.79-in) modèle F2 gun; 2 x 12.7-mm (0.5-in) machine guns; 2 x 7.62-mm (0.3-in) MGs
Armour: None

Boats carried: 1 x remote-controlled submersible for mine identification and disposal; 2 x rigid inflatables

The approximate Soviet equivalent of the "Tripartite" minesweeper was the "Natya" class, pictured here. Known to the Russians as the Project 266M Avkvamarin, the design evolved from the "Yurka"-class minesweeper with new minehunting equipment that included more advanced sonar and closed-circuit TV. A stern ramp made recovering sweeps easier. The hull was built of low-magnetic steel.

RUSSIAN MINEHUNTER: "NATYA"

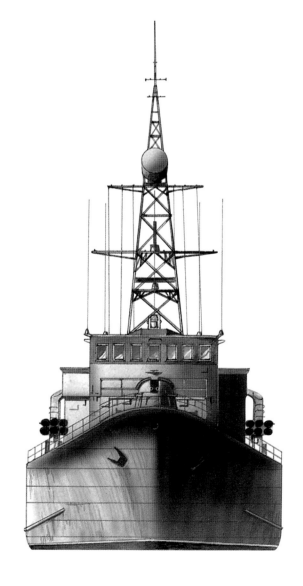

MINEHUNTING

Minehunting is a dangerous business, and this means that minehunting vessels must be as heavily protected as possible. Their hulls are designed with materials that reduce their own acoustic and magnetic signatures, two common forms of trigger for mines, and they are often soundproofed by having their machinery mounted on shock absorbers. Much of their work is done in confined waters, such as harbours or shipping channels, so they are fitted with an auxiliary propulsion system in the bow, enabling the engine thrust to be transmitted in any direction and so enhance manoeuvrability.

Seen here is an example of one of France's "Tripartite" vessels, designated M641 Eridan. *All of the French ships of this class were named after constellations, the final example being* M653 Capricorne.

In the early months of World War II, enemy magnetic mines were the main threat to British shipping in home waters. During September and October 1939 alone, such mines destroyed 53,550 tonnes (59,027 tons) of British coastal shipping.

A joint venture of the navies of France, Belgium, and the Netherlands, the "Tripartite" class of minehunter was conceived in the 1970s and built in the 1980s. France supplied the mine-hunting equipment, Belgium provided the electronics, and the Netherlands constructed the propulsion machinery. France and the Netherlands originally bought 15, and Belgium bought 10. All three countries' "Tripartite" ships contribute at times to NATO's Standing Maritime MCM capability groups (SNMCMG1 or SNMCMG2). Two hulls were also supplied to the Indonesian navy and the vessels were completed in Indonesia; five ex-Dutch vessels were sold to Latvia; one former Belgian vessel went to Bulgaria; and three ships were purchased by Pakistan, two of these being ex-French vessels, and the third built in Pakistan.

All the remaining Belgian vessels underwent an extensive upgrade during 2004–08, involving replacement of their anti-

mine warfare equipment. The Belgian ships in this class, referred to as *Chasseurs de Mines Tripartite* (CMT), are named after flowers, reminiscent of the Royal Navy's "Flower"-class corvettes of World War II fame.

The hull and decks of the "Tripartite" are constructed of approximately 163 tonnes (180 tons) of a glass weave polyester resin (GRP) compound, and the propulsion system is essentially the same as that fitted to the French *Circé* class of minehunter. "Tripartite" ships also carry the DUBM 21A minehunting sonar, an upgraded version of the equipment installed in the *Circé* class.

DISABLING MINES

Once located, mines can be disabled by a six-man diving detachment or by explosive charges laid by a remotely controlled PAP 104 submersible. These weigh 700 kg (1534 lb), are 2.7 m (8.9 ft) long and 1.1 m (3.6 ft) in diameter. Following the detection of a mine, the submersible is lowered over the side aft by a large hydraulic winch mounted on the centreline. The PAP is then guided towards the contact via a 500-m (1640-ft) cable. Once in the mine's vicinity, a TV camera in the nose is used to positively identify the target as a mine and a 100-kg (220-lb) HE explosive charge is released next to it. The PAP is then guided back to the mother ship, and recovered aboard. At this point an ultrasonic signal detonates the charge. To aid in the plotting and classification processes involved during a search, an automatic plotting table is installed in the sonar and operations control room, which is located in the superstructure forward of the bridge. The French "Tripartite" class also have a position for a second sonar control centre on the upper deck aft to provide facilities for a towed sidescan sonar system. Every ship of the

"Tripartite" type carries one light mechanical drag sweep to deal with any conventionally moored mines.

Some modern minehunters make use of the hulls of catamarans when detonating mines because they offer a large, stable working platform with minimal underwater contact. This reduces draught while lowering acoustic transmission as well as decreasing the fluid pressure generated by the moving hull that may otherwise detonate a mine that has been fitted with a hydraulic pressure trigger.

Close-up

The modern minehunter must be capable of clearing coastal and ocean waters, shore areas, and harbours of a range of mines, including pressure/contact, acoustic, and magnetic examples.

(1) **Sonar:** High-definition sonar detects the mines, which are then neutralized by a remotely controlled underwater vehicle.

(2) **Detonation Protection:** The ships were designed with exceptionally low magnetic and acoustic signatures to protect them against mine detonations.

(3) **Seabed:** The sonar display presents a view of the seabed with evaluation data on mine-like objects or features on, near or tethered to the seabed.

(4) **Data:** In the classification mode the system presents visual data based on the physical appearance of the complementary echo and shadow images.

(5) **Cradles:** Suspending machinery from glass-reinforced plastic cradles on deck isolates it acoustically.

(6) **Armament:** France's "Tripartite" minehunters are armed with three 12.7-mm (0.5-in) machine guns.

Giuseppe Garibaldi 1983

The *Giuseppe Garibaldi* was designed specifically to provide ASW support for naval task forces and merchant convoys, and as such is fitted with full facilities to act as flagship for a naval task group.

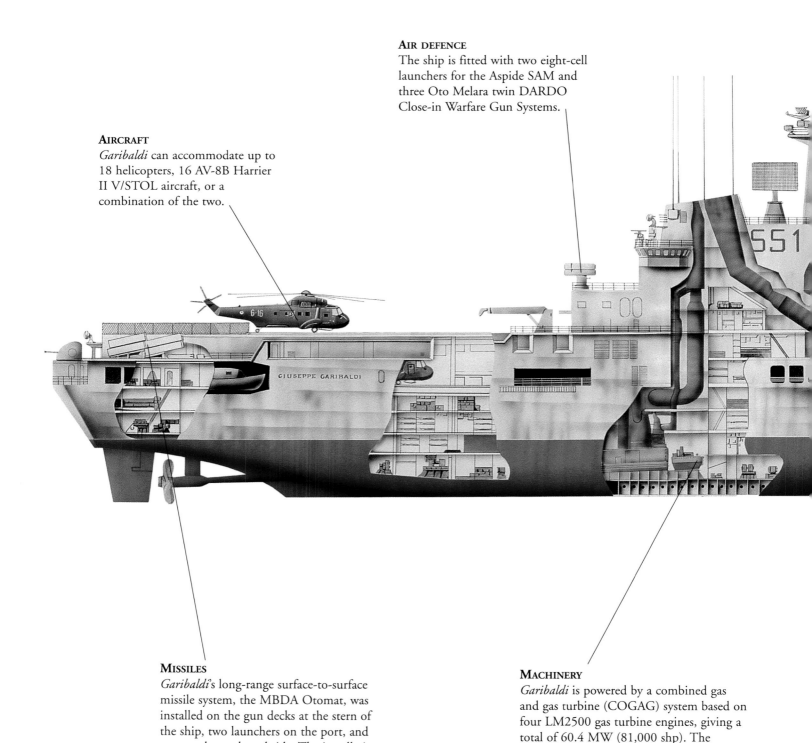

AIR DEFENCE
The ship is fitted with two eight-cell launchers for the Aspide SAM and three Oto Melara twin DARDO Close-in Warfare Gun Systems.

AIRCRAFT
Garibaldi can accommodate up to 18 helicopters, 16 AV-8B Harrier II V/STOL aircraft, or a combination of the two.

MISSILES
Garibaldi's long-range surface-to-surface missile system, the MBDA Otomat, was installed on the gun decks at the stern of the ship, two launchers on the port, and two on the starboard side. The installation was removed in 2003 to make room for new sensor systems.

MACHINERY
Garibaldi is powered by a combined gas and gas turbine (COGAG) system based on four LM2500 gas turbine engines, giving a total of 60.4 MW (81,000 shp). The engines produce a maximum speed of 30 knots and a range of 12,964 (7000 nm) at 20 knots.

COMBAT SYSTEM

The ship's IPN 20 command and control system gathers information from all sensors and from the communications and data networks and builds up a tactical display.

TORPEDOES

Two ILAS 3 triple-tube torpedo launchers from WASS (Whitehead Alenia Sistemi Subaqua) are fitted. The 324-mm (12.8-in) tubes are capable of firing the Honeywell Mark 46 or the A290 torpedo.

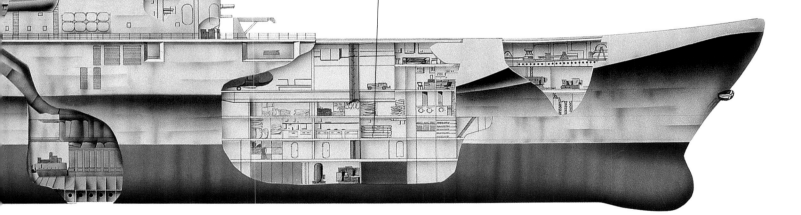

GIUSEPPE GARIBALDI – SPECIFICATION

Country of origin: Italy
Type: Aircraft carrier
Laid down: March 1981
Builder: Fincantieri
Launched: 11 June, 1983
Commissioned: 30 September, 1985. Still in service
Complement: 630 crew, 100 Fleet Air Arm, 100 C^4 (Command, Control, Communications, Computers) staff

Dimensions:
Displacement: (full load) 12,564 tonnes (13,850 tons)
Length: 180.2 m (591.2 ft); **Beam:** 30.4 m (99.7 ft);
Draught: 8.2 m (26.9 ft)

Powerplant:
Propulsion: 4 x GE/Avio LM2500 gas turbines, 60.4 MW (81,000 shp); 6 x diesel generators 9.36 KW (12.5 shp)
Speed: 30 knots
Range: 12,964 (7000 nm) at 20 knots

Armament & Armour:
Armament: 2 x Mk.29 octuple launcher for Sea Sparrow/Selenia Aspide SAM; 3 x Oto Melara Twin 40L70 DARDO CIWS; 2 x 324-mm (12.8-in) triple torpedo tubes
Armour: N/A
Aircraft: V-8B Harrier II fighter/bombers, Augusta SH-3D or AgustaWestland EH101 helicopters (ASW, ASH, and AEW)

***Charles de Gaulle*: Unlike Britain and Italy, whose relative small aircraft carriers are designed to operate a mixed complement of helicopters and V/STOL aircraft, France's nuclear-powered *Charles de Gaulle* operates conventional Dassault Rafale strike aircraft. She is the largest European aircraft carrier.**

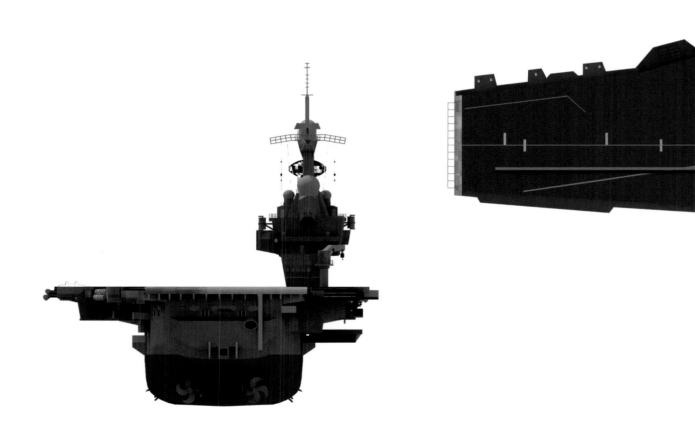

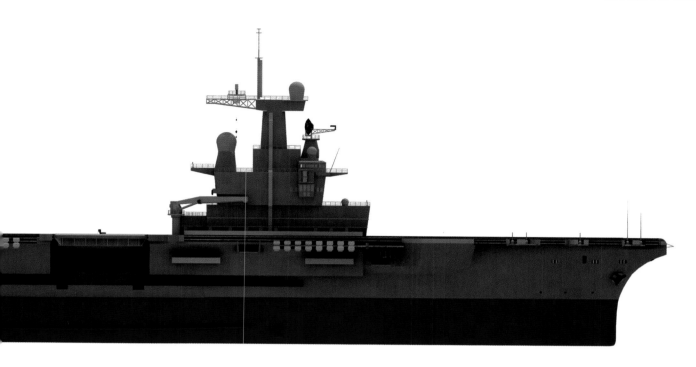

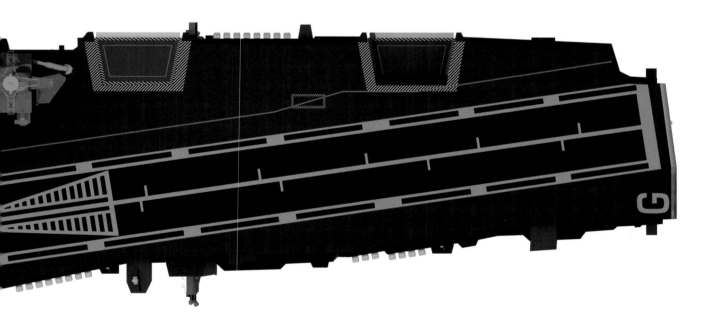

ITALIAN AIRCRAFT CARRIERS

During World War II Italy attempted to build two aircraft carriers, both converted from passenger liners. The first, named *Aquila* (formerly *Roma*), was nearly ready for sea trials at the time of the Italian armistice in September 1943; the other, *Sparviero* (formerly *Augustus*) was to have been completed as an escort carrier. Both were seized by the Germans after the armistice and scuttled. A treaty between Italy and the wartime Allies, concluded in 1947, banned the Italian navy from deploying an aircraft carrier with a complement of fixed-wing aircraft, so *Giuseppe Garibaldi* initially operated as a helicopter carrier. The rules were subsequently relaxed to permit the operation of the Harrier V/STOL aircraft.

Following her commissioning in 1985 the *Giuseppe Garibaldi* became the flagship of the Italian fleet, a position she held until the deployment of a new, larger carrier in 2008.

Built by Fincantieri at the Monfalcone shipyards in the Gulf of Trieste, *Giuseppe Garibaldi* – the fourth Italian warship to bear the name of the Italian hero – was laid down in March 1981, launched in 1983, and commissioned on 30 September, 1985. She was classed as an Anti-Submarine Warfare Aircraft Carrier (CVS–ASW) and based at Taranto. The peace treaty of 1947 banned Italy from having an aircraft carrier, so she was only able to operate helicopters and received the rather odd classification of *Incrociatore Portaeromobili* (Aircraft Carrying Cruiser). Although she occasionally accommodated Royal Navy Sea Harriers during

Close-up

Garibaldi's missions include anti-submarine warfare, command and control of naval and maritime air forces, area surveillance, convoy escort, commando transportation, and fleet logistic support.

(1) **Helicopters:** The ship can accommodate up to 18 helicopters, for example the Agusta Sikorsky SH-3D Sea King, seen here.

(2) **SAM Launchers:** Garibaldi's Albatros octuple SAM launchers are installed on the roof decks at the forwards and stern end of the main island.

(3) **Flight Deck:** This is the characteristic off-axis design with a 4-degree ski jump for V/STOL aircraft like the Harrier.

(4) **Landing Ban:** Until 1988 only Italian helicopters landed on her deck, as well as RAF Harriers during NATO joint maneuvers. The ban was eventually lifted.

(5) **Countermeasure Systems:** These included two SCLAR 20-barrel launchers for chaff, decoy flares, or jammers.

(6) **Bridge:** Garibaldi's bridge is well armoured and provides a good overview of the carrier's deck, even though it is situated a little lower than usual on the tower.

Giuseppe Garibaldi *pictured making a leisurely passage through the Mediterranean. Some of her Harrier V/STOL aircraft can be seen on the landing platform at the stern of the ship, and a Sea King helicopter is positioned at the rear of the flight deck.*

NATO exercises, it was not until 1989 that the ban was lifted and the Italian navy was able to acquire fixed-wing aircraft in the shape of the McDonnell Douglas/BAe AV-8B Harrier II.

OPERATING IN ALL WEATHERS

The *Garibaldi* was designed specifically to provide anti-submarine warship support for naval task forces and merchant convoys, and as such was fitted with full flagship facilities plus command, control, and communication systems for both naval and air force operations. In emergencies she can also carry up to 600 troops for short periods of time. Her extensive weaponry enables her to operate as an independent surface unit. A bow-mounted active search sonar has also been installed on the ship. To facilitate helicopter operations in heavy weather, the vessel has two pairs of fin stabilizers, and the aircraft maintenance resources are sufficient not only to service the ship's own air group but also the light ASW helicopters of any escorting warships. Harriers operating from her flight deck are able to use the characteristic "ski jump" modification, employed on the British *Invincible*-class carriers.

ASSISTING NATO AND THE UN

Garibaldi has been active in support of NATO and UN operations. In 1994 she deployed to the Adriatic for Operation Sharp Guard, her helicopters being employed to investigate commercial vessels sailing off the coast of the former Yugoslavia. Later in the year, and in 1995, she played an important part in support of Italian and UN troops operating in Somalia during Operation Restore Hope.

In 1996 the ship was once more in the Adriatic, this time with her complement of AV-8B Harrier IIs embarked, the aircraft carrying out air interdiction missions over Kosovo. Between November 2001 and April 2002, as part of a task group positioned in the Arabian Sea, her Harriers flew many missions, some of up to six and a half-hours' duration, in support of Operation Enduring Freedom, the air campaign in Afghanistan. During these operations the Harriers operated in packages with U.S. Navy F-14 and F-18 aircraft and were flight refuelled by USAF KC-135s.

In 2009, *Giuseppe Garibaldi*'s role as fleet flagship was assumed by a new carrier, *Cavour*. This was a larger vessel designed to combine fixed-wing V/STOL and helicopter air operations, command and control operations, and the transport of military or civil personnel and heavy vehicles. The *Cavour* was launched in July 2004 and commissioned on 27 March, 2008, following the successful completion of her sea trials.

Zeeleeuw 1987

The submariners of the Royal Netherlands Navy have a proud tradition. In the early part of 1942, Dutch submarines operating in the Far East sank more Japanese shipping than their American counterparts, and the expertise holds good today.

MACHINERY
Internal improvements over the *Zwaardvis* class include more powerful machinery. The diesel generators have SEMT-Pielstick PA4V200 12-cylinder engines.

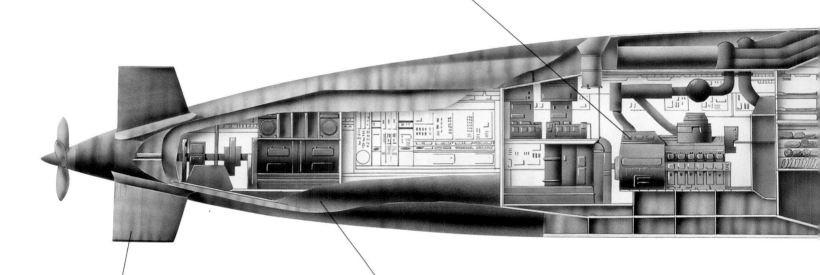

HULL
Zeeleeuw features a double-deck hull configuration of advanced "teardrop" form. It is constructed of high-tensile steel and has the minimum of apertures and welded joints.

DIVE PLANES
The dive planes and rudders of the *Walrus*-class submarines are arranged in an "X" configuration rather than a vertical-horizontal cross. The *Walrus* X-form after-plane configuration requires complex computerized control.

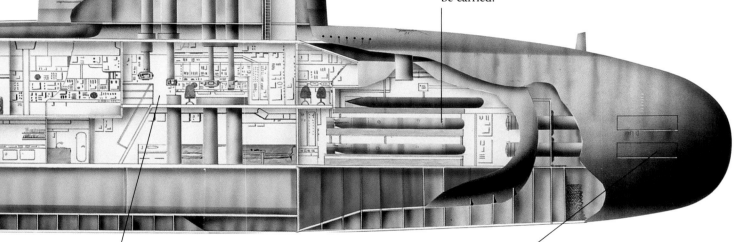

ARMAMENT
The *Walrus* class can carry 20 torpedoes or 40 mines. The Sub-Harpoon SSM can also be carried.

CONTROL CENTRE
A control centre below the fin houses the machinery control and surveillance consoles and an advanced Attack Centre for the data-handling and weapons control system.

SONAR
The *Walrus*-class boats are undergoing major upgrades to the sonar suite and periscopes, with the addition of a mine-avoidance sonar.

ZEELEEUW – SPECIFICATION

Country of origin: The Netherlands
Type: Attack submarine
Laid down: June 1979
Builder: RDM Shipyard, Rotterdam
Launched: 20 June, 1987
Commissioned: 1987. Still in service
Complement: 49

Dimensions:
Displacement: (surfaced) 2490 tonnes (2450 tons); (submerged) 2800 tonnes (2755 tons)
Length: 67.5 m (22 ft); **Beam:** 8.4 m (27 ft 7 in); **Draught:** 6.6 m (21 ft 8 in)

Powerplant:
Propulsion: 3 diesel engines delivering 4700 kW (6300 shp), 1 electric motor delivering 5150 kW (6910 shp) to one shaft
Speed: (surfaced) 13 knots; (submerged) 20 knots
Range: 18,520 (10,000 nm) at 9 knots

Armament & Armour:
Armament: 4 x 533-mm (21-in) torpedo tubes for 20 Mk 48 dual-role wire-guided torpedoes, or 40 influence ground mines, or Sub-Harpoon underwater-launched anti-ship missiles
Armour: N/A

The *Walrus*-class boats have an excellent balance of weapons and sensors, as well as good endurance. Their operational area is in the waters around Europe, but they have the capability to venture farther afield.

GERMAN PATROL SUBMARINE: *TYPE 209*

ITALIAN PATROL SUBMARINE: *ENRICO TOTI*

DUTCH PATROL SUBMARINE: *WALRUS*

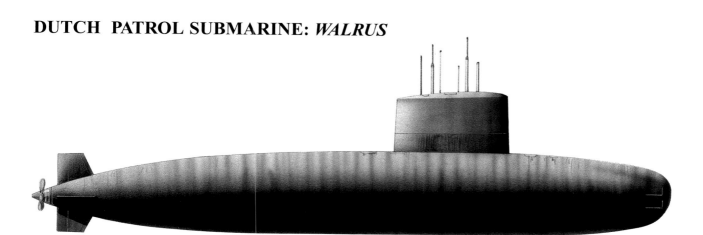

BRITISH PATROL SUBMARINE: *UPHOLDER*

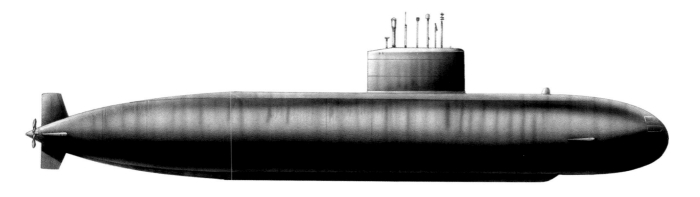

WALRUS-CLASS SUBMARINES

The *Walrus*-class submarines were originally fitted with indicator beacons that transmit a distress signal to trigger rescue operations in the event of the submarine getting into difficulties. In the interests of increased crew safety and enabling them to abandon the submarine as quickly as possible in case of an incident, these indicator buoys have been replaced with the new life-raft containers that can be deployed when required, each containing the inflatable raft, an automatically activated GPS search-and-rescue emergency beacon, and supplies. The life rafts remain tethered to the submarine so that the escaping crew can get on board.

The leader of the class to which *Zeeleeuw* belongs, *Walrus* acquired an altogether unjustified bad reputation when a fire that totally destroyed the combat system ignited while she was fitting out.

The Royal Netherlands Navy has made several unique contributions to submarine design, notably the *schnorkel* (snorkel), and this tradition continued after 1945. The *Dolfijn* class, built 1954–66, adopted an innovative triple-hull configuration, with two cylinders as the base. The upper cylinder accommodated the crew, control spaces, and weapons, while the two lower cylinders housed the diesel generators, electric motors, and batteries. In 1990, the sole survivor, *Zeehond*, was used as a test vehicle for the Spectre

Close-up

Walrus-class submarines were in high demand by NATO during the Cold War because they combined a highly skilled crew with a very silent boat.

(1) **Their silent running qualities and ability to operate close inshore means the *Walrus*-class boats have been tasked with intelligence-gathering operations.**

(2) **Snorkel Depth: The boats are fitted with many labour-saving devices; e.g., a single crewman can bring the boat to snorkel depth by pushing one button.**

(3) **Hull: A requirement to increase diving depth to 300 m (985 ft) led to the use of the French Marel high-tensile steel in the hull.**

(4) **Upgrades: These have all focused on their in-shore operations and modifications to their torpedoes.**

(5) **Sonar: The sonar systems comprise the Thomson Sintra TSM 2272 Eledone Octopus, GEC Avionics Type 2026 towed array, and Thomson Sintra DUUX 5 passive ranging and intercept array.**

(6) **Crews: The crews of the *Walrus* class are trained in a specially designed shore based replica called the Gipsy trainer.**

Walrus-class submarines provided a valuable asset to NATO's anti-submarine forces during the latter years of the Cold War and, in more recent times, found a new application in punitive and anti-terrorist actions.

closed-cycle diesel system. The two *Zwaardvis* class of 1966–72 were based on the U.S. *Barbel* diesel-electric design.

In 1972, the Royal Netherlands Navy identified a need for a new class of submarine to replace the elderly *Dolfijn* and *Potvis* classes. The new design evolved as the *Walrus* class, and was based on the *Zwaardvis* hull form with similar dimensions and silhouette, but with more automation, a smaller crew, more modern electronics, X-configuration control surfaces, and the French MAREI high-tensile steel hull material, which permits an increase of 50 percent in the maximum diving depth to 300 m (985 ft). What was intended as merely an improved *Zwaardvis* type consequently ended up as virtually a new design, resulting in massive cost overruns.

The first unit, *Walrus*, was laid down in 1979 for commissioning in 1986. However, in August that year while in the last stage of completion, she suffered a fire that was serious enough to make her hull glow white-hot. Despite the intensity of the blaze, luckily her hull escaped serious damage, although the combat system was destroyed and her finalization was delayed until 1991.

The accident to *Walrus* meant that it was now the second boat under construction, so *Zeeleeuw* (sea lion) was first to be launched, on 20 June 1987. She was followed by two more boats, the *Dolfijn* and *Bruinvis*. The four boats have proved very effective in service. Since 1988, they have

constantly proved their ability to operate far beyond Dutch territorial waters. Their operational radius of action includes the Eastern Atlantic Ocean, the North Sea, and the Norwegian Sea, as well as the Mediterranean. Their primary missions are anti-surface and anti-submarine warfare, carrying out surveillance, special operations, and minelaying.

Walrus-class submarines contain state-of-the-art electronics, the most sophisticated weapon systems available, and an integrated Sensor, Weapon, and Command system (SEWACO). The greatest improvement over the earlier class is found in the combat system, where a control center below the fin houses the machinery control and surveillance consoles and an advanced Attack Centre for the data processing and weapons control system.

LIFE RAFT SYSTEM TO SAVE LIVES

Zeeleeuw was the first of the *Walrus*-class boats to be fitted with the innovative containerized life raft system developed by Babcock Integrated Technology (Babcock Intec) for the Royal Netherlands Navy. The system is designed for deployment either sub-surface, from inside the pressure hull, or on the surface from outside the pressure hull with an external release mechanism, to save crew lives whether escaping from a stricken submarine underwater or on the surface.

"Duke" Type 23 1987

The Type 23 light anti-submarine frigate was conceived in the late 1970s to replace both the *Leander* class, developed in the 1950s, and the 1960s-vintage Type 21. The new type was intended to be the backbone of the British Royal Navy's surface ship anti-submarine force.

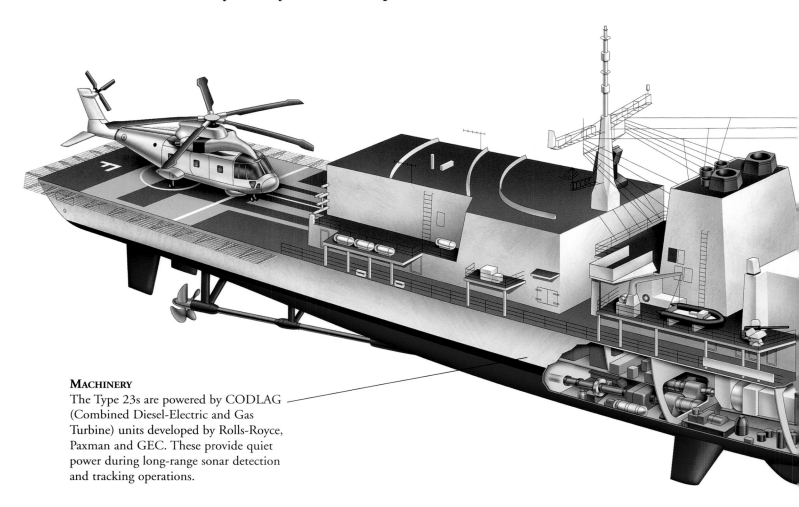

MACHINERY
The Type 23s are powered by CODLAG (Combined Diesel-Electric and Gas Turbine) units developed by Rolls-Royce, Paxman and GEC. These provide quiet power during long-range sonar detection and tracking operations.

"DUKE" TYPE 23 FRIGATE – SPECIFICATION

Country of origin: United Kingdom
Type: Frigate
Laid down: (First of type) 14 December, 1985
Builders: Swan Hunter and Yarrows
Launched: (First of type) 10 July, 1987
Commissioned: (First of type) 1 June, 1990.
    Still in service.
Complement: 181

Dimensions:
Displacement: (full load) 3810 tonnes (4200 tons)
Length: 133 m (434 ft 4 in)
Beam: 16.1 m (52 ft 10 in)
Draught: 7.3 m (24 ft)

Powerplant:
Propulsion: CODLAG (Combined Diesel-electric and Gas) with 4 x 1510 kW (2025 shp) Paxman Valenta 12CM diesel generators powering two GEC electric motors delivering 2980 kW (4000 shp) and 2 x Rolls-Royce Spey SM1A delivering 23,190 kW (31,100 shp) to two shafts
Speed: 28 knots
Range: 16,668 km (9000 nm) at 15 knots

Armament:
Armament: 2 x quadruple Harpoon launchers; 1 x Sea Wolf GWS.26 VLS; 2 x twin 324-mm (12.75-in) torpedo tubes; 1 x 11.4-cm (4.5-in) Mk 8 DP gun; 2 x DS 30B 30-mm (1.18-in) AA guns, 2 x CIWS
Aircraft: 1 x Lynx HMA8 or Merlin HM1 helicopter

SENSORS

The "Duke"-class frigates have a range of powerful sensors for communications and to detect the enemy in the air, on the surface or underwater. Information from the sensor suite is fed into the vessel's sophisticated BAeSEMA command system.

SUPERSTRUCTURE

Designed for an anti-submarine role, the ship's superstructure is angled to minimize radar reflections, shrinking her 133-m (434-ft) hull so that it has the radar signature of a fishing boat.

F A C T S

- All Type 23s are named after British dukes, and are consequently known as the "Duke" class.

- The first Type 23, *Norfolk*, was commissioned in 1990 and the sixteenth, *St Albans*, was commissioned in June 2002.

- Each "Duke"-class frigate carries either a Merlin or Lynx helicopter and most are fitted with advanced Type 2087 sonar.

- The design of the "Duke" class incorporates certain stealth features to reduce their radar cross-section.

GUNS

The frigates were originally equipped with a BAE Systems RO Defence 115-mm (4.5-in) Mk8 mod 0 gun with a range of 22 km (14 miles) against surface and 6 km (3.7 miles) against airborne targets. These were gradually replaced with the electrically driven Mk8 mod 1, *Norfolk* being the first to be so equipped in 2001.

MISSILES

The Type 23s are armed with two quadruple Harpoon launchers and were the first ships to be fitted with the vertical-launch Sea Wolf anti-aircraft missile, which is boosted vertically until it clears the ship's superstructure.

ACCOMMODATION

Much emphasis was placed on crew comfort and safety in the design of the Type 23s. For example, foam mattresses were replaced with sprung mattresses to reduce the risk of fire.

**In July 2006, the Type 23 frigate *St Albans*
assisted in the evacuation of UK nationals from
Beirut during the Israel/ Lebanon conflict, as
part of the Royal Navy Operation Highbrow.**

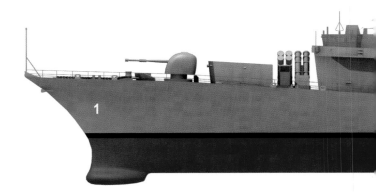

NORFOLK

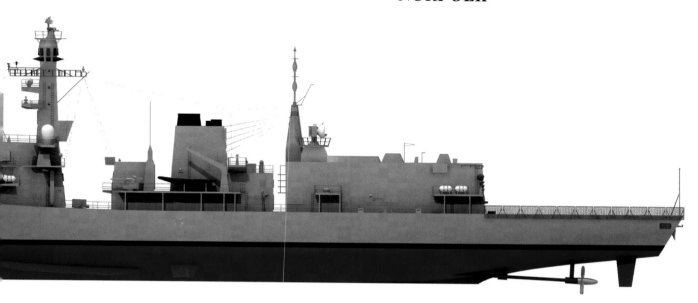

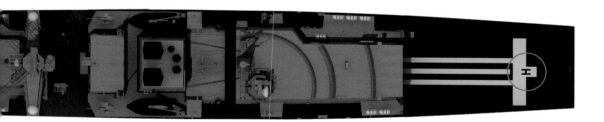

THE TYPE 23

The Type 23 is the latest in a long line of warships of a type that has formed an important element in the world's navies, ever since the frigate was conceived in the eighteenth century and its roles defined as reconnaissance and commerce raiding. Today, the name is applied to a wide variety of vessels, ranging from very expensive and highly specialized anti-submarine warfare ships like the Type 23 to cheaper ships like the U.S. Navy's *Knox* class, designed to escort convoys and amphibious warfare task groups.

Powerful and versatile, with the capability to operate anywhere in the world, the Type 23 frigate is the mainstay of the Royal Navy's modern surface fleet, forming half of the total frigate and destroyer force.

To counter the modern nuclear-powered submarine, with its high underwater speed, ASW frigates must be at the cutting edge of technology, a requirement that makes them prohibitively costly for smaller navies.

The Type 23 "Duke" class, in its originally designed form, was intended to be a relatively simple warship whose principal purpose was to detect Soviet submarines in the North Atlantic by means of a towed sonar array, but it would not mount any defensive armament. Instead, the Sea Wolf anti-aircraft missile system would be deployed on *Fort Victoria*-class replenishment oilers, one of which would typically accompany a group of four Type 23s. The oilers would also provide servicing facilities for the group's helicopters; the Type 23 would have facilities only for rearming and refuelling them.

The lessons learned in the Falklands War of 1982 altered this initial concept considerably, with the result that the design of the Type 23 grew in size and complexity to encompass the Vertical Launch Sea Wolf (VLS) system with

an extra tracking system as a defence against low-flying aircraft and sea-skimming anti-ship missiles. With the addition of Harpoon surface-to-surface missiles and a medium-calibre gun for naval gunfire support, the Type 23 evolved into a vessel that was optimized for general warfare, introducing many new technologies in the process. These included extensive measures to reduce the radar cross-section, automation to substantially reduce crew size, the installation of a CODLAG (Combined Diesel-electric and Gas) propulsion system providing very quiet running for anti-submarine operations together with excellent range, vertical launch missile technology, and a fully distributed combat management system.

VERTICAL BOOST MISSILE
The Vertical Launch Sea Wolf surface-to-air missile system was designed for and first deployed on the Type 23. Unlike the conventional Sea Wolf, the missile is boosted vertically until it clears the ship's superstructure and then turns to fly directly to the target. Consequently, the ship's structure does not cause no-fire zones that would delay or inhibit missile firing in a conventionally launched system.

Countermeasures systems include four Sea Gnat (Outfit DLB) decoys and a Type 182 towed torpedo decoy. The Sea

Gnats are mounted on Hunting Engineering 130-mm (5.1-in) six-barrel launchers. Type 23 frigates are being fitted with the BAE Systems Outfit DLH upgrade, which will allow the launch of the Siren Mk 251 active decoy round (which entered Royal Navy service in January 2004) as well as the Sea Gnat.

TOWED TORPEDO DECOY SYSTEM

The "Duke" class is fitted with the Type 2070 towed torpedo decoy system. This is being replaced with the Ultra Electronics surface ship torpedo defence (SSTD) system. *Westminster* was the first vessel to receive the system,

followed by *St Albans* in June 2008. The latter is the last of the 16 ships of the "Duke" class. Five Type 23 frigates, *Montrose*, *Monmouth*, *Iron Duke*, *Lancaster*, and *Argyll*, are employed across the normal range of standing strategic, home, and overseas commitments. These include Fleet Ready Escort duties around home waters, operational deployments to the Persian Gulf and Arabian Sea, and standing tasks in the South Atlantic, Caribbean, and within NATO's Standing Maritime Group in the Mediterranean. They will also continue to contribute to the UK's Maritime Joint Rapid Reaction Force (JRRF) held at high readiness for contingent operations.

Close-up

Much of the Type 23's operational task today involves anti-drug smuggling operations in various parts of the world, and authorized personnel working on the ships have made numerous arrests.

(1) **Merlin:** The ship's Merlin helicopter provides search-and-attack capability for ASW, as well as surface surveillance and over-the-horizon targeting for anti-surface warfare.

(2) **Decoy:** The "Duke" class is fitted with the Type 2070 towed torpedo decoy system, first fitted to *Westminster*.

(3) **Platform:** The Type 23's spacious landing platform can accommodate most types of naval helicopter in service with NATO.

(4) **Hangar:** The vessel was not originally intended to have a hangar, but one was incorporated into the design as a result of experience in the Falklands conflict.

(5) **Stealth:** Deck fittings and installations were reduced as much as possible to help reduce the warship's radar signature.

(6) Modern anti-submarine ships need to be quiet to avoid interfering with their own sonar systems, so the need to cut underwater noise was vitally important.

Kursk 1994

Prior to 12 August, 2000, the nuclear submarine *Kursk* was just another vessel in the Russian navy's fleet of "Oscar II"-class missile submarines. After that date, she was the focus of worldwide speculation and widespread condemnation.

STRUCTURE
The outer hull, made of high-nickel, high-chrome content stainless steel 8.5 mm (0.33 in) thick, has exceptionally good resistance to corrosion and a weak magnetic signature, which helps prevent detection by Magnetic Anomaly Detection (MAD) systems. There is a 2-m (6.5-ft) gap between the outer hull and the 50.8-mm (2-in) steel inner hull.

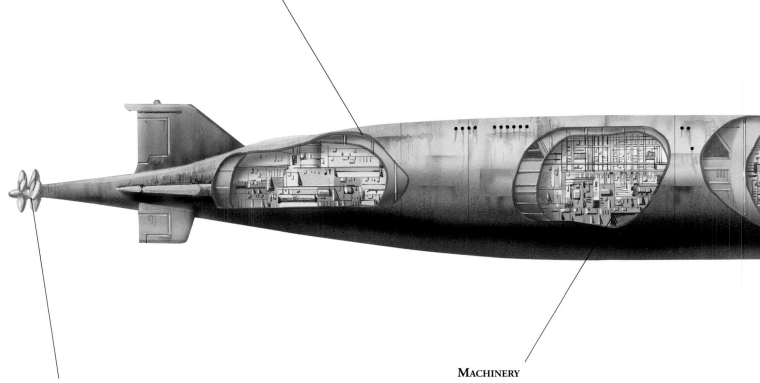

PROPELLER
The "Oscar II" is fitted with a seven-bladed propeller system, which makes it much quieter than the "Oscar I," which had a four-blade propeller.

MACHINERY
Two pressurized water-cooled reactors powering two steam turbines deliver 73,070 kW (98,000 shp) to two shafts.

ARMAMENT
The submarine-launched Granit cruise missile tubes are in banks of 12 either side of and external to the pressure hull and are inclined at 40 degrees, with one hatch covering each pair.

FIN
"Oscar II" boats have a larger fin than the "Oscar I," which makes for better handling and increases manoeuvrability when submerged.

BRIDGE
Like other Soviet submarine designs, the "Oscar" not only has a bridge open to the elements on top of the sail, but also an enclosed bridge forwards of this station in the sail for use in inclement weather.

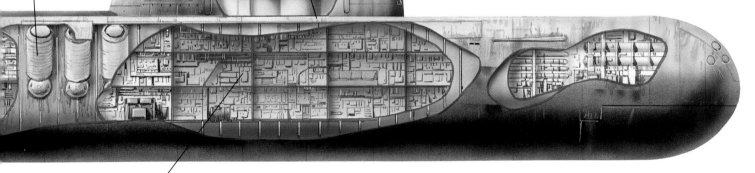

COMPARTMENTS
"Oscar II"-class submarines have at least 10 separate compartments that can be sealed off from each other in the event of accidents. The compartments are numbered in sequence from fore to aft.

KURSK – SPECIFICATION

Country of origin: Soviet Union
Type: Submarine
Laid down: 1992
Builder: Northern Machine Building Enterprise (SevMash), Severodvinsk, Russia
Launched: 1994
Commissioned: December, 1994
Fate: Sank 12 August, 2000, due to torpedo mishap
Complement: 44 officers, 68 enlisted

Dimensions:
Displacement: 14,878 tonnes (16,400 tons)
Length: 154 m (505 ft 3 in); **Beam:** 18.2 m (59 ft 9 in);

Draught: 9 m (29 ft 6 in)

Powerplant:
Propulsion: 2 nuclear reactors OK-650b, 2 steam turbines, 2 x 7-bladed propellers
Speed: (surfaced) 16 knots; (submerged) 32 knots
Range: Unlimited

Armament & Armour:
Armament: 24 x SS-N-19/P-700 Granit; 4 x 533-mm (21-in) and 2 x 650-mm (25.6-in) bow torpedo tubes
Armour: N/A

Kursk was one of 11 "Oscar II" boats built at
Severodvinsk, and was one of five assigned to the
Northern Fleet. The other six were assigned to
the Pacific Fleet. Three more were planned, but
construction was halted.

SOVIET SSBN: "DELTA I"

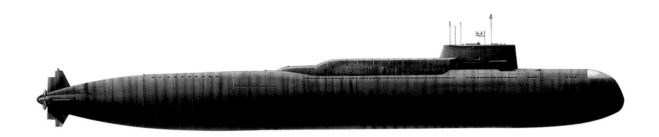

SOVIET SSBN: "DELTA III/IV"

SOVIET SSBN: "YANKEE"

"OSCAR" CLASS

The underwater equivalent of a *Kirov*-class cruiser, the first "Oscar I" class cruise missile submarine (SSGN) was laid down at Severodvinsk in 1978 and launched in the spring of 1980, starting sea trials later that year. The second was completed in 1982, and a third of the class, which became the first "Oscar II," completed in 1985, was followed by a fourth, fifth, and sixth at yearly intervals. The primary task of the "Oscar" class was to attack NATO carrier battle groups with a variety of submarine-launched cruise missiles.

The Russian designation for the "Oscar II" boats was Project 949A Antei (Anteus). *Kursk* was named after the Battle of Kursk, the largest tank battle in history, which took place in July 1943.

Kursk was laid down in 1990 at Severodvinsk, near Archangel'sk, and was one of the first vessels to be completed after the collapse of the Soviet Union. On commissioning in 1994 she was assigned to the Northern Fleet, most of whose boats were laid up at that time because of a serious lack of funding. Little work had been done to maintain anything but the most essential frontline equipment, including search-and-rescue equipment, and Northern Fleet sailors had gone unpaid in the mid-1990s. However, the end of the decade saw something of a renaissance for the fleet, with ocean deployments getting

Interior view

The largest and most heavily armed attack submarines in the world, "Oscar II"-class boats were, theoretically, able to survive one or even two torpedo hits.

1. **Periscope:** Those fitted to most Russian submarines were developed by the Lomo Company of St Petersburg.

2. **Commander:** The commander is carrying out a sweep of the horizon, an essential move before the boat surfaces.

3. **First Officer:** The first officer is in contact by telephone with another department of the boat, possibly the engine room.

4. **Crew:** A senior naval rating is standing by in case he is required to carry out a specific task.

5. **Equipment:** Even in the most modern Russian submarines, equipment has not reached the level of sophistication found in their Western counterparts.

6. **Nickname:** The "Oscar II" boats were nicknamed "Mongo" because of their size and firepower.

An "Oscar II"-class boat is pictured on the surface in a northern Russian inlet. During the Cold War, keeping track of Soviet submarines slipping out into the Atlantic consumed huge resources.

under way once more, and in 1999 *Kursk* deployed to the Mediterranean on attachment to the Russian Fifth Eskadra, where her task was to track the movements of the U.S. Sixth Fleet during the Kosovo conflict.

DISASTER IN THE BARENTS SEA

August 2000 saw *Kursk* operating in northern waters again, and in August she sailed to take part in a major exercise – the first since the collapse of the Soviet Union nine years earlier. The exercise involved four attack submarines, the Northern Fleet flagship *Pyotr Velikiy*, and many smaller craft in the Barents Sea. On 12 August, at 11:28 local time, there was an explosion while the crew prepared to fire torpedoes. The officially accepted explanation was that the explosion was caused by the detonation of high-test peroxide (HTP), used as a torpedo propellant. This was followed by a second, more powerful explosion, equivalent to between 4.5–6.3 tonnes (5–7 tons), which hurled large pieces of debris back through the submarine.

The submarine sank in relatively shallow water at a depth of 108 m (350 ft), about 135 km (85 miles) from Severomorsk. As news of the accident became known in the West, Britain and Norway immediately offered to send rescue teams, but this offer was declined by the Russian leadership. The Russians claimed that all 118 crew had been killed, but it was later established that 24 men had survived for some time, as notes found on the body of an officer testified.

The Russian admiralty issued some extraordinary statements in the immediate aftermath of the disaster, even claiming that it had been caused by a collision with NATO submarine said to have been in the area.

The salvage operation that took place in September 2001 was a delicate one. There were fears that the essential process of cutting away the bow using a tungsten-carbide studded cable before the boat could be lifted might trigger further explosions, as the tool could potentially ignite any pockets of volatile gas such as hydrogen that remained trapped inside.

The operation was successfully completed, however. The recovered portion of the *Kursk* was towed to Severomorsk and placed in a floating drydock where extensive forensic work was carried out. The bow section was raised by the Russians, who at last were forced to admit the real reasons behind the accident.

Seawolf (SSN-21) 1995

Seawolf-class submarines were designed to operate autonomously against the world's most capable submarine and surface threats. The primary mission of the *Seawolf* was to destroy Soviet ballistic missile submarines before they could attack American targets.

ELECTRONICS
Seawolf's electronics suite can integrate into a naval battle group's infrastructure, or shift rapidly into a land-battle support role.

PERISCOPES
Seawolf has two main periscopes, mounted in a sail that is specially strengthened for operations under the Arctic ice cap.

ARMAMENT
Seawolf has an eight-tube, double-deck torpedo room, enabling the boat to engage multiple threats. *Seawolf* has twice as many torpedo tubes and its weapons magazine is one-third larger in size than the earlier *Los Angeles*-class submarines.

SPECIAL OPERATIONS
The third *Seawolf*-class submarine, *Jimmy Carter*, is capable of supporting Special Operations Forces with provision for operating the Dry Deck Shelter (DDS) and Advanced SEAL Delivery System (ASDS). The DDS is an air-transportable device that piggybacks on the submarine and can be used to store and launch a swimmer delivery vehicle as well as combat swimmers.

MACHINERY
Seawolf is powered by one S6W reactor and is an extremely quiet boat with a very high tactical speed (the speed at which a submarine is still quiet enough to remain undetected while tracking enemy submarines effectively).

HULL
Construction of the *Seawolf*-class submarines relies on a new welding material to join the steel into plates, hull subsections, and large cylindrical sections. Their hulls are made entirely of high-pressure HY-100 steel. Previous submarine classes were made with HY-80 steel.

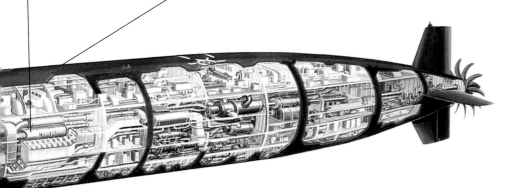

SEAWOLF – SPECIFICATION

Country of origin: USA
Type: Submarine
Laid down: 25 October, 1989
Builder: General Dynamics Electric Boat, Connecticut
Launched: 24 June, 1995
Commissioned: 19 July, 1997. Still in service
Complement: 15 officers, 101 enlisted

Dimensions:
Displacement: (surfaced) 7802 tonnes (8600 tons); (submerged) 8290 tonnes (9138 tons)
Length: 108 m (353 ft); **Beam:** 12 m (40 ft);
   Draught: 11 m (36 ft)

Powerplant:
Propulsion: One S6W pressurized water-cooled reactor powering steam turbines delivering 33.6 MW (45,000 hp)
Speed: (submerged) 35 knots; (silent) 25 knots
Range: Unlimited

Armament & Armour:
Armament: 8 x 660-mm (26-in) torpedo tubes (with up to 50 Tomahawk cruise missiles; Mk 48 ADCAP torpedoes or 100 mines)
Armour: Unavailable

The approximate equivalent of *Seawolf* in the British Royal Navy is *Astute*, which was launched in 2007. She is armed with Tomahawk cruise missiles and, because her systems can purify both air and water, she can theoretically circumnavigate the globe without surfacing. In fact, her endurance is limited only by the amount of supplies she can carry.

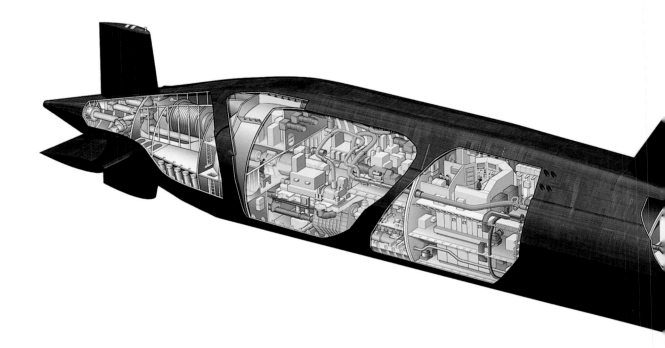

BRITISH SSN: *ASTUTE*

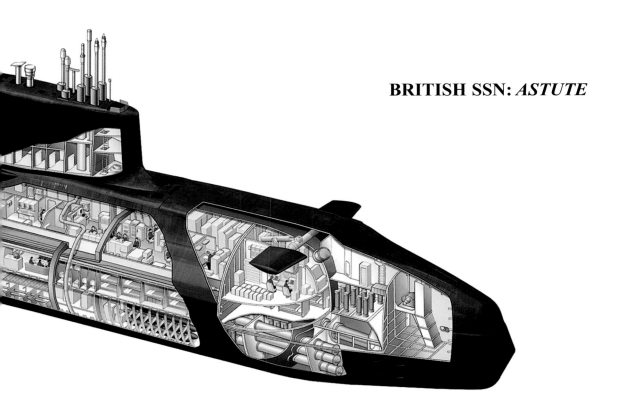

SEAWOLF CLASS

The *Seawolf* class was originally designed to counter the rapidly increasing capabilities of the Soviet submarine force projected for the 1990s and beyond. Quiet, fast, and well armed with advanced sensors, their primary purpose was to deploy to forward ocean areas to search out and destroy enemy submarines and surface ships, and to attack land targets. The robust design of the submarines enables them to perform a variety of crucial assignments from underneath the Arctic ice pack to littoral regions anywhere in the world. Their missions include surveillance, intelligence collection, special warfare, covert cruise-missile strike, mine warfare, and anti-submarine and anti-surface ship warfare.

The Seawolf *(SSN-21) is photographed travelling at speed on the surface. As indicated by the massive and turbulent wake, nuclear submarines are not meant for surface travel; their true environment is deep underwater.*

When Ronald Reagan became president in 1981, he was determined to reverse what most military people regarded as the decline in America's ability to defend itself against the Soviet Union.

The commanders of the U.S. Navy's submarine fleet advised the new president to go on the offensive. This meant penetrating the "bastions" of the USSR to engage Soviet submarines, rather than waiting behind defensive barriers until the Russians chose their moment to attack.

One result of this new policy was the development of *Seawolf*. The design that emerged had eight launch tubes, positioned just ahead of the forwards bulkhead of the pressure hull, and stowage for 50 torpedoes or anti-ship missiles. Its machinery was much quieter than that installed in the earlier *Los Angeles* class (with which U.S. submariners had expressed much dissatisfaction), and it

was more compact. The pumpjet propulsor would reduce cavitation (the formation of bubbles in the wake), reducing noise levels and still leaving the new SSN capable of 35 knots underwater. The new S6W reactor produced a power output of 33.6 MW (50,000 hp), while the electronics suite included the new BSY-2 command system, a spherical receiving sonar array, a linear transmitting array wrapped around the bow, the new TB-16E and TB-29 towed arrays, and other sensors.

FULLY INTEGRATED COMBAT SYSTEM
The BSY-2 is the U.S. Navy's first fully integrated submarine combat system, with all the sensors, data processors, consoles, and weapon controls riding the same high-capacity fibre-optic databus. The consoles can be switched among the various command and control tasks, and the bus can handle 1000 messages per second. The whole system is so complex that it requires nearly 600 litres (157 gallons) of chilled water per minute to cool it.

Seawolf is claimed to make less noise at a tactical speed of 25 knots than *Los Angeles* does when laid up beside a pier. Originally, 29 *Seawolf*s were planned for production, but with the end of the Cold War, the cost was judged to be prohibitively high and only three were built in favour of the smaller *Virginia* class, which are about 10 percent cheaper.

UNPRECEDENTED SPEED

Seawolf was launched on 24 June, 1995, and began initial sea trials in July 1996. She demonstrated unprecedented speed during her first trial. Following delivery, *Seawolf* began acoustic trials, which were completed in November 1997. The second boat in the class, *Connecticut* (SSN-22) went to sea in 1998. The third and final *Seawolf*-class submarine, *Jimmy Carter* (SSN-23), was launched in 2004 and is outfitted with an additional hull section. This lengthens the ship for special missions and research and development projects. *Jimmy Carter* is roughly 30 m (98 ft) longer than the other two ships of her class. This is due to the insertion of a plug (additional section) known as the MMP (Multi-Mission Platform), which allows the launch and recovery of remotely controlled vehicles and special forces. *Jimmy Carter* also has additional manoeuvring devices fitted fore and aft that allow it to keep station over selected targets in odd currents. In the past, submarines fitted with these devices were used to intercept communications by tapping into underwater cables.

Interior view

Nuclear submarines are generally fitted with two escape trunks, one situated forward and the other aft. Each trunk can accommodate two crew members at a time.

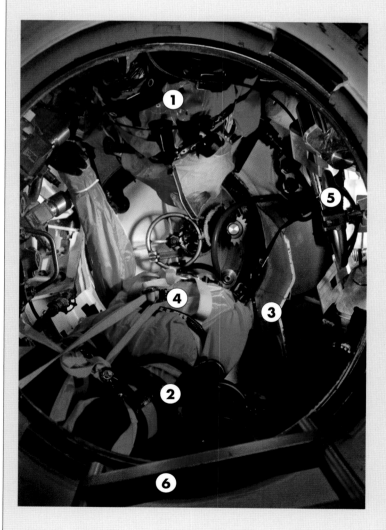

1 **Pressure Vessel:** The escape trunk is composed of a pressure vessel about 2.4 m (8 ft) tall and 1.5 m (5 ft) in diameter, which is something of a tight squeeze.

2 **Immersion Suits:** The crew are provided with immersion suits, bright red in colour for ease of identification and location.

3 **Steinke Hood:** Crew members use a "Steinke hood," a combination of life jacket and breathing apparatus that fits over the head.

4 **Hatch:** The top is a hatch capable of withstanding the same pressure as the hull of the boat.

5 **Air port:** There is an air port on the side of the trunk from which sailors charge their Steinke hoods prior to escape.

6 **Supplies:** In harbour, supplies and equipment are often loaded in the boat by way of the escape trunks.

Ocean 1995

Designated as an Amphibious Assault Ship or LPH (Landing Platform Helicopter), *Ocean* is the only vessel of her class in the British Royal Navy and is currently the largest vessel in the fleet. She will remain so until the deployment of the new *Queen Elizabeth*-class aircraft carriers.

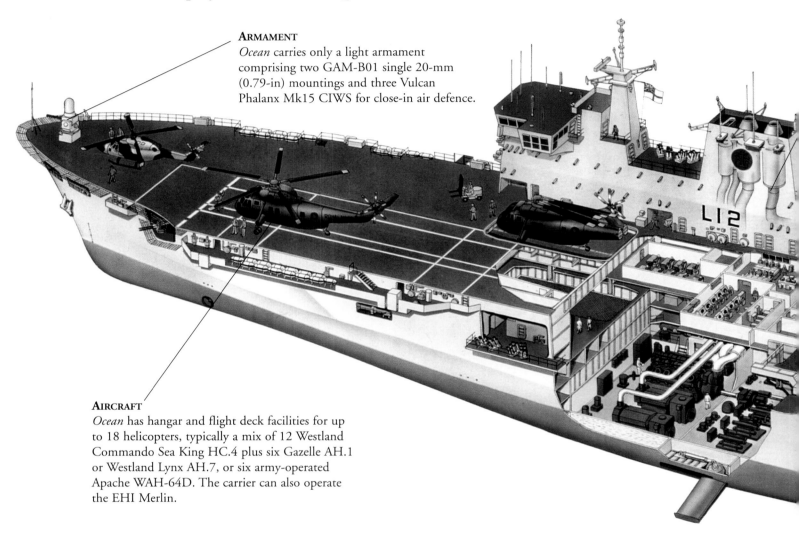

ARMAMENT
Ocean carries only a light armament comprising two GAM-B01 single 20-mm (0.79-in) mountings and three Vulcan Phalanx Mk15 CIWS for close-in air defence.

AIRCRAFT
Ocean has hangar and flight deck facilities for up to 18 helicopters, typically a mix of 12 Westland Commando Sea King HC.4 plus six Gazelle AH.1 or Westland Lynx AH.7, or six army-operated Apache WAH-64D. The carrier can also operate the EHI Merlin.

OCEAN – SPECIFICATION

Country of origin: United Kingdom
Type: Amphibious assault ship
Laid down: 30 May, 1994
Builder: Vickers Shipbuilding and Engineering Ltd, Scotland
Launched: 11 October, 1995
Commissioned: 30 September, 1998. Still in service.
Complement: 284 officers and crew, 206 Fleet Air Arm

Dimensions:
Displacement: 19,575 tonnes (21,578 tons)
Length: 208 m (682 ft 3 in)
Beam: 34.4 m (112 ft 10 in)
Draught: 6.6 m (21 ft 8 in)

Powerplant:
Propulsion: 2 x Crossley Pielstick diesel engines
Speed: 18 knots
Range: 12,964 (7000 nm)

Armament & Armour:
Armament: 2 x GAM-B01 single 20-mm (0.79-in) mountings; 3 x Vulcan Phalanx Mk15 CIWS
Armour: N/A
Boats and landing craft: 4 x Mk 5B Landing Craft Vehicle Personnel (LCVP)
Aircraft carried: Up to 18 helicopters (typically Westland Commando and Lynx, but also Merlins, Boeing Chinooks, Westland Apache); capable of carrying up to 15 Harrier II

COMMAND CENTRE
The operations complex amidships comprises three primary tactical areas: the Operations Room (where the real-time tactical picture is compiled and displayed); the Amphibious Operations Room; and the Main Communications Office (MCO).

ACCOMMODATION
When fully loaded *Ocean* can accommodate 803 troops plus their equipment, artillery, vehicles, and stores, supported by 12 support helicopters, six attack helicopters, and four Landing Craft Vehicle Personnel (LCVP) Mk 5 landing craft.

F A C T S

- Built in the mid-1990s by Kvaerner Govan Ltd on the River Clyde.

- Commissioned in September 1998 at Devonport, Plymouth, Devon.

- Has a normal maximum speed of 18 knots.

- Underwent a long refit in 2007.

- Is capable of limited anti-submarine warfare tasks in addition to her primary role.

MACHINERY
Ocean is powered by two Crossley Pielstick 16PC2.6 V 400 two-shaft diesels developing a sustained output of 17.8 MW (23,904 hp). The vessel has Kamewa fixed-pitch propellers and a bow thruster.

HULL
The hull is based on that of the *Invincible* class with a modified superstructure. The deck is strong enough to take RAF Chinook helicopters. The are six landing and six parking spots for helicopters. The hull was built on the River Clyde by Kvaerner Govan Ltd and sailed under its own power to Vickers at Barrow in November 1996 for fitting out and the installation of military equipment.

One of *Ocean*'s main functions to date has been to provide relief in disaster areas. For example, while undergoing her warm-water trials in the Caribbean, she provided humanitarian assistance to hurricane-devastated Honduras.

AMERICAN ASSAULT SHIP: *IWO JIMA*

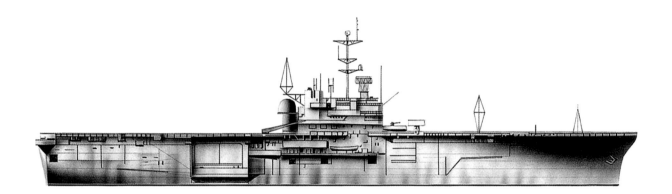

FRENCH ASSAULT SHIP: *MISTRAL*

SOVIET AIRCRAFT CARRIER: *KIEV*

ITALIAN HELICOPTER CRUISER: *VITTORIO VENETO*

OCEAN

The 1982 Falklands War proved that the amphibious task force was still one of the most effective methods of projecting power over long distances, just as it was in the Pacific during World War II. Indeed, in the case of the Falklands it was the only means of force projection at Britain's disposal. That conflict also highlighted one major disadvantage of the amphibious assault – it was relatively slow in its approach to its objective, and vulnerable in the disembarkation phase. The answer was to provide the fleet with one or more vessels classified as Amphibious Assault Ships Helicopter, like *Ocean*.

Because *Ocean* was built to commercial standards, in order to save money, she has a projected operational life of only 20 years. This is significantly less than that of other warships.

The Amphibious Helicopter Carrier was originally conceived in the mid-1980s to provide the sort of amphibious assault capabilities previously fulfilled by the commando carriers *Albion* and *Bulwark*. *Ocean* was commissioned on 30 September, 1998, completing her trials programme and initial basic operational sea training in the spring of 1999. The ship's primary role is to carry an Embarked Military Force (EMF) supported by 12 medium-support helicopters, six attack helicopters, and four Landing Craft Vehicle Personnel (LCVP) Mk 5 landing craft. Her secondary roles include afloat training, a limited anti-submarine warfare platform, and a base for anti-terrorist operations.

Vehicles and stores are loaded through a starboard quarter ramp, and the deck can take six 105-mm (4.1-in) light guns and up to 40 assorted military vehicles. A ramp from the vehicle deck to the flight deck allows equipment

Interior view

Ocean's role within NATO is illustrated in this photograph, which shows U.S. Marines on board during a NATO exercise.

① **Elevator:** *Ocean's* massive elevators give ready access to the flight deck for personnel, equipment, and stores.

② **Marines:** The U.S. Marines here belong to the 26th Marine Expeditionary Unit (Special Operations Capable), which operates closely with British commando forces.

③ **Uniform:** The marines are kitted out for a NATO exercise in Turkey, code-named Northern Approach.

④ **Group:** The function of this group of marines is to go ashore and secure the landing areas. The group is designated Lima Company, Battalion Landing Team 3/8.

⑤ **Structure:** The structure of *Ocean* is designed to meet the requirements of Lloyds Register of Shipping, pioneering the use of commercial standards in the Royal Navy.

⑥ **EMF:** The bulk of the Embarked Military Force (EMF) is accommodated forwards, with assault routes running directly to the hangar assembly areas.

All aspects of Ocean*'s capability are to be seen in this photograph, with a Sea King helicopter overhead and landing craft in the water around the Landing Platform Helicopter (LPH).*

to be flown ashore by helicopter. At anchor, vehicles can also be unloaded through the ship's stern ramp onto Mexifloats, then transferred ashore.

SECONDARY ROLE

In her secondary role, *Ocean* can embark, support, and deploy an anti-submarine warfare helicopter squadron of up to 12 Merlin or Sea King helicopters when operating in close conjunction with an *Invincible*-class carrier. Alternatively, she can be used as a base for maritime counter-terrorist operations, to support afloat flying training or as a ferry for Sea Harrier aircraft. However, she is not equipped to fly the Harrier in an operational role.

Ocean's first operational deployment was in 2000, when her Embarked Military Force (EMF) supported operations in Sierra Leone, aiding the suppression of rebel activity and providing support facilities for the Spearhead battalion ashore. On 17 February, 2002, *Ocean* made some rather unfortunate headlines when a unit of her Royal Marines engaged in a night exercise mistakenly landed on the beach at the Spanish town of La Linea instead of

neighbouring Gibraltar, where they were supposed to be, causing a minor diplomatic incident. In the following year, she deployed as part of a large Royal Navy task force in support of Operation Telic, the UK contribution to the invasion of Iraq.

BUDGETARY CONSTRAINTS

An invitation to bid for the building of the new helicopter carrier that was to become *Ocean* was tendered in 1992, but the project was almost immediately threatened with cancellation because of budgetary constraints. She was reprieved mainly because of Britain's involvement in NATO operations in the Balkans, during which the Royal Fleet Auxiliary's aviation training ship *Argus* was pressed into service as a Landing Platform Helicopter. *Argus* proved totally unsuitable in terms of accommodation and facilities needed for a large Embarked Military Force. This fact emphasized the need for a purpose-built platform. As a result, on 29 March, 1993, the defence procurement minister announced that development of the new Landing Platform Helicopter was to proceed.

Visby 2000

The *Visby*-class corvette is the latest class of corvette to be deployed with the Royal Swedish Navy after the *Göteborg* and *Stockholm* classes. The vessel has many stealth features, and the first two ships became operational early in 2010.

AIRCRAFT
Visby can carry one helicopter such as the AgustaWestland A109M. A helicopter hangar was originally planned, but was deleted because it was considered too cramped.

STRUCTURE
The hull is constructed with a sandwich design consisting of a PVC core with a carbon fibre and vinyl laminate. Its angular design reduces its radar signature.

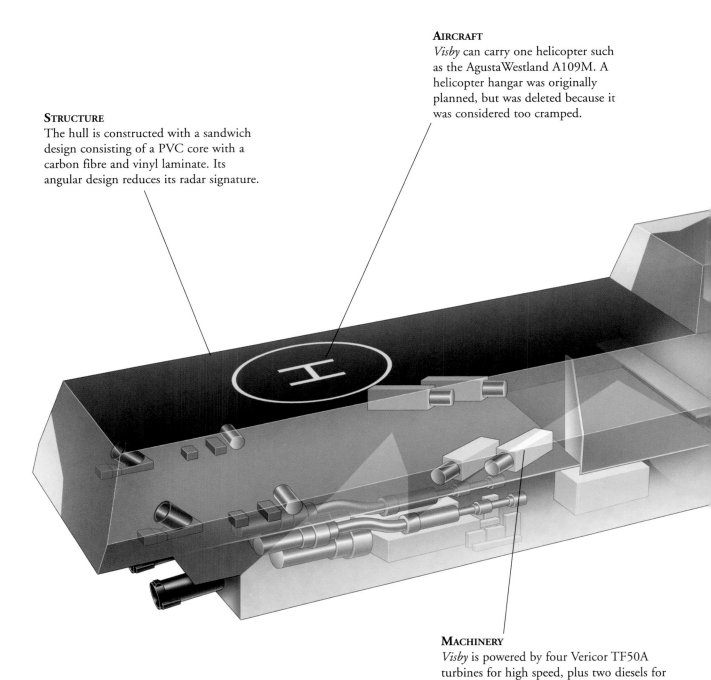

MACHINERY
Visby is powered by four Vericor TF50A turbines for high speed, plus two diesels for low speed with double flexible mountings, with encapsulated noise-absorbant housings.

SYSTEMS
Visby carries hull-mounted, variable-depth and towed-array sonar systems. The vessel is fitted with a Condor CS-3701 Tactical Radar Surveillance System and a Ceros 200 fire control radar system.

ARMAMENT
Visby was designed to carry eight RBS15 anti-ship missiles, mines and depth charges, and vertical-launch surface-to-air missiles, but it was decided not to install the latter. A rapid-firing 57-mm (2.24-in) Bofors gun is mounted.

F A C T S

- *Visby* is named after the principal city on the island of Gotland.

- The class was originally designed to be divided into two subcategories where some ships were optimized for surface combat and others for submarine hunting.

- *Visby* was launched in 2000.

- There are five ships in the class, the others being *Helsingborg*, *Härnösand*, *Nyköping*, and *Karlstad*.

- There was a delay of almost 10 years between the first ship being launched and the first two being delivered.

ROVs
The corvette is equipped with a compartment for housing and launching remotely controlled vehicles (ROVs) for hunting and destroying mines.

VISBY – SPECIFICATION

Country of origin: Sweden
Type: Corvette
Laid down: 17 February, 1995
Builder: Kockums AB, Sweden
Launched: 2000
Commissioned: N/A
Complement: 27 officers, 16 conscripts

Dimensions:
Displacement: 590 tonnes (650 tons)
Length: 72.6 m (238 ft)
Beam: 10.4 m (34 ft)
Draught: 2.5 m (8.2 ft)

Powerplant:
Propulsion: CODAG, 2 x Honeywell TF 50 A gas turbines, total rating 16 MW (21,446 shp), 2 x MTU Friedrichshafen 16V 2000 N90 diesel engines, total rating 2.6 MW (2385 shp)
Speed: 40 knots
Range: Not specified

Armament & Armour:
Armament: 1 x 57-mm (2.24-in) Mk3 gun; 8 x RBS15 Mk 2 anti-ship missile; plus mines and depth charges
Armour: N/A
Aircraft: Helicopter pad

The *Visby* class experienced exceptional delays between launch and delivery. By 2008, the only weapons system that had been integrated and tested on the *Visby* was the Bofors gun.

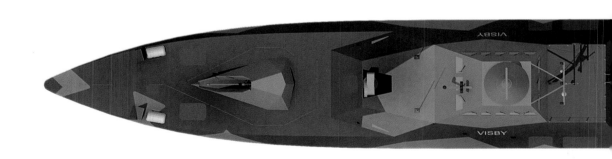

VISBY

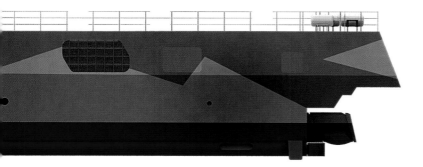

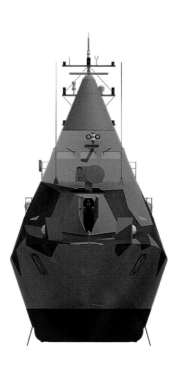

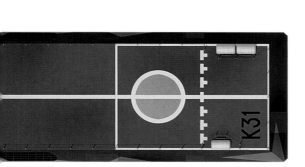

SWEDISH SURFACE WARSHIPS

Since the 1980s, Swedish surface warships have been named after Swedish cities, hence the nomenclature of *Visby* and her sister ships. Submarines are named after Swedish provinces, and minehunters after Swedish lighthouses. The surface ships are mostly small, a configuration dictated by the relatively shallow and confined waters of the Baltic Sea, relying on agility and flexibility to fulfill their tasks. In 1972 the Swedish government decided to scrap all military protection of merchant shipping to enable the decommissioning of destroyers and frigates. This limited the endurance of the navy considerably, but the use of smaller short-range ships was at the time deemed adequate by the government for anti-shipping missions along the coast and in the archipelago.

Looking very futuristic, the Helsingborg *(K32) is pictured slicing through the Baltic in a plume of spray. The barrel of the gun is folded back into the turret. The hull is constructed with a sandwich design consisting of a PVC core with a carbon fibre and vinyl laminate.*

Construction began in 1996 at Kockums' Kalrskrona yard. The *Visby* (K31) was launched in June 2000 and was delivered to the FMV (the Swedish Defence Materiel Administration) in June 2002 for fitting with weapons and combat systems.

From the outset, the design of the *Visby*-class corvettes placed heavy emphasis on stealth technology. *Visby* was the lead vessel and was launched in 2000. However, the entire progamme was immediately beset by a succession of delays, caused not least by a reduction of funding caused by the apparent end of the Cold War. It was not until 2009 that *Visby* and a second vessel, *Helsingborg* (K32), were delivered to the Royal Swedish Navy. Even then, they lacked some of their planned weapon systems, resulting in a much reduced operational capability.

Much of the design of the *Visby* class was based on experience gained with an experimental ship, *Smyge*. The hull consists of a sandwich design comprising a PVC core with a carbon fibre and vinyl laminate, and its angular design greatly reduces the radar signature. Stealth

technology is also applied to other areas. For example, the barrel of the 57-mm (2.24-in) Bofors cannon can be folded into the turret to reduce its cross-section.

The *Visby* class was originally intended to be divided into two subcategories, one optimized for surface combat and the other for submarine hunting, but the roles were combined because of funding economies. The corvettes are equipped with a helicopter platform for operating general purpose/ASW helicopter such as the AgustaWestland A109M. A helicopter hangar was originally planned, but was deleted during the design phase because it was considered to be too cramped.

INTEGRATION AND TESTING

Fitting out and completion of the *Visby* corvettes has been slow. By 2008, eight years after launch, the only weapon system that had been integrated and tested on the *Visby* was the Bofors gun. The weapon has a fully automatic loading system containing 120 rounds of ready-to-fire ammunition and fires up to 220 rounds a minute to a maximum range of 17,000 m (10.5 miles). The integration and testing of the torpedo system remained incomplete when *Visby* was delivered in 2009, as was integration of the vessel's intended anti-ship missile, the RBS-15. The missile has a high subsonic speed, Mach 0.9, and is armed with a 200-kg (441-lb) warhead. The missiles will be installed belowdecks and fired through special hatches to maintain the vessel's stealth. The missiles' exhaust plumes will be dispersed in separate canals.

MINEHUNTING ROLE

The *Visby* class is equipped to carry Saab Bofors Underwater system ROVs (remotely operated vehicles) for mine hunting, and the Atlas Elektronik Seafox ROV for mine disposal. The minehunting ROVs are a development of the Double Eagle Mk III. The *Visby* corvettes are being fitted with the Hydra multi-sonar suite from General Dynamics Canada (formerly Computing Devices Canada), which integrates data from a Hydroscience Technologies passive towed array sonar, C-Tech CVDS-26 dual-frequency active variable depth sonar (VDS), C-Tech CHMS-90 hull-mounted sonar and data from the ROVs.

All systems were expected to be fully integrated in 2010–13, but full operational capability was not expected until 2013.

Interior view

A key feature of the *Visby*-class corvettes is their fully automated control centre, designed to reduce the number of crew members and cut costs.

(1) Command and Control: The vessel's CETRIS C³ (command, control, and communications) system consists of the Saab Systems 9LV Mk3E combat management system.

(2) Open System: The 9LV Mk3 is based on open system architecture and uses the Windows NT operating system.

(3) Communications: The communications system has a high-capacity digital communications switch, developed by Danish company Maersk Data Defence.

(4) Radio Links: The system provides internal communications or open conference lines and access to external communications with various radio links.

(5) TRSS: The CS-3701 tactical radar surveillance system (TRSS) provides electronic support measures (ESM) and radar warning receiver (RWR) functions.

(6) Integration: The SaabTech CEROS 200 fire control system will be fully integrated into the combat management system.

Daring Type 45 2006

The Type 45 destroyer is a state-of-the-art air defence destroyer programme, designed to replace the Type 42 destroyers in service with the British Royal Navy. The Type 45s are also known as the *Daring* class after the lead ship of the same name.

STEALTH FEATURES

The Type 45 incorporates signature reduction features, including the elimination of right angles and reduced equipment on deck. The infrared signature is reduced by cooling devices on the funnels.

AIR DEFENCE

The Type 45 design uses the Principal Anti-Air Missile System (PAAMS), a joint British, French, and Italian design. The PAAMS system is able to control and coordinate several missiles in the air at once.

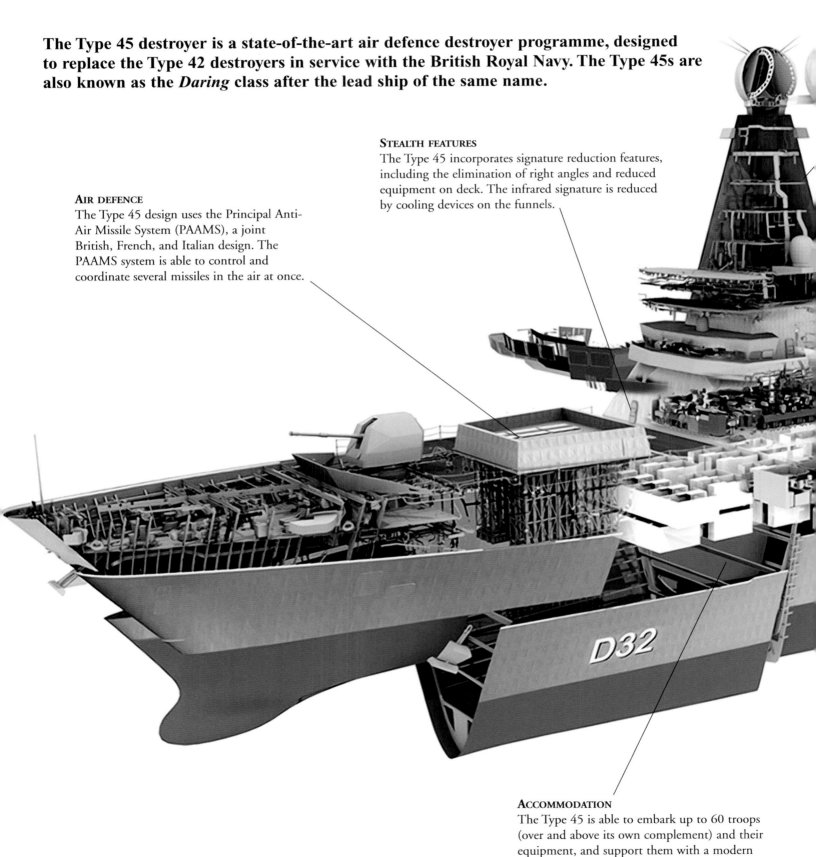

ACCOMMODATION

The Type 45 is able to embark up to 60 troops (over and above its own complement) and their equipment, and support them with a modern medical facility that can provide surgical capability.

RADAR

Daring's SAMPSON radar is said to be capable of tracking an object the size of a tennis ball traveling at three times the speed of sound.

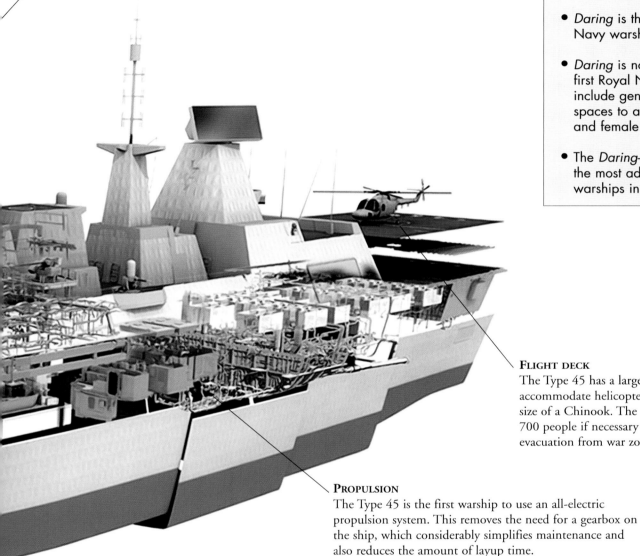

FLIGHT DECK

The Type 45 has a large flight deck that can accommodate helicopters up to and including the size of a Chinook. The ship can also take up to 700 people if necessary to support a civilian evacuation from war zones or natural disasters.

PROPULSION

The Type 45 is the first warship to use an all-electric propulsion system. This removes the need for a gearbox on the ship, which considerably simplifies maintenance and also reduces the amount of layup time.

DARING TYPE 45 – SPECIFICATION

Country of origin: United Kingdom
Type: Guided missile destroyer
Laid down: 28 March, 2003
Builder: BAE Systems Surface Ships
Launched: 1 February, 2006
Commissioned: 23 July, 2009
Complement: 190

Dimensions:
Displacement: (deep load) 8092 tonnes (9000 tons)
Length: 152.4 m (500 ft)
Beam: 21.2 m (69.5 ft)
Draught: 7.4 m (16.4 ft)

Powerplant:
Propulsion: 2 x Rolls-Royce WR-21 gas turbines producing 21.5 MW (28,819 shp), 2 Converteam electric motors producing 20 MW (26,808 shp)
Speed: 29 knots
Range: 12,964 km (7000 nm) at economical speed

Armament & Armour:
Armament: 1 x PAAMS Air Defence System SYLVER CLS of Aster 15 and Aster 30 missiles; 2 x Phalanx CIWS; 1 x BAE 115-mm (4.5-in) Mk 8 mod 1 gun; 2 x 30-mm (1.18-in) guns
Armour: N/A
Aircraft: 1 x Lynx HMA8 or 1 x Westland Merlin HM1 helicopter

The Type 45 may be fitted with cruise missiles in the future, should the need arise. The most likely candidate is a naval version of the Storm Shadow missile, already operated by the RAF.

EVOLUTION OF THE DESTROYER

Since World War II, the destroyer has evolved from a torpedo-armed, all-gun surface warfare vessel into a specialist anti-air or anti-submarine ship, capable of either independent operations for a short time or of operating as an escort in a task force. The losses suffered by the Royal Navy's destroyers during the Falklands War proved to NATO that the UK's minimally armed warships, which had been constructed to satisfy constraints imposed by the UK Treasury, were extremely vulnerable in a conventional war, let alone the nuclear scenarios that were then proposed for any future conflict in the North Atlantic theatre of operations. Any new design would have to be completely fit for purpose, as the Type 45s are.

TYPE 45

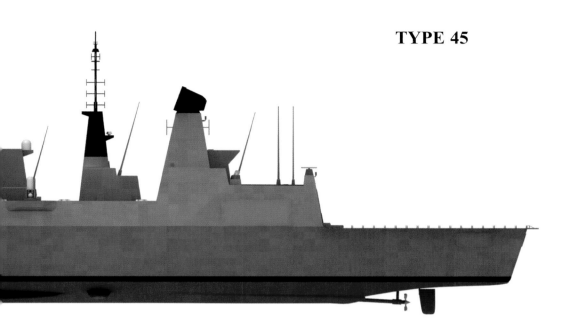

The *Daring* class destroyers are significantly larger than the Type 42s that they replaced, displacing about 7350 tonnes (8101 tons) compared to 5200 tonnes (5732 tons) of the Type 42. Their range is also about one-third greater, thanks to their advanced propulsion system.

Launched on 1 February, 2006, *Daring* (D32) successfully completed her stage one sea trials in 2007. Of the other ships in the class, *Dauntless, Diamond, Dragon*, and *Defender* were respectively launched between 2007 and 2009, with the sixth, *Duncan*, expected to follow in October 2010. The Type 45 destroyers will provide the backbone of the Royal Navy's air defences for the first half of the twenty-first century, and will be able to engage targets simultaneously and defend aircraft carriers or groups of ships against the strongest future threats from the air.

Close-up

Daring is seen here under construction at BAe Systems, Scotstoun, on the River Clyde. She is claimed to be the most advanced air defence warship in the world.

(1) **Gantry:** The warship is surrounded by a large gantry, or cradle, that is a prominent feature of every ship construction yard.

(2) **Main Armament:** *Daring*'s main gun armament of one 114-mm (4.5-in) gun is being lowered into position at the forwards end of the ship.

(3) **Secondary Armament:** *Daring*'s gun armament also comprises two 30-mm (1.18-in) weapons, mounted on either side amidships.

(4) **Radar:** The Type 45's SAMPSON radar system is slowly taking shape. The structure will eventually be fully enclosed.

(5) **Stealth:** Even at this stage in her construction, *Daring*'s angular stealth features are clearly visible.

(6) **Missile Launch:** Just behind the forwards gun turret mounting, not visible here, is the vertical launch system for the ship's short- and long-range missiles.

Despite their angular appearance, the Daring-*class Type 45s are handsome vessels. Throughout the years, seven classes of warship have carried the name* Daring.

A versatile design, the Type 45 will provide unprecedented detection and defence and will contribute to worldwide maritime and joint operations in multi-threat environments, providing a specialist air-warfare capability.

Daring's main armament is the Principal Anti-Air Missile System, a surface-to-air missile system developed under a tri-national programme by France, Italy, and the UK. This advanced weapons system will defend the Type 45, her consorts, and other task force vessels against highly manoeuvrable hostile incoming aircraft approaching at subsonic and supersonic speed, individually or in salvoes. The Type 45 could also accommodate cruise missiles and anti-ballistic missile systems should this requirement be identified in the future. The Type 45 will be able to operate a helicopter up to the size of a Chinook or Merlin, but will initially operate with Westland Lynx HMA.8 helicopters armed with Stingray torpedoes.

ALL-ELECTRIC PROPULSION SYSTEM
The Type 45 is the first warship to use an all-electric propulsion system. This removes the need for a gearbox on the ship, which considerably simplifies maintenance and should thus reduce the amount of layup time the ships experience. It also means that either of the turbines can be used to run the ship alone at a lower speed; higher speeds are achievable by simply starting up the other turbines. Combined with the use of highly efficient WR21 gas turbines, this is expected to make the Type 45s highly fuel-efficient, reducing their life cycle costs. As a result of this engine efficiency, the Type 45 has a range of some 12,964 km (7000 nm), as compared to the Type 42's 7408 km (4000 nm). During sea trials in August 2007, *Daring* reached her design speed of 29 knots in 70 seconds and achieved a speed of 31.5 knots in 120 seconds.

DESIGNED FOR STEALTH
Operationally, one of the Type 45's outstanding attributes is stealth. The design of the Type 45 brings unprecedentedly low levels of radar signature to the Royal Navy. Deck equipment has been reduced to produce a very clean superstructure similar to that of the French *La Fayette* class of frigates. Berthing equipment and life rafts are concealed behind superstructure panels and, externally, the mast is very sparingly equipped, reducing the clutter that increases the radar signature.

Glossary

AA Anti-aircraft, as in 'anti-aircraft artillery' (AAA); air-to-air, as in 'air-to-air missile' (AAM).

Ahead; Astern Forward; backward (in reverse).

ASW Anti-submarine warfare.

Axial fire Gunfire ahead or astern, along the major axis of the vessel.

Ballast The weight added to a ship or boat to bring her to the desired level of floatation and to increase stability. Originally in the form of gravel, later metal and sometimes concrete, now more commonly water, which latter has the advantage of being easy to remove and replace.

Barbette Originally an open-topped armoured enclosure, inside which a gun was mounted on a turntable. The addition of an armoured hood, which rotated with the gun mount, turned it into a turret. Latterly, the fixed (armoured) cylinder upon which a turret rotated.

Battlecruiser The made-up designation for a hybrid warship armed like a battleship but sacrificing passive protection in the form of armour plate for speed.

Battleship Originally the biggest and most powerful ships of the fleet, mounting guns of usually 10 in (254 mm) or larger calibre (the biggest were those of the Japanese Yamato class, which were 18.1 in (460 mm), and heavily armoured.

Beam The width of a ship's hull.

Bofors A Swedish armaments manufacturer, best known for its 40 mm anti-aircraft gun. First produced in the 1930s and adopted widely from 1942, the recoil-actuated 40mm L/60 Bofors was the most effective weapon of its type; improved versions were still in production at the end of the 20th century.

Boom A spar used to extend the foot of a sail; also a floating barrier, usually across the entrance to a harbour.

Breech block The removeable part of a gun's breech, through which projectile and charge could be loaded.

Calibre The diameter of the bore of a gun barrel; the number of times that diameter fits into the length of the barrel, expressed as 'L/(calibre)'; eg, a gun of 10 in bore with a barrel 300 in long would be described as '10 in L/30', or just '10 in/30'.

Clipper An ultimately meaningless term used to describe any fast sailing ship, particularly one engaged in the grain, opium or tea trades, widely used in the mid-19th century.

Cruiser A warship, larger than a frigate or destroyer, much more heavily armed and often armoured to some degree, intended for independent action or to act as a scout for the battlefleet.

Displacement A measure of the actual total weight of a vessel and all she contains obtained by calculating the volume of water she displaces.

Draught (also Draft) The measure of the depth of water required to float a ship, or how much she 'draws'.

Dreadnought The generic name given to a battleship modelled after HMS *Dreadnought*, the first with all-big-gun armament; it fell into disuse once all capital ships were of this form.

Forecastle Originally the superstructure erected at the bows of a ship to serve as a fighting platform, later the (raised) forward portion and the space beneath it, customarily used as crews' living quarters. Pronounced fo'c'sle.

Frigate Originally, fifth- or sixth-rate ships carrying their guns on a single deck, employed as scouts, and the counterpart of the later cruiser.

Gundeck The name given to the main deck in sailing warships of the British Royal Navy.

Ironclad The contemporary name for wooden warships clad with iron, and by extension, to the first iron warships; it continued in use up until the arrival of the dreadnought.

Jib A triangular sail (usually loose-footed) set on a forestay.

Knot Internationally, the measure of a ship's speed – one nautical mile per hour.

Lee/Leeward The side of the vessel away from the wind, but a coast onto which the wind is blowing.

Liner A ship carrying passengers to a fixed schedule, usually on trans-oceanic routes; the term became current from the mid-1800s. A cargo liner also operates on fixed schedules, with space for a limited number of passengers.

Magazine Secure storage for explosives.

Nautical mile Internationally, the measure of distance at sea which has become standardised at 6080 ft (1852 m).

Poop The short raised deck at the stern of a vessel, originally known as the aftercastle. The word is derived from the Latin *puppis*, stern.

Quarterdeck That part of the upper deck abaft the mainmast (or where the mainmast would logically be in a steam- or motor ship), traditionally the reserve of commissioned officers.

Radar An acronym for Radio Direction and Range – a means of using electromagnetic radiation to locate an object in space by bouncing signals off it and measuring the time elapsed before they return to the plane of the emitter, the orientation of the receiving antenna provides directional data.

Ram A strengthened, usually armoured, projection from the bow of a warship, designed to allow her to pierce the hull of an adversary with relative impunity. Widely used in the age of the galley, it fell into disuse with the coming of sail, but enjoyed a brief revival after the Battle of Lissa in 1866, and was found on most major warships from just after that date until the coming of the dreadnoughts, even though it actually figured in more peacetime disasters than ever it did in wartime successes.

Reefer A refrigerated cargo-carrier.

Reserve Warships not in active commission are said to be in reserve; this may be a temporary measure, in which case maintenance work will be kept fully up to date, or a long-term measure, in which case the ship will be "mothballed" – effectively sealed up, with precautions taken to ensure that any machinery liable to deteriorate is well protected.

Rifle/Rifling The practice of cutting a series of grooves in a spiral the length of a gun's barrel, in order to impart spin to a projectile and thus stabilise it in flight. The system was widely adopted for naval ordnance from the mid-1800s; see also smooth-bore.

SAM Surface-to-air missile.

sc single class.

Schnorkel/Snorkel A tube with a ball-valve at its upper extremity, which allows a submarine to take in air, and thus continue to operate its internal-combustion engines, while remaining below the surface. Invented in the Netherlands in the 1930s, it was not used extensively until the German navy took it up during World War II, but since then it has been universal.

Sheer The upward curve of a ship's upper deck towards bow and stern.

Smooth-bore A gun with a smooth (ie, unrifled) barrel, used as naval ordnance until the second half of the 19th century.

Sonar An acronym for Sound Navigation and Ranging, a technique of using sound waves to detect objects underwater, and by extension, to the hardware employed.

Sponson A platform built outside the hull, at main or upper-deck level, usually to allow guns on the broadside to be sited so as to allow them to fire axially.

Squadron In the British Royal Navy, originally an organised unit of (usually eight) major warships – cruisers and capital ships, but in the US Navy (and the practice became widespread), an organised unit of ships of any type, from minesweepers upwards, the term having taken over from flotilla.

Square-rigged A sailing vessel whose sails are set on yards, which when at rest are at right angles to the longitudinal axis of the hull.

SSM Surface-to-surface missile.

SSN Nuclear-powered submarine.

Standing rigging That portion of a ship's rigging – stays and shrouds, for example – which is employed to steady her masts.

Steam turbine A rotary engine in which steam is used to drive turbine blades arranged upon a shaft; invented by Parsons at the end of the 19th century.

Stem The foremost member of a ship's frame, fixed at its lower extremity to the keel.

Stern post The aftermost member of a ship's frame, fixed at its lower extremity to the keel.

Strake A structural timber running the length of a ship or boat's hull, along the major axis.

Submarine Properly speaking, a vessel capable of indefinite (or at least very prolonged) underwater operation; early submarines were in fact submersibles, and it was not until the advent of air-independent propulsion systems that true submarines were constructed.

Tack The lower forward corner of a fore-and-aft sail; a reach sailed (in a sailing vessel) with the wind kept on one side.

Tiller A wooden or metal bar attached rigidly to the rudder and used to control its movement.

Tonnage The load-carrying capacity of a merchant ship or the displacement of a warship.

Topmast The second section of a mast, stepped above the lower mast, carrying the (upper and lower) topmast yard(s).

Topping lift A rope or wire tackle by means of which a spar is lifted.

Transom A squared-off stern form, adopted both because it saved weight and resulted in better hydrodynamic perfromance.

Turret Originally an armoured shell or covering for a gun, which rotated with the platform upon which the gun is mounted; later the armoured cover became an integral part of the rotating mounting, and itself supported the gun or guns.

VLCC/ULCC Very/Ultra-Large Crude Carrier; the biggest oil tankers, with a deadweight capacity of over 200,000 tons (VLCC) and over 300,000 tons (ULCC).

Index

Picture Credits

Art-Tech/Aerospace: 7, 99, 104, 128, 129, 134, 135, 141, 181, 193, 235, 236

Art-Tech/MARS: 8, 123, 187, 198, 247

BAE Systems: 313

Cody Images: 6, 9, 20, 21, 33, 38, 39, 56, 63, 68, 69, 74, 75, 80, 81, 86, 87, 92, 93, 98, 105, 110, 111, 116, 117, 122, 140, 152, 153, 158, 159, 168, 180, 186, 223, 228, 229, 240, 253, 258, 264, 265, 276, 277, 283, 289, 312

De Agostini: 51

Kockums: 163, 306, 307

Library of Congress: 44

Mary Evans Picture Library: 62 (Suddeutsche Zeitung)

Photo 12: 27

Photos.com: 26, 50

Rex Features: 288 (Action Press)

TopFoto: 45 (Granger Collection)

U.S. Department of Defense: 57, 146, 147, 160, 161, 162, 169, 174, 175, 192, 199, 204, 205, 210, 211, 216, 217, 222, 234, 241, 252, 259, 270, 271, 282, 294, 295, 300, 301

Wikipedia Creative Commons Licence: 14 (Musee Marine)

All artworks courtesy of Art-Tech/Aerospace and De Agostini except for the following:

BAE Systems: 292/293

John Batchelor: 290/291

Kockums: 302/303

Military Visualisations Inc: 214–215, 250–251, 268-269, 280–281, 298 bottom, 304–305, 310–311

Navy News: 278/279, 296/297, 308/309

Tony Gibbons courtesy of Bernard Thornton Artists, London: 12–13, 18–19, 36–37, 42–43, 54–55, 66–67, 126–127